WEDDINGS BY DESIGN

WEDDINGS

BY

DESIGN

A GUIDE TO THE NON-TRADITIONAL CEREMONY

Richard Leviton

HarperSanFrancisco
A Division of HarperCollinsPublishers

HarperSanFrancisco and the authors, in association with
the Rainforest Action Network, will facilitate the planting
of two trees for every one tree used in the manufacture of
this book.

FIRST EDITION

Library of Congress Cataloging-in-Publication Data
    Leviton, Richard.
        Weddings by design : a guide to the non-traditional
    ceremony / Richard Leviton. - 1st ed.
            p. cm.
    Includes bibliographic references.
    ISBN 0–06–2501007–X (pbk. : alk. paper)
    1. Weddings—Planning.   I. Title.
    HQ745.L47 1993
    395².22—cd20   92–53058
                                                  CIP

93 94 95 96 97 ❖ RRD(H) 10 9 8 7 6 5 4 3 2 1

This edition is printed on acid-free paper that meets the
American National Standards Institute Z39.48 Standard.

for

JUDY "CLARISSA" LEWIS,

Darl of Dahls

CONTENTS

1

THE

RAVISHING

LOVE AND THE WORLD CULTURE WEDDING

Oh, hasten not this loving act,
Rapture where self and not-self meet:
My life has been the awaiting you,
Your footfall was my own heart's beat.
—Paul Valéry, Poems in the Rough

When I was young, I had elaborate daydreams of my wedding. First I would be ravished by love. Then I'd concoct a public ceremony big enough and plush enough to reflect this ravishment. It would be an opulent three-day Elizabethan extravaganza of food, flowers, music, entertainments, and poetry set in an impossibly idyllic country estate. When I readied myself to marry at midlife, however, not only was there no script to match my fantasy, but neither I nor my partner wanted anything to do with conventional wedding rites.

When we thought of the conventional Western format for getting married, we just wanted to walk away from the whole subject: it wasn't for us. These rituals are somebody else's idea, not ours; inherited rules of behavior that seem unrelated to the gender realities and spiritual iconoclasm of the 1990s. This is empty and anachronistic, we thought, and we'll have no part of it.

When we started to plan our wedding, we couldn't imagine ourselves feeling comfortable and authentic moving toward this state along the standard wedding track. Bridal showers, rings, bachelor parties, fancy invitations, best man, bridesmaids, tuxedos, lace tulle, walking down the aisle, the altar ceremony, the big cake, confetti, old shoes, tin cans, the catered reception, the relatives, the honeymoon . . . not for us. That's just another page out of any issue of *Bride's* magazine, we told each other. But then, what instead? How could we design a ceremony that reflected our feeling that marriage was a profound expression of relationship, yet didn't make us feel as if we'd bought our wedding out of a catalog?

The Plight of the Lapsed

Unfortunately our backgrounds offered us nothing practical for designing a wedding. My partner, raised Catholic, grew up in Australia with nuns for schoolteachers. I'm a Protestant-trained American who paid no attention whatsoever to all attempts at indoctrination, and topped it all off with an early defection to Zen Buddhism. None of this translated into any kind of tradition, lineage, or nuptial format that felt meaningful.

Most of our friends were already married, and had been for ten or fifteen years. Their marriages back in the 1970s were part of that post-hippie laissez-faire New Wedding milieu of bare feet, embroidered dhotis, petunia-strewn beards, brown rice, and guitar-picking in the pasture. That wouldn't do; in fact, remembering these youthful shenanigans brings a blush of embarrassment.

We had fallen apostatically out of the ranks of convention into the "Bohemia of the lapsed," as one cheeky friend told me. We were lapsed, a man and woman without an official religious context. I was a Buddhist at eighteen, lapsed at thirty, unclaimed by any dogma at forty; she was a good Catholic girl at eight, self-excommunicated at twenty, a spiritual freelancer at thirty-five—and both godless ever since, or so people would think. But we aren't atheists or agnostics. Between us we've had our share of numinous encounters and wordless insights. If you asked us to name our brand of spirituality, I don't think we could satisfy you with any recognizable tag: we're not only not Protestant, Catholic, or Buddhist, but we're not New Age, Gnostic, Sufi, pagan, Wiccan, Muslim, Jewish, Quaker, Baha'i, either; nor are we particularly Australian or American, at least not at the level of living ritual. But nonidentification doesn't spell rejection. If anything our sentiments are pluralistic and inclusive, multiculturally eclectic,

globally spiritual. That's why, when we decided to cast around for inspiration, we were drawn to examine the matrimonial customs of other cultures. Not being exclusively of one tradition, we feel pulled toward what is living in all traditions and faiths, with the hope that we might reverse the cultural deconstructionism of iconoclasm and help birth a new nuptial icon out of the numerous matrimonial folkways. But first we began to wonder what the mainstream was up to these days.

Stretching the Rules

According to *New York Times Magazine* bridal journalist Linda Wells, the mainstream is stretching the rules. Independent-minded couples are incorporating the personal touch into their ceremonies. "Many women and men are rejecting the textbook wedding," Wells writes. "The event is still grand and festive, but it tends to be infused with quirks and personal style."

Wells cites ample evidence of convention bending: a bride negotiating the church aisle in a blushingly scarlet gown (rather than the traditional white), her bridesmaids done up in black velvet (instead of pastel), her groom frilled out in a brocade vest (where's the tuxedo?). One bride, who fancied motorcycles but wanted to please her grandmother, wore a leather cyclist's jacket over her virgin white gown.

Wells reports that couples are opting to hold their wedding ceremonies and receptions at the same location, such as on a barge moored in Brooklyn with a splendid view of the downtown urban skyscraper forest of Manhattan. "It seems that as the rules disappear, many wedding receptions are dissolving into big whoop-de-doos," reports Wells. This is good news for the guests, especially if they haven't eaten much beforehand

and anticipate a decent spread; in the new "whoop-de-doo" they're likely to get hors d'oeuvres and champagne nonstop, starting the minute they walk in the door—or onto the barge.

Intrigued, I began to make a Sunday-morning ritual of studying Lois Smith Brady's "Vows" column in the *New York Times*, eager to learn which unusual, intriguingly different wedding she had visited this past week for my edification. Kathy, thirty-one, and Jake, thirty-three, got married on a posh midtown roof, part of a rentable loft called the Biodome, according to a script mostly self-written. "Your journey together has often been bumpy and especially in the last couple of weeks," proclaimed their officiant. "This marriage is truly a testament to the effectiveness of the psychoanalytic process," he added, referring—with a grin, I hope—to the fact both bride and groom had been in group and individual therapy for some time. Several of their psychoanalysts attended, offering reflective toasts on their analysands' behalf after a dinner of vegetarian lasagna, Caesar salad, and carrot cake.

Josefa, thirty-four, and William, thirty-two, staged their wedding in the backyard of her childhood home in the middle of a spring downpour. They had figured on the rain, and fortunately they had enough umbrellas on hand for their ninety guests. "The wedding was a mix of the traditional, the alternative, the mystical," commented Brady. The bride's dress was so billowy it knocked over chairs as she wafted through the tent. As the ground turned muddy and the tent dripped along the seams and the umbrellas turned inside out in the wind, a Gnostic minister and Tarot reader (she'd been reading the couple's Tarot cards for the eight years of their relationship, a theme she worked into her wedding oration) performed the joining ritual.

Brady also witnessed the modest Manhattan wedding ceremony of a Japanese couple from out of town—from Tokyo, in fact. Kyoko, twenty-seven, and Shuji, thirty-two, wanted a New York wedding so much that they were willing to fly non-stop from Japan to New York to shell out $3,000 to an American company that sells wedding packages (including a white stretch limousine for two hours) to make it happen. They had hardly any guests, barely understood the English-language service, and staggered around with jet-lag; but for them the Western wedding was far preferable to the ornate, meticulously scripted Japanese formality. "In Japan the marriage ceremony is family to family, a big occasion," said Shuji. "In New York it is individual to individual. We like it that way. We need only two to get married."

"The Eternal Bliss Machine"

It's true that couples may need only "two to get married," but it may cost them $13,310 if they do it American-style. According to *Modern Bride*, that's the average wedding tab for an American wedding circa 1990 with all the trimmings, including $850 for music, $2,575 for rings, and $6,150 for the reception. Approximately 2.4 million American couples spent an estimated $31 billion annually on American nuptials, between $534 million and $1.8 billion for wedding gowns, $5.9 billion for receptions, and $2.7 billion for honeymoon travel.

Weddings with all the elegant extras are more popular than ever, commented *Nation's Business* in June 1990. Big-checkbook weddings are back, declared *Time* in 1986, an observation no less true in 1993. In 1985 the wedding industry raked in $10.9 billion, a 43 percent increase over the previous decade. The "big blowout" is the posh repudiation of the "free form tribal rites of the Love and Me decades," explained *Time* magazine's Jay Cocks. Celebrity and royalty weddings became *the* style worth copying. "They are all fair game for emulation in a democracy where a plastic card can grab you a piece of anyone else's dream and an extra piece of wedding cake."

If you have a lot of plastic and don't watch the bills too carefully, you might end up spending $60,000 for your big blowout, as one not particularly wealthy San Francisco couple did. Between "I do" and "I pay," Andrea Debo and Mark O'Brien had pledged to pay for, among other things: engagement ring, $25,000; reception, $11,500; wedding gown, $2,500; cathedral rental, $2,042; honeymoon trip, $3,000; limousines, $1,450; wedding party gifts, $1,250; trousseau, $1,000. The twenty-seven hours between rehearsal and reception—a major "cash hemorrhaging" in which "bills stretched like mozzarella"—cost the couple about $20 a minute. But at $60,000 the Debo-O'Brien "whoop-de-doo" was still a rather tastefully modest nuptial compared to the 1981 wedding of Mohammed, son of Shaik Zayid ibn Sa'id al-Makhtum, to Princess Salama in Abu Dhabi. That cost $33 million.

The biggest danger to getting married American-style is the "Wedding Mafia" that seemingly controls all the money spent in the United States during the month of June, the year's most prolific time for marriages, explains the groomsman's adviser, Peter Nelsen, in his witty manifesto, *Marry Like a Man.*

Nelsen, recently married and no doubt exposed to the mercantile strategies of caterers, florists, and consultants, nails the Wedding Mafia forthrightly to the wall: "A huge bloodsucking conspiracy of liars and thieves who lure you in when your brain isn't working and your defenses are down and soak you for every penny you have because they know you're going into your wedding believing it's a once-in-a-lifetime event wherein money, they will try to convince you, should be no object." If the money doesn't get you, then the mystery will, adds Nelsen. "If love is a mystery, the wedding is its Mystery Play"—a drama not unlike death, quips Nelsen. Death and marriage loom perpetually in our midst as possibilities, but we never take either seriously until we suddenly realize, it *could* happen

to us. "It's not death we fear," Montaigne said, "but dying, not the state but the stroke of it. Not marriage, but weddings."

But why should we fear our own grandest fantasy, our designer wedding, our personal shot as actors in the perennial nuptial drama? "The American wedding is nothing if not profoundly romantic, pure magical fantasy," explained Marcia Seligson twenty years ago in her critical and fascinating look at American nuptials, *The Eternal Bliss Machine.* Whatever the simplicity or exorbitance, it's theater, she said—the same plot, characters, and costumes, while only the sets change, depending on the style of the pageant. "It can be a musical comedy, a Wagnerian opera, a rodeo, or a carnival or a vaudeville or burlesque. The wedding to us, is really a panacea, a mini-microcosm of all the dreams and goals and fantasies and promises that American life has to offer."

The matrimonial operetta, says Seligson, turns on the quintessentially American themes of Love and Money, so watch out for "the ever-spiralling web of detail and expenditure and obsession in which the participants are caught . . . a ritual event of ferocious, gluttonous consuming, a debauch of intensified buying never again to be repeated in the life of an American couple." Seligson was intrigued to note that Americans, despite the hippie free-form and precocious New Weddings, are getting married pretty much the same way our forebears did a century ago. Why? Because, despite the iconoclasm and individuality on which America, at least legendarily, was founded, we crave ritual, we demand prescribed formal systems of observance and sanctified public ceremonial.

Whether we're Boy Scouts or Zen Buddhists, the prescripted ritual is deeply comforting and fulfilling. It transfers our personal biography into a grander, multipersonal, even archetypal context. Rituals, says Tom Driver in *The Magic of Ritual,* make three great gifts to social life. They help establish order, deepen communal life, and assist in "the dynamic of social change through ritual processes of transformation." Rituals may be agents of transformation, but they are themselves transformed by the times in which they flourish. "Weddings, of course, are rites of passage in which the status of two persons, and the community's expectations concerning them, are transformed; but the rites themselves undergo change as they are employed in shifting circumstances."

These shifting circumstances involve major shifts in demographics, not least of which is the radical upheaval in gender relations and the massive departure of women from the household to the marketplace. The image of the traditional bride gowned in virginal white is "downright disingenuous," remarked Holly Brubach in *The New Yorker* a few years ago. Women entering marriages today are older and have established careers, often arriving with a truckload of household furniture, a backlog of marital and romantic memories, and increasingly with children from previous husbands. Weddings may pick up where fairy tales end, comments Brubach, but it's no longer true that an American woman's future is sealed on her wedding day. "Somewhere between the spun-sugar vision of the Sleeping Beauty awakened by the Prince's kiss and the fact of the matter—which is that, married or single, a woman is responsible for herself—lies a narrow aisle that is difficult to negotiate."

That narrow aisle, lying somewhere between *Bride's* and *Ms.*, between *GQ* and *Man!*, is what I call the world culture wedding.

Shedding the Old Wedding Ways

If our Western wedding rituals impress us personally as empty formulas and anachronistic gestures, what is their relationship with our culture? The more we examined this question, the more it seemed clear to us that the basic sociological reasons for the conventional wedding format are no longer relevant to our social circumstances. It troubled me, as a twentieth-century American contemplating the marriage ritual at the close of the millennium, that my social and psychological milieu, and probably that of many readers, simply isn't the one out of which these rituals arose. To spiritually empower the new world culture wedding, we must identify some understanding that enlivens our eclectic rituals; otherwise we are doing nothing more than cleverly moving cultural museum pieces around like stage props on a performance stage.

Our Judeo-Christian wedding customs are astoundingly patriarchal, paternalistic, and, some will argue, misogynist as well. This isn't surprising when you stop to consider that the wedding ritual essentially arose out of a paternalistic, male-dominant, and probably antifeminist approach to gender relations. Its origin was a cultural milieu in which the economic power and secular authority of the family, meaning the parents, was predominant and unassailable. Marriage in late adolescence marked a coming of age, a crucial rite of passage, a pivotal social initiation supervised and approved by one's community elders on behalf of one's parents. In traditional cultures marriage had a rationale; its rituals emerged to catalyze and chaperone important transformations in the life cycle of its members.

First, marriage facilitated the graduation of sons and daughters from the parental home into adulthood, independence, and the new conjugal home. Second, it shepherded young virginal women, the family's valuable yet problematic "property," along the passageway from puberty to motherhood without any detours (what we casually call extramarital sexual relationships today). Third, it guaranteed the continuity and stability of family life through the continual generation of children; it sanctioned fertility and controlled sexuality (legally and spiritually) through the vehicle of the family. Fourth, it assured the survival and integrity of one's social unit, the tribe, ethnic clan, affinal kinship network, and extended community. As a corollary, each marriage created a new household, which for many centuries was the fundamental social unit; through the wedding the community bound (and legally sanctioned) the husband and wife to this solemn duty of maintaining a household for the good of the larger community.

The traditional marriage ceremony was (and in many parts of the world, still is) the successful articulation of these conformist, regulative pressures through socially meaningful rituals. Of course there's love, that melting, transcendent kiss of Aphrodite that compels anything—but we don't need marriage to cultivate love, do we? "Love is the flower, marriage is the fruit," says the Finnish proverb. Overall the protocols of marriage were based on an entrenched paternalism that assumed young men and women were insufficiently mature and responsible to conduct their own passage from unawakened puberty to adult sexuality without disaster, and required rigorous, programmatic chaperoning by parents, adult family members, and other authority figures.

For many of us, especially those who are members of that precocious demographic "pig in the python" called the Baby Boom generation, this is all irrelevant. We find ourselves in a social circumstance in which these standard, supposedly perennial factors are no longer operative. People marry much later in their lives, long after they've left home, finished college, and begun careers. So we don't require marriage to graduate us from our parent's nest; we are sufficiently psychologically mature to look after ourselves as we engage in the problematic terrain of gender relations.

The idea of sedulously protecting a daughter's virginity until marriage is no longer meaningful. The worldwide pressures of overpopulation have reversed the rationale about sanctioning fertility; if anything we want to curtail fertility. We don't need big broods because we don't base our livelihood on labor-intensive agriculture in which a few extra (and free) pairs of hands can make the difference between crop failure and a full silo. The trend among many dual-career Baby Boomers is toward smaller families, or no family, delayed until a couple's thirties, even forties.

For those who take the views of the established feminist and emerging men's movements seriously, male-dominant rituals such as the traditional wedding format are inappropriate and anachronistic; clearly we need to reformat our primary bonding ritual to reflect true gender equality. We need to create a new wedding ritual that is free of the nineteenth-century matrimonial ideal of tamed, nurturing woman and wildly adventurous man. The new world culture wedding honors (and probably requires) that both woman and man be psychologically independent and well on the way to self-completion and individuation, so that the wedding joins together two whole people, not spare parts.

We don't need marriage to permit us to express our sexuality, certainly not after the "sexual liberation" of the 1960s. It becomes harder to accept the premise that only the family can commission sexuality; after two decades of feminist analysis of Western culture, it's also glaringly irrelevant. Nor do we need the family as a sanctioned context for raising children: simply consider single mothers, either unwed or separated, parents who don't marry, and lesbian and gay parents.

The rule of the priesthood is also waning. Internal contradictions, improprieties, and fundamentalist rigidity continue to weaken the authority of established Western religions, while sexual, financial, and patriarchal issues corrupt the imported exotic Eastern beliefs. We iconoclasts are swept up in a new form of Protestantism that says: no priests, no religious intermediaries, gurus go home. When we want Spirit, we'll go straight to the Source. Clan loyalty, too, has lost a lot of its potency, which paradoxically accounts for the intensity of worldwide ethnic conflicts. It's the last violent paroxysm of a dying attitude. Today many of us marry widely: interracially, interethnically, interdenominationally, globally; we mix homelands, religions, and folkways; we marry as individuals, as planetary citizens.

The Aquarian Basis of Ritual

One of the names of this new post-traditional atmosphere is Aquarius. Admittedly a great deal of nonsense, both inaccurate and millennialist, has been published on behalf of the nascent "Age of Aquarius." Aquarian, however, isn't so much New Age platitudes as it is radical change in the form of the rampant ethnic, nationalist, and gender strife we see virtually everywhere.

The ubiquity of tumult and conflict in today's world, despite its grim visage and bleak extrapolations, is actually the signature of a powerful, positive Aquarian catalyst churning up all the old, encrusted forms. Transformation and transmutation—old forms are burned up, releasing new energies for fresh forms along a different line. Gender equality, multiculturalism, globalism, undifferentiated spirituality, planetary awareness: that's Aquarius. The astounding degree of upheaval around us is directly proportional to the amount of resistance these outmoded forms are exhibiting. Resistance is natural, but the changes are inevitable; they're transmuting the old world with the inexorable force of a cultural evolutionary imperative. And that includes wedding rituals.

One of the positive hallmarks of Aquarian energy is the cultivation of strongly individuated women and men who derive their identity not from their tribe, their ethnicity, nationality, or other ephemeral social distinctions, but from their mature humanity and the vast planet itself. The Aquarian is a citizen of the world, a global individual, a person who wears insignias of all the world's cultures, religions, and folkways on a coat of many colors, yet doesn't rigidly identify with any of them. Such a person is in effect *self*-excommunicated from his or her religious fold.

Aquarius is strongly antihierarchical, antisacerdotal, antiecclesiastical, yet not antispiritual. But it's a spirituality acquired *directly*, without mediation or filtration. We are all potentially Prometheus stealing the spark of celestial fire from the gods for our colleagues. As the Quakers realized several centuries ago, we are all, equally, Friends "in the presence of God." So not priest, lama, minister, roshi, imam, or rabbi can ultimately intercede on our behalf—or should want to. We each make the connection on our own, directly; we each learn the language of Spirit and work out for ourselves the rites and utterances appropriate for future reiterations of the numinous contact. That's Aquarius, too.

Virtually all ethnic cultures are represented in the United States. You can buy their foods, walk through their neighborhoods, learn their languages, listen to their sagas of emigration, study their folkways in college. If you belong to an electronic data base or computer bulletin board, you're already a cross-cultural communicator, downloading messages to correspondents in St. Petersburg, Capetown, Bucharest, Darwin, and Brasilia. And the communication also goes the other way. An estimated 2 billion people, for example, watch America's Academy Awards ceremony beamed around the planet by television satellite from Hollywood each March. Concurrent with this prodigy of globally distributed information is a loosening of our own folkways, religions, and our ethnic, even national, identity. If any culture will do it, America is likely to first shed its nationalistic skin and emerge

UNITED STATES

as a world culture. That delicate spring green growing tip of cultural evolution often presumptuously called the New Age is what will bring us into world culture.

Exciting as this may be, it's also unsettling. As our culturally entrenched forms lose potency and relevance, many of us find ourselves culturally unmoored, ritually uprooted. Our social identities, rituals, and forms are loosening their hold on many of us because what fuels them, the Judeo-Christian ethos itself, is also steadily dissolving. Somehow the cultural identity of being an American—or Canadian, or Australian, and of perhaps any English-speaking culture—doesn't provide any innately *American* forms for weddings. That's because, culturally, America is a pluralistic polyglot of world cultures. It's almost tautological to say "an American form of wedding," despite our distinctive "big blowout" style of spending princely dollars for our nuptials. That's not ritual; that's just personality.

And that turns out to be a good thing where weddings are concerned. For the American who no longer identifies with his or her traditional ethnic, social, religious, even national background (or for one who wishes to deepen or supplement what this tradition offers) the particularities of world cultures, spiritualities, folkways, and mythopoeic ritualism can become the motherlode for components in the new, self-designed world culture wedding.

In the 1990s sensitive men are realizing that if they opt for the traditional wedding, it means a de facto endorsement of outmoded, single-gender attitudes. That's why we need new forms that emerge from world culture. In addition to its roving cultural eclecticism and insistence on self-authenticated spirituality, our new "wedding-by-design" reflects the emerging redefinition of gender relations. In the world culture wedding, we marry by design, not by habit.

So Why Get Married?

According to a 1992 U.S. Census Bureau study, there are more Americans saying "I don't" than there are saying "I do," contributing to a marriage-rate decline that has accelerated since 1965. Compared to a peak of 16 marriages per 1,000 people, the rate in 1992 was only 9 per 1,000. An estimated 22.6 percent of Americans of the age of 18 or older have never been married (about 41 million people), compared to 16.2 percent in 1970; of men between the ages of 35 and 39, 17.6 percent had never married, a 7.8 percent increase since 1980. Of women in the same age group, 11.7 percent are unmarried, a 5.5 percent increase. And the median age for first marriage is also rising, from age 21 (women) and 23 (men) between 1950 and 1969 to 24 and 26, respectively, in 1991. Sociologists speculate that demographic shifts and a prolonged recession might have produced the low marriage rates.

There's an insider's joke among Jungian analysts when they speak about relationships and marriage. The minister asks the groom, "Do you take this woman to be your lawfully wedded anima, to project onto until death do you part?" The *anima*, in Jungian parlance, is a man's inner experience of his soul in the guise of a woman; hence, the anima represents the mutable face of a man's inner, and usually unintegrated, uncultivated feminine. Since men tend not to integrate their animas, they remain incomplete and dependent on "outside" women to carry for them the missing feminine aspects of their own psyches. Those missing parts get there by way of subconscious projection; it's as if men deftly pin the mask of a different woman upon the face of the actual woman they are in relationship with. Inversely it's the same with women: their uncultivated, unclaimed inner masculine is called the *animus,* and this too, can be projected onto the face of lover or husband. We're not irrevocably doomed to a life of anima and animus projections. Rather, recognition of this dynamic can serve as the catalyst that sparks a long-term and complex, but ultimately vastly rewarding, process of inner work and integration that Jungians call individuation—growing into psychological wholeness and the innate integrity of the Self.

Powerful psychological undercurrents, expectations, and inadequacies may fuel our relationships. Unless we take things consciously in hand and willingly undertake a process of individuation, says Jung, when one anima figure has been integrated and the outer mask (projection) stripped from our female partner, we may find our relationship suddenly parched, possibly irrelevant. It is not a pleasant experience, but it happens a lot: we find that we haven't been in love, but in projection, and when the projector stops spinning its reels, we often find ourselves on the way to separation or divorce. Many marriages fail on account of these uncovered projections; men grow out of one anima and demand a new one, and women outgrow one animus and want another. But things needn't be this way; there is a positive side to marriage, provided we're willing to work at it.

According to marital therapist Liberty Kovacs, Ph.D., who was recently profiled in *Psychology Today,* marriage is essential for growth and individuation. "Only stable enduring relationships allow individual growth to take place. We need to develop enough trust in a partner for the hidden parts of ourselves to surface. It takes years into a relationship." Kovacs suggests that marriage evolves through six distinct stages as a couple grows toward intimacy and mutuality; each stage has unique difficulties and opportunities. First comes romance, honeymoon, and fusion, which is a piece of cake; expectation and compromise, the second phase, isn't too bad: here we relinquish our family of origin and establish firm boundaries and self-esteem, says Kovacs. The next two stages see us in conflict, struggling for control and power, experiencing that archetypal "seven-year itch"; suddenly our partner is no longer a seamlessly grafted extension of ourself, but a separate, somewhat problematic individual. If we make it through these difficult straits, says Kovacs, the marriage can open out into the expansiveness of reconciliation, cooperation, acceptance, and collaboration.

The key is to construe marriage as a project of "duration." Kovacs's sequential model of marriage helps couples abandon the notion of instant gratification, explains Hara Estroff Marano in *Psychology Today.* "It clues them that you need to go through life making changes—designing your own marriage."

Marriage—understood as committed relationship—can be a dynamic catalyst for individual growth, expansion, and insight. Some traditions use the word "precipitation" when discussing the interpersonal dynamics of a marriage; suppressed, unresolved issues are precipitated into awareness by the force of the relationship. Living together with a commitment to communication and self-growth can precipitate issues quickly and forcefully. Through an honest mirroring of our flaws, projections, and illusions, our partner can help us become aware of the quirks and passions and waywardness of our inner life. Sometimes an intimate, frank relationship is the only way to precipitate the tightly knotted issues and attitudes that only live *in* relationship because that's where they were originally created.

So why get married? Marriage is an opportunity for intense psychological growth and self-fulfillment—one of the best opportunities a secular, worldly life offers. Marriage is a profound way of salvation and deliverance, suggests Adolf

Guggenbühl-Craig in *Marriage: Dead or Alive.* It's hard, painful, and troublesome work, marked by suffering and sacrifices, yet it offers joys and "the deepest kind of existential satisfaction." A marriage works when we open ourselves to what we'd never have the nerve to ask for otherwise—intense growth, change, and transformation through relationship. "Only through rubbing oneself sore and losing oneself is one able to learn about oneself, God, and the world."

Indeed the Hindu marriage encourages husband and wife to help each other realize the divine in the context of their human relationship, thereby conceiving of matrimony as an inherently spiritual affair. The woman mirrors Shakti, or the divine feminine, while the man transmits the quality of Shiva, or the cosmic masculine. In recognition of this, the bride and bridegroom perform the seven steps of Saptapadi, in which they promise mutual fidelity and lifelong devotion. As contemporary yoga teacher Swami Sivananda Radha puts it, "Those who seek a higher life of Cosmic Consciousness are willing to prepare for it by creating a good partnership and being friends in their marriage."

Creating a New Matrimonial Icon

And that brings us back to our original question: What form should our nuptial rituals take?

As we have seen, wedding folkways were born out of a social circumstance that no longer exists as part of the experience of many contemporary Westerners. The dynamics of family, gender, sexuality, fertility, clan loyalty, sacerdotal authority, and individual responsibility have all changed dramatically, disqualifying, in the view of many, the traditional wedding rituals from contemporary relevance.

We would be mistaken, however, to disregard traditional matrimonial folkways without a careful, penetrative analysis. Implicit within these archaic rites of behavior and scripted styles of relationship exists a profound, unacknowledged sacramental core. We need to rediscover this spiritual rationale as our first step in a reanimation of the Western wedding ritual. Wedding customs grew out of a core sacramental reality that perceived bride, groom, and community as actors in a divine drama about humanity. As such this core sacramental dimension establishes the archetypal basis for the world culture wedding. The fact that we can't see it doesn't mean it's not there; we simply need to look back to an earlier day, when what we now call spirituality, occultism, and magic were integral to society.

Wedding customs ultimately derive from a magical, supersensible, and spiritual perception of male-female relationships. Rites that impress us as superstitious—such as using astrology to fix the wedding date, or employing all sorts of ruses to protect the bride from evil influences—turn out to have a rational basis within this worldview. Rites that strike us as antiquated, obscure, or simply curious—such as the use of the nuptial crown or throwing rice—have numinous significance, evoking the spiritual pith of the event. Other elements, such as betrothal, bridal shower and bachelor's party, the wedding processional, and the reception, hold spiritual riches awaiting our rediscovery.

When we remove the paternalistic, patriarchal, misogynistic layers of our inherited wedding customs, there remains a profound, transformative core spirituality still viable today—in fact, *especially* viable today. When we identify the stages of this divine dramaturgy, we can incorporate ritual elements as we wish drawn from a variety of cultures into the new, living context of the world culture wedding.

Weddings by Design reveals a core sequence of transformations and observances derived from the tremendous amount of information about wedding customs available from ethnographic, anthropological, and folklore research. These transformations and observances yield an almost infinite number of variations from which you can construct the new world culture wedding. On this basis you can construct a dynamic wedding ritual appropriate to you and your time, yet which incorporates the wisdom and depth of spirituality of the world's cultures.

As you'll see, the wedding process can be perceived as eight stages. This eightfold process is a sublime drama that articulates the relations between the genders set against the archetype of the Divine Couple. The rituals usher the partners through two transfigurations, from man/woman to groom/bride, and then to husband/wife. As individuals they enact the allegory of the primal separation and unification of the sexes as the two parts of the enduring Human from whom both sexes originated.

The first stage, the Ravishing, is this chapter's discussion of reconstruing love, commitment, and wedding rituals in the context of changed social circumstances and psychological realities. In chapter 2, The Mysterious Force, we reevaluate the discredited role of astrology in determining the compatibility of our partner and in finding the best time for our wedding. In chapter 3, The *Yuino*, we examine rituals for announcing and formalizing the relationship with parents, friends, or family as witnesses, thereby finding the basis for reanimating betrothal on a new key. Chapter 4, The *Sagun*, explores the way of inner purification and self-preparation as essential prewedding work. Chapter 5, *Hieros Gamos*, sets our individual wedding within the archetypal model of the divine marriage, shows us how to include the earth in our ceremonies, and explains why the right location can be as important as the right time. Chapter 6, The *Chuppah*, highlights the outer public celebration, in which the community itself forms a holy altar and wedding canopy for the joining of the bride and groom. In chapter 7, The *Cununie*, we discover

that what truly marries us is an experience of transfiguration, blessing, and grace. The spiritual "presence" that created us and now marries us is publicly honored in chapter 8 as the *Confarreatio*, the celebratory opulence on behalf of the pristine couple.

A Minimalist Ritual with Two Yellow Roses

Unfortunately, my wife and I didn't know any of this when it was time for us to get married. We were still in the query phase. But for various personally important reasons, we went ahead with the date our astrologer had indicated was opportune for a wedding. We had a minimalist ceremony, with the fewest elements possible.

So when our neighbor Bill O'Riordan, a justice of the peace, arrived at our lakefront cottage in the cloistered hills of western Massachusetts in mid-February, there wasn't a lot for him to do. We sat at the kitchen table and enjoyed the view of the frozen, snow-packed lake. We had tea and biscuits, admired the two yellow roses in the vase on the kitchen table, discussed brands of champagne, horses, the prospects for more snow, the potholes in the road, and the cost of gas fuel versus hardwood.

Bill is a quiet, friendly, family man in his forties with snow-white hair. He's been marrying couples since 1976—over seven hundred ceremonies, he guesses—in all kinds of exotic, original venues: in a small airplane circling our town, in a running suit for sports shop owners, in a boat on the Connecticut River, in a hot air balloon, in a hospital recovery room when he was disabled and his matrimonial clients—loyal fans no doubt—assembled around him to make their vows, in outdoor parks and gardens, in farmhouse living rooms, on a mountaintop at sunrise. Sometimes his couples write their own programs, script their vows, and hand him a list of unusual scriptures to read; other times they rely on him to know what's correct and legal.

What's legal, at least in Massachusetts, is almost anything; you simply need a J.P. as an official witness, says O'Riordan. No ring, no church, no guests, no ceremony—the minimalist joining ritual is an oral acknowledgment by the couple of their consent to marry and the J.P.'s signature on the marriage license. But you can build on the minimum foundation of course, and if we had something more elaborate in mind, O'Riordan said he'd be glad to witness unobtrusively (on behalf of the state and church) as we conducted our own services.

As he signed our marriage certificate around five o'clock on a Tuesday afternoon, I contemplated the fact that this scribble on a piece of parchment meant we were married. Our relationship, cultivated so attentively over the last fifteen months in California, France, England, and New England, was hereby somehow transformed and socially sanctioned by this small gesture. We were married, and we were glad. But we felt something was missing, something more than the obvious absence of a church processional and Mendelssohn's wedding march. No, we hadn't wanted that. We didn't know what to call it at the time, but we wanted the world culture wedding.

Our lack of suitable multicultural rituals or an understanding of the core sacramental aspect of the wedding precipitated this book. Now that we have a bookful of options, maybe we'll get married again and put it all into practice. Or maybe you will.

2

THE

MYSTERIOUS FORCE

THE AUSPICIOUS DATE AND THE COUNSEL OF ASTROLOGY

Forty days before the creation of a child, a voice proclaims in heaven:
"So-and-so's daughter for so-and-so's son!"
—*Talmud*, Sotah, *2a*

Marriages (at least good ones) are made in heaven. That's the nearly worldwide sentiment about the destiny of relationships, whether you ask the Matyos of Hungary, who believe a "mysterious force, Love, draws the couple to each other," or Hollywood's Alan Rudolph, whose *Made in Heaven* film characters—one recently dead, the other an unborn virgin soul—meet in heaven and discover they were "made for each other." That's the easy part; once incarnate, they have to find each other again against formidable obstacles, mostly psychological. In Rudolph's view the fact that these two pledged their troth before birth guarantees a profoundly satisfying, even blissful, match once they are born as man and woman—providing they can find each other again. As their presiding angelic *genius locus* tells them, if they don't meet each other by age thirty, they'll each marry someone else and remain unhappy for life.

Folk wisdom of nearly all cultures has perennially acknowledged that certain matches are meant to be. The couple is right and the time is right. When these two factors are simultaneously "right," then the marriage is auspicious.

Astrology—Advance Information on Relationship Dynamics

Astrology is the science of auspiciousness that puts folk wisdom into precise, predictive terms. Despite centuries of ridicule by mainstream science, in recent decades astrology has regained a measure of respectability and acknowledged practicality in the West. Many people consult qualified astrologers for background information on important decisions, from stock investment to travel plans—and an increasing number of intellectually adventurous couples are using this powerful tool to gauge the appropriateness of a match and the best time for the wedding ceremony.

Astrology quantifies what folk wisdom suggests: that certain times in the year, month, and day may be more favorable for weddings. As eighteenth-century British moralist William Cowper put it: "Misses! the tale that I relate / This lesson seems to carry—Chose not alone a proper mate / But proper time to marry." Implicit in the folkways of traditional peoples who honor this view is the belief that starting a marriage off at the right time and with the right understanding can make all the difference in the quality of its outcome.

Marital unions may be conceived in heaven, but we commonly overlook a crucial question in our late-twentieth-century approach to wedding plans: *Between whom* and *when* can marriages be most auspiciously formalized? We assume that because we're in love, our partner is unarguably perfect for us. Perhaps. But when the initial ravishment wanes and the practicalities of living together emerge, the relationship becomes more realistic. Astrological analysis of one's proposed partner before the wedding, even before betrothal, can pro-

vide invaluable advance information about the possible shoals and waves and delights the relationship is likely to generate. It's then not a question of abandoning the proposed match, but rather appreciating the old bromide that forewarned is forearmed. A competent astrologer can provide accurate information one step ahead of your intuition or actual experience in the relationship, articulating the hidden issues for the benefit of both partners. In a sense astrological analysis is another form of marriage counseling, except that it's undertaken (one hopes) at the beginning of a relationship or marriage and not after it has become bumpy and fraught with inexplicable difficulty.

Astrology provides a predictive vocabulary that assesses potential compatibility between mates, so that choosing a partner is based on more than initial attraction and shared interests. In the same way, astrology teaches that there is more to setting the date than what weekends are convenient for aunts and uncles from out of state. The wedding customs of many of the older folk cultures preserve this awareness, offering the world culture wedding a valuable resource. Crucial questions need to be answered: Is this person I've fallen in love with the right match for me? What is the right time, the most auspicious moment, for the wedding? The answers to these questions are the focus of this chapter, as we draw first from Western folk traditions of timing and mate selection, then delve deeper into the science of astrology in Chinese, Hindu, and Western cultures.

Naming the Day—Moving from Profane to Sacred Time

For most contemporary couples, the proper time to wed is largely a matter of convenience:

when the parents, relatives, and friends can come (usually a weekend); when the weather will be user-friendly (usually summer); when churches are available (usually Saturday); and when it's most popular and socially correct (typically June through September). But according to world folklore wisdom and Eastern spiritual traditions, establishing the correct time for a wedding may be a bigger, more vital subject, more profound than the arguments of convenience suggest.

When the question of timing comes up in the Western Judeo-Christian culture, suitable wedding dates have usually been determined with respect to preexistent liturgical calendars that mark holy days. Secular wedding celebrations must not interfere with the hieratic, ecclesiastical cycles of the year. Therefore, to prevent nuptial contretemps, it's been customary within the tight folds of orthodox established religions for the priest, minister, or rabbi to take responsibility for "naming the day."

The folklore constellated about the theme of naming the day is complex, sometimes contradictory, but consistently intriguing. If the plethora of customs and traditions we're about to examine has one common theme, it's the inference that ordinary, calendrical time—yearly, seasonal, monthly, weekly, daily, hourly—has a sacred as well as a mundane dimension; and that a major life transition ritual such as a wedding properly takes place within sacred time. A correctly placed event thus becomes auspicious.

The sacrality of time and the appropriateness of the moment were once cornerstones of an entire cosmological view of the world, human life, and the universe; in fact, all human social activities, from agriculture to marriage, were undertaken within this sacralized context. According to scholars of myth, this context of sanctified time was the fertile soil from which all human ritual observance sprouted. The core rituals of human life, says Mircea Eliade, were originally offered in imitation of stages of the Creation for the "continuous regeneration of time." If the perennial wisdom implicit in folklore is to be trusted, it's telling us that our choice of day and hour can have an import that surpasses what convenience, personality, and conventionality would reasonably dictate.

Never at Saturday High Noon

A spiritual imperative may inform our marriage, but in some cultures the union must find its proper place within the social context of time. In the Hebrew tradition, for example, suitable dates for weddings arise not so much out of the interpersonal time of astrological horoscopes, but from historical, social, *liturgical* time. Weddings, declares Hebrew tradition, must be inserted within the yearly spiritual cycle of meaningful Jewish or suprapersonal time. This view sets individual weddings against a larger, more profound background: the religious calendar. It seems at first glance as if it might straitjacket our spontaneity; but when we understand what days are acceptable and which are abjured—and *why*—we begin to sense a cyclic numinosity to the unending stream of days.

A host of calendrical proscriptions surrounds the Orthodox Jewish wedding, and planning the date requires careful consideration. Some rabbis encourage marriages during the waxing phase of the moon as a sign of blessing because love and good fortune grow with the moon. Many couples elect Rosh Hodesh, the first day of the new moon cycle, excepting the month of Nisan (or Aries, March 20–April 19), the eight days of Hanukkah (December 20–28), the fifteenth of Av (Leo, July 22–August 22), Shevat (Aquarius, January 20–February 19), or the day after Shavuot (Christian Pentecost or Whit-Sunday).

That's just the top of the Hebrew list of nuptial interdictions. Virgins should marry only on Wednesdays, widows on Thursdays; and Orthodox couples often choose Tuesday, because in the biblical creation story, God praised this day as "good." Jews must not marry on the Sabbath, which means from sundown Friday to dusk on Saturday. Weddings shouldn't be scheduled on formal Days of Joy, which include Rosh Hashanah, Yom Kippur, Sukkot, Purim, and Pesach, because as the Talmud puts it, "one should not intermix rejoicing with rejoicing." Jewish couples are also enjoined against weddings on Days of Sadness: the fast days of Tishah be-Av (ninth of Av, July 22–August 21), Gedaliah (third of Tishri, Libra, September 22–October 22), and Esther (thirteenth of Adar, Pisces, the day before Purim); tenth of Tevet (Capricorn, December 21–January 20) and seventeenth of Tammuz (Cancer, June 20–July 22). The entire three-week period between seventeenth of Tammuz through ninth of Av, which marks the mourning period for the destruction of the Temple of Jerusalem, is contraindicated for any celebrations of personal happiness. Similarly the forty-nine-day period from Passover to Shavuot is reserved for mourning the death of the renowned Rabbi Akiva's students and followers.

The cross-cultural rationale for proscribing weddings on holy days is that humans must not superimpose their comparatively mundane activities upon special days already weighted with spiritual significance, probably because it's either too presumptuous or because the gods are distracted on these days with other projects and will not be available for nuptial blessings. In other cases men and women are expected to observe holy days in an attitude of reverence, piety, and respect for the patriarchs, saints, or antediluvian event commemorated on that particular day.

Moroccan tribes commonly celebrate weddings in the autumn at the end of harvest, when the granaries are stocked with corn. Weddings are avoided in Muharram, the inaugural "sacred month" of the Mohammedan year (June 21 in 1993). Weddings performed during pilgrimages are considered invalid. Egyptians believe that marriages performed during Muharram will be unhappy, but those undertaken in Shawwal (the tenth month "of hunting," immediately following Ramadan) will be most propitious.

In Bali the *pedanda,* or high priest, determines the propitious day for the wedding festival. Marriages based on *mapadik,* the traditional old form of marriage, take place in the fourth or tenth month of the year. For the newer style of elopement, *ngorod,* the marriage is scheduled for the *ingkel wong,* a good day of the week—but that's only one out of every six weeks. Other weeks are reserved as favorable for affairs concerning domestic animals, birds, fish, and bamboo, but not marriage.

The rural Greeks in older days scheduled their weddings according to the convenience of agricultural events. Favorite seasons included the last several weeks before Lent in late winter (the month of Gamelion in their traditional calendar; late January, early February in ours), the late autumn after the vintage and olive gathering, and the last Sunday before the Christmas fast begins. The etymological root of the month called Gamelion, in fact, is *gamos,* the Greek word for marriage itself—a clear indication of the high connubial favor in which it was held. Hesiod claimed that the fourth day of the month was the most favorable, which in a lunar month would mark the appearance of the first crescent of the new moon. Proclus declared that the day when sun and moon meet in the same quarter of the sky is the day when a couple will best meet in wedlock.

The Finnish people found that Midsummer Day (June 24) and Christmas (December 25) were the most popular times for weddings, based on agricultural factors. Midsummer Day was associated with the fertility and life-renewal ceremonies of high summer; and Christmas, in addition to its strictly Christian connotations, was a time of enforced rest, when the year's harvests were gathered and no further outdoor work could be done.

The Jews and Muslims were not alone in having formal opinions about the correct use of days. The Roman proscriptions against weddings were also based on a liturgical calendar. Unlucky days for marrying include the Calends, Nones, and Ides, and the day immediately after each. The Calends are the month's first day, sacred to the Goddess Juno. Nones are the ninth day before the Ides, or the seventh day of March, May, July, and October, and the fifth day of the other months; and the fifth of the seven canonical hours of the day, approximately 3:00 P.M. The Ides is supposedly the day of the full moon, sacred to Jupiter; but they're also reckoned as the eighth day after Nones, specifically the fifteenth of March, May, July, and October, and the thirteenth day of the other eight months. The anniversary of an unhappy political memory, such as a defeat in battle, was also judged unfortunate for weddings. The early days of June were off-limits for weddings for the Romans; they were *dies religiosi* for the worship of Vesta. So were the days of *mundus patet* (August 24, October 5, and November 8), three days in which the doors to the underworld were dangerously open.

In the sixteenth century, the Catholic church began publishing its own liturgical calendar of suitable days for weddings. Eventually "unsuitable" came to mean "prohibited," up until the Reformation. The proscriptions against nuptials on Christian holy days was precise, thorough, and daunting. Marriage was forbidden during the following canonically important times: from Septuagesima ("seventieth," third Sunday before Lent) Sunday until the octave of Easter (its seven succeeding feast days); the three weeks before the feast of St. John the Baptist (June 24); from the first Rogation Day (three days before Ascension) until the

LUCKY MONTHS FOR WEDDINGS— FROM FOLKLORE

Married in January's *hoar and rime,*
Widowed you'll be before your prime.
Married in February's *sleepy weather,*
Life you'll tread in time together.
Married when March *winds shrill and roar,*
Your home will lie on a distant shore.
Married 'neath April's *changeful skies,*
A chequered path before you lies.
Married when bees o'er May-*blossoms flit,*
Strangers around your board will sit.
*Married in month of roses—*June—
Life will be one long honeymoon.
Married in July *with flowers ablaze,*
Bitter-sweet memories in after days.
Married in August's *heat and drowze,*
Lover and friend in your chosen spouse.
Married in September's *golden glow,*
Smooth and serene your life will go.
Married when leaves in October *thin,*
Toil and hardships for you begin.
Married in veils of November *mist,*
Fortune your wedding-ring has kissed.
Married in days of December's *cheer,*
Love's star shines brighter from year to year.

Folk rhyme, from Urlin,
A Short History of Marriage

MOROCCO
EGYPT
GREECE
FINLAND
CAMBODIA
ENGLAND
SUDAN
JAPAN
INDIA
MEXICO
NEPAL
FRANCE
CHINA

octave of Whitsuntide (Pentecost) or Trinity Sunday; and from the first Sunday in Advent (first Sunday after November 30) until the Epiphany (January 6). Additional holy days were judged ill-omened for weddings: Maundy Thursday (the day before Good Friday), St. Swithin's Day (July 15), St. Thomas's Day (December 21). As early as 1008, the Council of Laodicea had forbidden marriages during Lent, during Ember Days, from Advent until the octaves of Epiphany, and from Septuagesima until fifteen days after Easter. In the mid-nineteenth century, the Roman Catholic church prohibited marriages from the first Sunday in Advent until after the twelfth day, and from the beginning of Lent until Low Sunday. A popular saying in eastern England advised: "Marry in Lent, and you'll live to repent."

As a final note, Edward J. Wood, in his mid-nineteenth century compendium *The Wedding Day in All Ages and Countries,* noted that more Scottish weddings occurred on December 31 than in any other week in the year; but unions on December 28, once acknowledged as Childermas or Holy Innocent's Day, were discouraged. Childermas was once regarded as a day of ill portent because it commemorated Herod's massacre of the children when he was seeking the death of the Christ child. At one time European superstition advised avoiding most activities on the day of the week on which the previous year's Childermas had fallen.

Or in the Merry Month of May

The "pagan" cultures have their own overlay of propitious and circumscribed months and days on the yearly round. We noted above that Orthodox Jews discourage marriages between

Passover and Pentecost. That period includes all of May, a month that is off-limits for nuptials in many cultures. May may be the merry month, but the merriment mustn't include weddings, if Western folklore is to be trusted.

The Romans strongly opposed May weddings, regarding them as highly inauspicious; this belief was echoed throughout Celtic folk culture. May for the Romans is a month for purification, and that means the Lemuralia. The days between May 9 and May 12 mark the Lemuralia, the Feast of the Dead, a time when sacrifices were offered to purge each home of hostile, unclean spirits, called *Lemures* or *Larvae.* During Lemuralia, so the Romans believed, the passages between the world of the living and dead open up and familial spirits are able to revisit their old haunts. During Lemuralia the master of each household banishes the unwanted spirits of the dead in-laws and ancestors in a special midnight ritual. He washes his hands in spring water, then spits black beans at the offending spirits. All affairs of state—political, juridical, even military—pass into abeyance during Lemuralia; no business is transacted and no marriages performed.

In classical times, May was the month for the strictly women's festival of Bona Dea. This is the feminine convocation of "the Good Goddess," who might have been Fauna, Damia, or Vesta, and no men could be present. During Bona Dea, women abstained from the bath and from all cosmetics. A superstition held that May is the month of old men but June, its successor, is the month of the young, and thus far preferable for matrimony. Later the Catholic church dedicated May to Our Lady the Virgin Mary, thereby strengthening the month's associations with chastity, virginity, and purity, and reinforcing the folk embargo on marriages.

What's wrong with May? After all, the exuberant seventeenth-century British poet Robert Herrick sang its praises without hesitation in "Corinna's Going A-Maying": "A thousand virgins on this day / Spring, sooner than the lark, to fetch in May." According to the ancient Celtic tree alphabet called *ogham,* May 13 through June 9 is the month of hawthorns, or Uath, the sixth of twenty-five trees in the Beth-Luis-Nuin Druidic arboreal calendar. In Greece and Britain, Uath is the time when people go about clad in their old clothes, knowing they must "Ne'er cast a clout ere May be out," which means, don't wear any new clothes until May/Uath is over. During the hawthorn month, Celtic people ritually abstained from sexual intercourse. During May in Greece and Rome, the temples were cleaned and the images of the gods were purified; the concurrent Terebinth fair at Hebron had the same intention. When asked why the Romans didn't marry in May, Plutarch declared: "Is not the reason that in this month they perform the greatest of purification ceremonies?" Ovid reports that the oracular priestess of Jupiter, advising him about his daughter's forthcoming nuptials, said: "Until the Ides of June there is no luck for brides and their husbands. Your daughter will have better luck in marriage when Vesta's fire burns on a cleansed hearth."

The white-blossomed, thorny hawthorn was regarded as the "tree of enforced chastity," explains Robert Graves in *The White Goddess.* The object behind the taboos on new clothes and sexuality was "the washing and cleansing of the holy images." May is the month of the Greek goddess Maia, whose name means "grandmother"; Maia, Graves tells us, is another face of the polymorphous White Goddess—"a malevolent beldame." She's also Cardea (mistress of two-headed Janus), who casts unlucky spells with the hawthorn. "The Greeks propitiated her at marriages—marriage being considered hateful to the Goddess—with five torches of hawthorn-wood and with hawthorn blossom before the unlucky month began," says Graves.

One-liner adages from European folklore capture the disinclination for May nuptials. May clearly is unfavorable for fertility: "The girls are all stark naught that wed in May"; "From the marriages in May all the bairns die and decay"; "May never was ye month of love"; "Who marries between the sickle and the scythe will never thrive"; "Marry in May and you'll rue the day." When Mary Queen of Scots ignored this interdiction and married Bothwell on May 15, 1567, she was silently upbraided by her folklore-conscious public. She found this judgment from Ovid pinned to the gates of Holyrood Palace: "Wantons marry in the month of May."

February is traditionally another ill-favored month for weddings, especially among the Greeks and Romans, and for fairly substantial reasons. For the Greeks this is the time of their Anthesteria (February 11–13), a festival of ghosts in honor of the resurrected wine-god, Dionysos, whose darker side is Lord of Souls. It is a time to placate and purify, to feast then banish the lingering, noisome dead. The name February itself comes from the Latin *februare,* meaning "to make pure"; instruments of purification were called *februa.* The days of Anthesteria, said Lucian, are unlucky and require "complete idleness and cessation of business." Friends abstain from socializing and even the sanctuaries are closed during these gloomy days, as the Greeks concentrate on self-purging and offering sacrifices to the dead spirits.

On the heels of Anthesteria came the Parentalia (February 13–21), another purificatory festival of the dead. Temples were closed and altar fires extinguished, as Roman society emphasized family tombs. At Parentalia Romans inspected their ancestral graves, held love-feasts, and made offerings to the deceased of flowers, water, wine, oil, milk, and honey, all within the ambiance of spring-cleaning and purification. After Parentalia came the Feralia (February 21–22), the last of the spectral rites for the dead. Feralia was an occasion for family reunions and celebration of the Lares, the benevolent family ancestral spirits of the

MOROCCO
EGYPT
GREECE
FINLAND
CAMBODIA
ENGLAND
SUDAN
JAPAN
INDIA
MEXICO
NEPAL
FRANCE
CHINA

MOROCCO
EGYPT
GREECE
FINLAND
CAMBODIA
ENGLAND
SUDAN
JAPAN
INDIA
MEXICO
NEPAL
FRANCE
CHINA

household. When you calculate the ritual impact of Anthesteria, Parentalia, and Feralia, it's no surprise that at least for the ancient Greeks and Romans, February was a write-off for weddings.

The Native American *kachinas* don't approve of February weddings, either. Among the Hano, a contemporary Tewa Indian community in Arizona, marriages usually take place in January and August, the traditional months of gaiety and social dances, but not, taking their cue from the neighboring Hopis, during the Kachina season, from February through July. The Hopi recognized over five hundred different kinds of supernatural beings, or kachina, who included the spirits of nature and Hopi ancestors. During the Kachina season, the Hopi performed numerous

kachina dances as the centerpiece of their ceremonial life.

The Goddess Looks Favorably Upon a June Bride

As much as May is abjured for marriage, so is June favored as the optimal month for nuptials. In popular Western understanding, June *is* weddings. In 1989 12.1 percent of all registered American marriages—about 291,000, the largest number for the year—took place in June. Unarguably for

AMERICA'S MOST POPULAR WEDDING DATES

1989	Number of Marriages	Percent of Total
January	117,000	4.9
February	126,000	5.2
March	159,000	6.6
April	185,000	7.7
May	228,000	9.5
June	291,000	12.1
July	217,000	9.0
August	245,000	10.2
September	231,000	9.6
October	210,000	8.7
November	188,000	7.8
December	208,000	8.6
TOTAL	2,405,000	

Source: National Center for Health Statistics, quoted in *Nation's Business*, June 1990.

AUSPICIOUS DATES FOR THE WORLD CULTURE WEDDING

In the expanded context of the world culture wedding, annual dates that have a spiritual, liturgical, occult, historical, or astronomical "charge" might be considered as auspicious for weddings. Here's a partial listing of possibilities:

January 6	Traditional date of Epiphany, revelation of the Christ to the Magi; the original Christmas
February 2	Candlemas (or Imbolc, Oimele), Celtic holy day of lights and burning candles, St. Bridget's Day of the coming Light; one of four quarter-points in the year
February 4	Chinese New Year (variable date)
February 14	St. Valentine's Day
March 1	Matronalia, Roman festival in honor of Juno Lucina, patroness of marriages, women, and childbirth; originally the Roman New Year
March 17	St. Patrick's Day, patron saint of Ireland
March 21	Vernal equinox
April 12	Festival of the Buddha's birthday
April 23	St. George's Birthday, a geomantic holiday for British patron saint and "dragon slayer"
April 26	Florialia, Roman spring festival honoring Flora, Goddess of flowers (through May 3)
May 1	Beltane, May Day, Celtic quarter-point and start of summer
May 16	Wesak, full moon (variable date) Buddhist esoteric convocation in the Himalayas and Triple Blessing of the Buddha
June 21	Summer solstice
June 24	Midsummer Day, St. John's Tide, celebrated in Shakespeare's *A Midsummer Night's Dream*
July 6	Birthday of His Holiness, Tenzin Gyatso, the 14th Dalai Lama of Tibet
August 2	Lammas (or Lughnasa), Celtic quarterly turning day in honor of Lud, God of Light
September 22	Autumnal equinox
September 29	Michaelmas, holy day honoring the Archangel Michael, patron of Grail Knights and geomancy
December 7–9	Rohatsu, traditional Japanese meditation intensive honoring the Buddha's enlightenment
December 13	St. Lucia's Day, celebrated in Sweden in honor of Lucia, Queen of Light, crowned with garlands and candles
December 21	Winter solstice

Westerners June is the most favored month for marriages. An excursion into mythology suggests the reasons behind it.

June honors the Roman Goddess Juno, Queen of Heaven, and partner to Jupiter (the Greek Zeus), King of the Gods. Juno is the goddess of fecund marriage, the hearth, and childbirth, and the monthly Calends were her sacred time. For Roman women Juno was their lifelong guardian and mentor, from birth to death, presiding over their femininity in all its phases and expressions. Juno was womankind's role model for dignity and matronly honor, which was why women called her Juno Moneta, giver of good counsel. Her annual festival, the Matronalia, was observed on March 1. Juno's totem animals were the peacock, goose, goat, and the crow, which symbolized fruitful marriage.

Behind Roman Juno stands Greek Hera, her mythological antecedent. "I sing of Hera on her golden throne, immortal queen" sang the poet of the Homeric Hymns, "eminent indeed: she was the sister and the wife of great Zeus, the thunderer; glorious is she, honored on Olympus, revered of all the gods, the equal of Zeus, wielder of lightning." Hera (wife to Zeus, the Greek Jove, King of the Gods of Olympus) represents the "primordial feminine trinity," says Barbara Walker in *The Women's Encyclopedia of Myths and Secrets;* she also signifies the triple aspects of the moon: Hebe/new moon, Hera/full moon, and Hecate/old moon, "otherwise personified as the Virgin of spring, the Mother of summer, and the destroying Crone of autumn." Or as the second century A.D. Greek geographer Pausanias catalogued it, Hera is Child, Bride, and Widow.

As Juno or Hera, she regulated every aspect of marriage through her network of priestesses. Here's how the Roman nuptial pantheon assigned the responsibilities: Juno Pronuba arranged marriages; Juno Domiduca escorted brides across the threshold of the conjugal home; Juno Cinxia loosened the bride's virgin-girdle; Juno Lucina presided over the newly pregnant wife; Juno Ossipago nurtured the bones of the infant; Juno Sospita tended women in labor; Juno Rumina encouraged mother's milk to flow; and Iris (the Rainbow), Juno's messenger, left radiant multihued traces of her swift passage across the sky on behalf of her Goddess. Marriage rites under Juno's aegis were in the hands of women. "In marriage and family matters, women ignored God and appealed to their own Goddess," comments Barbara Walker. "The idea that a male priest should preside alone over a marriage ceremony was unthinkable—which is one reason why Christians didn't think of it." So not only does June mean weddings, June means brides: *Juno's* brides, in *matri*monial triumph.

Only the Unlucky Marry on Saturn's Day

Not only are the months tagged for or against weddings, but so are the days of the week. A brief multicultural survey reveals an array, sometimes contradictory, of recommendations about individual days. In the time of the Romans, it was customary to mark off your calendar: black letters for *dies altri* (unlucky days), white characters for *dies albi* (auspicious days). Then you could see the year ahead in straightforward black-and-white terms. There's no definitive list of proscriptions and recommendations for the best marrying days of the week, but this folklore saw from England makes the attempt: "Monday for wealth. Tuesday for health, Wednesday the best day of all; Thursday for crosses, Friday for losses, Saturday no luck at all."

Saturday Let's begin with luckless Saturday. For Orthodox Jews, the week *begins* on Saturday; for

Christians, the week *ends* on Saturday. Whither Saturn? In a sense Saturday is oroboric, both beginning and end, the cosmic snake eating its own tail—on Saturday. What's at stake is a metaphysical view of the world that sees in the seven-day week a concentrated, potentized recapitulation of the seven stages in the creation of the world, from Saturn to Venus, Saturday through Friday. To make any sense of the numerous folklore opinions about the weekdays, we must in effect entertain a cosmogony that continues to inform and inspire our human time. In other words we may find the secrets (and energies) of cosmogenesis living among us, in the ordinary working-world days of the week.

Saturday—or *Saeter-daeg* in Old English, *Setern's*-day in Saxon, *Dies Saturni,* the Romanized form of the Greek Cronus, Father Time—gets such bad press because of its association with Saturn, the dense planet of material restrictions, limitations, and finite time. Astrologers often regard Saturn as the "greater malefic," the grim harbinger of ruin and sorrow. Saturnian energy is ultradisciplinarian, reminding us of our duties, obligations, and earthly responsibilities. Saturn throws tests of endurance and unexpected obstacles in our path. It forces us to surrender our illusions and misconceptions in the face of material reality, inciting incessant small deaths of the personality. Saturn's instrument of "torture" is Time, the experience of unbounded spirit caught in biological matter. In human physiology we find Saturn in the process of ossification; Saturn lives in our bones, teeth, and joints, producing congestion and the arthritic tightening. Saturn's colors are gray, black, and dark browns, shades of old earth. Insofar as it expresses what astrologers call a Planetary Age of Man, Saturn is the end of the line, from age sixty-eight to death.

On the other side of the world, in Cambodia, we find their calendrical color for *Thngai sau,* or Saturday, is black, highly appropriate for the compacted density of Saturnian time and matter.

For the Cambodians Saturday is favored only by demons and spirits, which makes it a good day if you want to appeal to them, but not if you're trying to avoid them.

But not everybody follows these philosophical dictates. Saturday, as we know, is a favored day for connubials. "In the 1950s, when most of my friends were getting married, between 2:30 and 3:30 on a Saturday afternoon was the most popular time," reflects Britisher Ann Monsarrat in *And the Bride Wore—The Story of the White Wedding.*

Sunday The marriage proverb quoted above doesn't mention Sunday in its catechism of good and bad days for weddings probably because all "good" Christians are supposed to be in church on Sunday, and a Sunday wedding would be mixing rejoicing upon rejoicing, to paraphrase the Hebrew stipulation. Astrologically Sunday means the day of the sun's influence, or in Hebrew *Ashahed,* meaning "the all-bountiful fire." The Sun symbolizes the Self, the spirit, the individuality, the fire and light of the cosmic Father from the first day of Creation that generates and vitalizes the planets and all life.

In Elizabethan England Sunday was the wedding day of first choice, whether it was Londoners or countryfolk. Shakespeare's *The Taming of the Shrew* showcased this custom's prevalence throughout England. In this drama Petruchio explains to his imminent father-in-law "that upon Sunday is the wedding day," and expatiates even further on this theme: "Father and wife, and gentlemen, adieu, I will to Venice, Sunday comes apace; We will have rings and things and fine array; And kiss me, Kate, *we will be married o' Sunday.* " The British exuberance for Sunday lost its spunk with the advent of the Puritan "Directory for Publick Worship" in 1644, which advised that wedlock not be solemnized on "the Lord's day."

This attitude persisted throughout Victorian England so that Sunday, once among the most popular days for nuptials, became too sacrosanct

for marriages. "Victorian Englishmen," observed John Cordy Jeaffreson in his *Brides and Bridals* in 1872, "very generally concur in holding a particular day of each week, i.e., a seventh of the entire year, as too sacred for bridal mirth. A fashionable wedding, celebrated on the Lord's Day in London, or any part of England, would now-a-days be denounced by religious people of all Christian parties as an outrageous exhibition of impiety." The Church of England further inconvenienced Victorian weddings by banning marriages on their premises after midday—which meant the ritual splendors had to take place in the morning, often at hours far earlier than the Victorian gentlewoman preferred to countenance, as Jeaffreson noted.

The Moroccans contend that Sunday is a good time to commence married life because it's the start of the new week, but don't introduce the bride to your home on Tuesday (say the Tsul tribe) or Friday (advise the Ait Waráin). In the early eighteenth century, Sunday betrothals and weddings were actually banned in some areas of Scotland for their "Sabbath-daye enormities." In 1711 one northern Scottish parish decreed that "there be no marriages hereafter upon Monday," for the better preservation of the sanctity of the Christian Sabbath, Sunday. In nineteenth-century Norway and Sweden, marriages were customarily performed on Sunday, and the nuptial partying would continue for several days, "a sober bridal being almost unknown." In Ethiopia weddings are generally held on Sunday, with the couple's sexual consummation reserved for midnight. Greeks too favor Sunday for first-time weddings (Saturday evening for remarriages), although it's the culmination of feverish prenuptial rituals that begin on Wednesday but never extend to Monday.

Monday   As the Greek proverb cautions regarding the Day of the Moon: "Everything was wrong, and even the wedding was on Monday." Aside from the obvious inconvenience of Monday in terms of the standard workweek, and despite the gloom of the proverb, Monday's association with the moon and the moon's positive associations with marriages suggest that this might after all be an auspicious day for weddings.

That's the conclusion suggested by the ancient science of swara yoga, which correlates the rhythmic cycles of sun and moon with daily human breathing cycles, energetic flows in the body, and cerebral hemisphere and nostril dominance. The major flow of our breathing (and hemispheric activity) shifts cyclically from left to right to left nostril (and hemisphere) about every two hours. According to swara yoga expert Harish Johari in his *Breath, Mind, and Consciousness,* Monday (Wednesday, Thursday, and Friday, too) is good for marriage because it begins (at ninety minutes before sunrise) with an ascending (growing) moon cycle and a right-brain cerebral dominance, which has lunar, magnetic, feminine, receptive, and peaceful attributes. "Before deciding to undertake an activity," writes Johari, "one must consider the nature of the activity and whether or not the moment is right to act. Swara Yoga clearly states that certain activities are best performed when a particular nostril is operating."

Tuesday   Tuesday may be the Day of Mars the aggressor, the standard-bearer of fiery masculine energy, but still awards "health" to men and women marrying under its auspices, if folklore can be trusted. Perhaps the combative quality of Mars is overstated and misconstrued, as astrologer Alan Oken suggests. "Mars is the force which creates matter out of the primal energy of spirit," says Oken in his *Complete Astrology.* "Thus Mars is seen as a great creative impetus to the individual . . . as the vehicle of new outpourings of energy into the material world." Mars, as son of the Sun and husband to Venus, embodies the active male force of virility and procreative potency, and "the force of Man asserting his individual desires upon his environment."

Weddings among the Breton villagers of northwestern France always took place on Tuesday mornings. The Scottish middle and lower classes married on Tuesday or Friday—except the villagers at Forglen, who accounted Friday unlucky; while the upper classes preferred Monday marriages.

Wednesday Woden's-day or Dies Mercurii, the day of Mercury, the fleet-footed messenger of the Gods—Wednesday, the "best day of all," is about balance. Its color is green, its position the fulcrum of the week, the fourth color in the spectrum, and the color of the heart chakra, the mediator between mind and body. Wednesday's Mercury energy emphasizes active intelligence and the faculties of reason, intellectual and inventive abilities, writing, speaking, oratory, message-giving, and the healing arts. Mercury's equivalents in other mythic systems include Thoth, the Egyptian "Lord of Divine Books and Scribe of the Company of the Gods"; Hanuman, the Hindu monkey-god, "whose feats are great and his wisdom unrivaled"; Hermes, the Greek god of the "persuasive tongue"; and Buddha, the awakened one of divine wisdom. "Mercury's function is to separate Man from the animal kingdom through the use of the faculties of reason," explains Oken.

Sudanese villagers determine the proper time for the betrothal contract signing (the *'agid*) based on a chance divination from the Koran. About a week before the desired time of the *'agid*, on a Wednesday, for example, the bride's father reads a selection at random from the Koran. To decide whether the next Wednesday augurs well for signing the marriage contract, he examines the first letter of each word in the passage before him. If he discovers that many of the words begin with *shiin*, this is an evil portent for next Wednesday because the word for devil, *shaytaan* (the Western Satan), begins with the letter shiin; but if his chance selection turns up lots of words beginning with *kha*, this is favorable because the word *khiir*,

meaning "good," begins with this letter. Sometimes, however, it all works out more simply. As most villagers observe Friday as a holiday, the crucial rituals of 'agid and *Al Yawm ad Dukhla* ("Day of the Entry," in which the groom first crosses the threshold of his bride's family house) occur on Thursday.

Thursday "Thursday for crosses." Perhaps the origin of this intimidating expression can be laid at the feet of Jupiter (the Roman Zeus), King of the Gods. Jupiterian energy emphasizes the suprapersonal realm of divine law, the solar Father as grand vizier and temporal lord. Jupiter, according to esoteric tradition, is the cosmic seat of the ascended human masters. Jupiter signifies mature compassion born through wisdom, human contact with the universal mind, and to some degree cognition of the Plan that underlies earthly and solar life. Even this modest degree of comprehension of the essentially ineffable can stagger our human sense of proportion and significance; we see both our responsibility and its minor role in the unfolding of a vast intention—hence the "cross" of awareness and service we bear under Thursday's influence. But for a couple whose relationship aspires to aid the self-evolution and awakening of each partner, Thursday's higher-mind imperative may be the best news of the week, despite folklore's caution.

In Tangier Thursday is the most suitable day for collecting the bride from her home (but never Saturday, which is the best day for writing charms for evil purposes). In Tripoli and Egypt, Thursday night is favored; Saturday and Tuesday are evil days, entirely inappropriate for marriages. But among tribes in other regions of Morocco, it's Sunday, Monday, or Thursday. For the Scottish islanders of the Orkneys and Shetlands, engagements are formalized Saturday night, the banns (or marriage vows) are proclaimed on the next three Sundays, but the wedding ceremony is performed on Thursday, considered the week's luckiest day.

MOROCCO
EGYPT
GREECE
FINLAND
CAMBODIA
ENGLAND
SUDAN
JAPAN
INDIA
MEXICO
NEPAL
FRANCE
CHINA

THE WEEKLY NUPTIAL CAVEAT, DAY BY DAY

Marry Monday, marry for wealth

Monandaeg: moon's day: from *Lunae Dies;* Old Man in moon; karmic relationships; the eternal Great Mother; moon

Marry Tuesday, marry for health

Tiwesdaeg: Mar's Day, *Dies Martis;* Tiu, Tyr, Norse war-god; Mars

Marry Wednesday, the best day of all

Wodnesdaeg: Woden's Day, sphere of communication, the mind, conductor of souls; midweek, fourth day, heart pivot of the cosmic cycle; *Dies Mercurii,* Mercury

Marry Thursday, marry for crosses

Torsdaeg: Thor's-day, Thor the Thunderer; Roman Jove, *Dies Jovis,* Jove's-day, King of the Gods; Jupiter

Marry Friday, marry for losses

Freya's-day: Frigg, wife of Odin/Woden; *Dies Veneris,* "pagan" day of fertility, Aphrodite, the Goddess, much unwarranted bad press from Christian church; Venus

Marry Saturday, no luck at all

Saeterndaeg: Saturn's-day; Old Father Time, the black, contractive density of matter and time; Jewish sabbath

Sunday—(take the day off)

Sunnandaeg: Sun's-day, rest and repose; eternal solar Father

Friday Friday for losses? In Western European folklore, Friday, May 13, is certainly the most opprobrious, unluckiest day for a wedding in the entire calendar. It's a day of triple jeopardy, at least for patriarchs who dread the Feminine. Consider its terrors as recounted in the popular imagination: the day of Venus/Aphrodite, mistress of love, beauty, and desire, in the concupiscent, floral month of May/Taurus on the day of the witch's number of magic, thirteen. Recent feminist mythographic research and antipatriarchal polemic have reinvested Friday with its legitimate sanctity as a day of the Goddess. Friday the thirteenth need no longer strike terror into our hearts; it's merely an invocation to Venus (on Freya's-day) and her now abandoned thirteen-month lunar calendar. Viewed differently, this date could be among the most auspicious in the week—promising a triple blessing from the triple Goddess, as virgin, mother, and wise crone—for those who respect the Feminine.

Among the Jews of the Middle Ages, Friday—the seventh, concluding day in their week, and Sabbath's eve—was favored for weddings. Marriage was forbidden on the Sabbath, but the proximity of Friday to the day of rest, and the opportunity to dovetail the wedding ceremony with the synagogue services, gave Friday a strong attraction. As a variation—and possibly to appease purist rabbis—the betrothal ritual was celebrated on pre-Sabbath Friday, and the wedding ceremony was observed on post-Sabbath Sunday.

Consulting the Shadchan— *The Traditional Matchmaker*

In many traditional societies, individual men and women proposing to become married—or, more often, their parents acting as their proxies—were not expected to understand the subtle complexities of auspicious timing and mate selection. Instead they would consult a matchmaker. The traditional role of matchmaker, marriage broker, or official "go-between" in various cultures preserves the understanding that great care must be given to establishing conjugal relationships. The matchmaker didn't always have the tools for precise calculation of the best and most favorable dates, as did the astrologer (and soothsayer, fortuneteller, and witch-doctor); but the survival of this folk institution indicates an awareness of factors beyond the apparent infatuation of a young woman and man—or the dictates of their parents—in arranging a viable marriage.

In Jewish culture the matchmaker is called *shadchan,* derived from the Talmudic Hebrew verb *shedach,* meaning "to persuade, to influence." The shadchan customarily took a fee for *his* services, typically 2 percent of the bride's dowry (3 percent if the parties lived more than ten miles apart), which was more than the average business broker got (1 percent or less). Even though the role of marriage broker generated income, many shadchanim viewed their work as a pious task—a *mitzvah*—on behalf of God. In the Middle Ages, the profession of shadchan was highly esteemed, especially among Jews in Germany, and was practiced by many prominent European rabbis. As one seventeenth-century observer noted, "In earlier times, none but scholars were shadchanim." The reputation of rabbinical shadchan Jacob Molin as a masterful marriage-agent extended throughout the Rhineland of central Europe; he supported himself on his matchmaker's income so he could donate his rabbinical salary to his students for their support.

In many cases the rabbi was acutely well-suited to this complicated job of matching the destinies of young men and women and assessing the compatibility of the couple and their families. Rabbis often had acquaintances all around the country, and with their deep understanding of human nature and their upright, morally unassailable character, they enjoyed great public confidence and authority in matters of matchmaking. Eventually the public integrity of the shadchan deteriorated into a somewhat caricatured figure. It didn't help matters that traveling merchants and opportunists started taking over the shadchan's position; they were hungry for fees and as ready to hawk hearts as trinkets if it meant a sale. In Jewish folklore the matchmaker's portrait was drawn unflatteringly: an affable chatterbox, sometimes impudent, and usually willing to gloss over his client's physical and personality defects if it meant securing his broker's fee. In the twentieth century, shadchanim still flourished in Eastern Europe, and even America, where in 1929 they formed a special trade association in New York City.

Among the Egyptians the mother of a young man desiring to marry consulted a *khát'beh,* a woman who professionally arranged marriages. As recently as the 1820s in Cairo, it was customary for a man's mother, several of her female companions, and the khát'beh to visit a harem to scout out possible female partners. Or if she went alone, afterward the khát'beh would give the mother a confidential report: one woman is "like a gazelle, pretty and elegant," another is "not pretty, but rich," according to the notes of a British visitor to Egypt in 1825. If the young man was satisfied with the report, he would award the khát'beh a present and dispatch her to the family of the designated bride, where she could be counted on to give an exaggerated description of his personal, family, and financial attractions.

In Japanese villages the matchmaker, called *naishokiki* ("secret finder-out"), was often a family friend, usually a woman. When the family judged

MOROCCO
EGYPT
GREECE
FINLAND
CAMBODIA
ENGLAND
SUDAN
JAPAN
INDIA
MEXICO
NEPAL
FRANCE
CHINA

the time was nearing for their son to marry, they engaged the naishokiki to scout out likely mates. She arranged "chance" meetings between the young man and woman in her company; afterward she weighed the qualities and expressed opinions of both to decide whether to carry matters any further. The naishokiki also investigated the medical history of both families for such defects as madness and leprosy; and she evaluated their economic and social status, especially if the family was from a distant village.

Another type of Japanese matchmaker was known as *nakodo* ("one between both houses"). The nakodo, often a husband and wife team, organized the matrimonial connections. Sometimes families employed a famous person to act as nakodo purely for the celebrity status it brought to the announcement party—even if sometimes the nakodo couldn't remember the names of the man and woman he was praising in his "table speech."

In Morocco's Islamic world, a young man's marriage proposal (*hotba*) is usually preferred by male mediators called *hattâbin,* who are influential family friends. Female matchmakers, or *hattâba,* are also engaged for the preliminary arrangements, particularly by men without a family. Among the Manuvu of the Philippines, marriage proposals are initiated by the parents of the young man who engage the *melaw,* a go-between called to bring gifts and solicitations when visiting the family of the prospective bride.

The Punjabi of India had at least two categories of matchmaker. When parents sought to arrange matches among distant relatives to preserve family ties, they employed a *bichola,* or female matchmaker who was herself a relative, to perform *sak liai,* or "bringing a relation." More typically the Punjabi barber was dispatched as intermediary to a proposed match. The bride's family often hired the family barber to give *sagan* (ritually auspicious gifts) to the groom.

Among the Mayas of southern Mexico, it was considered mean-spirited for a young man to seek a wife on his own. That's why young Mayan men employed a professional matchmaker, the *ah atanzahob,* to seek a partner for him "in good time and of good quality," as one sixteenth-century Spanish bishop remarked. The ah atanzahob worked out the details of the dowry, then put the man in contact with a priest, an *ah kin nec chilan,* who consulted his astrologic "book of days" to see whether the names, birthdays, and date of the proposed marriage fell on unlucky or auspicious days.

Marriages among the Peruvian Incas were often arranged by the *tucui-ru-cuc,* ("he-who-sees-all"), the village chieftain. Old women were the *cihuatlanque,* or marriage-brokers, among the Mexican Aztecs, called in to negotiate the arrangements after a soothsayer gave his recommendation. The Aztec cihuatlanque visited the parents of the young woman, using fancy rhetoric and "fine language" to make their case. Later, during the wedding ceremony—the tying of the *Tilmantli*—the husband and wife listened to homilies delivered by at least two of the matchmakers. In Quetzaltenango, Guatemala, the groom's father seeks out a *tertulero* to act as go-between to find a suitable wife for his son. This tertulero must be resourceful; the father may literally expect him to jump over a high wall as a sign that he's able to surmount all obstacles in accomplishing his job.

For the Limbu of Nepal, the day on which a young man sets out to find a wife is itself determined by his priest, the *fedangma*. Once a prospective partner has been identified, the *ingmiva,* or go-between (usually one of the man's relatives), takes up the responsibility for completing the arrangements between the families.

Among the bourgeoisie of nineteenth-century France, marriage by introduction was arranged by matchmakers, typically elderly spinsters, cousins, or close friends of the family with impeccable reputations. These French marriage-brokers set up meetings between young people whom they judged were likely to get along. (Ironically the parents of the renowned French feminist author Simone de Beauvoir met in this paternalistic way.) In Breton village life, the time-honored function of the male marriage-broker (*le bazvalan*) and female matchmaker (*an gomer goz*) started to wane by the 1920s. But even into the 1930s many families still employed somebody—it might be the tailor, verger, bagpiper, oboist, traveling draper, the ragman, or "some old 'missus' desperately anxious to mate people," recalls Pierre-Jakez Helias in *The Horse of Pride*—to act as intermediary suitor and conjugal diplomat between the interested parties.

Among the upper-class Greeks of Macedonia, the professional matchmaker was either male (*stroinikote*) or female (*stroinikitza*). With their neighbors, the Bulgarians, the *swaty* was the intermediary commissioned by the young woman's family to procure a suitable husband. For the Romans the *pronuba* was the woman who attended the bride and assisted in the arrangements and ceremonies of marriage. The Roman pronuba saw herself working under the aegis of Juno, Goddess of marriage, whose epithet was Pronuba, divine patroness of nuptials.

The role of the matchmaker, or *svatun'ka*, was respected and precisely delineated in late-nineteenth-century Russia. Although the groom's close male relatives, eldest female relative, or father could act as matchmaker, more often it was a professional woman. Some of them evidently had a formidable reputation judging by the nicknames they acquired: Battle-Ax and Tar Brush are among the most evocative. In Kaluga the most accomplished matchmaker was called Toporikha, and her speciality was with the families of merchants. Toporikha, say the legends, knew the personal and financial particulars of all the eligible young people in her district, including the contents of each proposed dowry. She would provide this data on demand to the groom's father. When the deal was secured, the Russian matchmaker was paid handsomely, in rubles and a cashmere shawl, which became the imprimatur of the trade. The more shawls, the more competent the matchmaker—so it was said of Toporikha: "If you turn to her you will not fail; she has gained a chest full of shawls by her matchmaking."

In Eastern cultures, from Mongolia, Tibet, Korea, and China to India, Laos, Vietnam, and Malaya, timing is taken seriously. What determines the appropriateness of one date as against another for a wedding is personal and individual—and that means astrologically specific. In these cultures preparing a horoscope (or natal chart based on the disposition of the stars and planets at the moment of one's birth) for the bride and groom is essential, one of the first practicalities in planning a wedding. Couples consult their astrologer—who might also be called soothsayer, diviner, witch-doctor, medicine woman, sorcerer, fortuneteller, lama, or living Buddha—to find out if their proposed union is favored by the stars and planets and what day is most auspicious for its celebration. Sometimes even the charts of invited wedding guests are analyzed for unfavorable configurations. Horoscopic law was so precise in preinvasion Tibet, for example, that often guests whose zodiacal signs clashed with either the bride or groom and whose mere presence could invite astrological disaster were asked to remain outside the ceremonial chambers while the wedding was held *in camera.*

MOROCCO
EGYPT
GREECE
FINLAND
CAMBODIA
ENGLAND
SUDAN
JAPAN
INDIA
MEXICO
NEPAL
FRANCE
CHINA

MOROCCO
EGYPT
GREECE
FINLAND
CAMBODIA
ENGLAND
SUDAN
JAPAN
INDIA
MEXICO
NEPAL
FRANCE
CHINA

Astrology Vindicates the Pronouncements of the Matchmaker

We don't often encounter this kind of sophistication—some would call it superstition—in contemporary Western marriages. The folkways of the traditional European cultures still preserve fragments of a sacral calendar in which individual days and months of the year bear numinous import, either benefic or inimical, with regard to one's marital intentions. In this view all human acts are performed within a transpersonal celestial context, under the influence of the stars and planets, and (according to some traditions) the angelic kingdom as well.

In today's mass media, astrological information is at best entertaining, superficial filler for the back pages. But the role of the "heavens" in naming the time for a wedding isn't entirely forgotten. *Bridal Guide,* one of America's three magazines for prospective brides, published a one-page "Horoscope Star Guide" in its January/February 1992 issue, offering a "wedding day forecast" by telephone in which an expert would inform callers what the stars have in store for them on their wedding day.

The survival of this nuptial folkway tells us that behind our mundane sense of time—a sequence of neutral numbered days on a decorative calendar—there is another sacred calendar based on cosmological rhythms. In this sacred calendar, the divisions of time have spiritual import for human activities; and as any astrologer will tell you, they have an effect whether or not you're looking in that direction. In this older view, human time is numinous, suprapersonal, and nodal: for each moment or node of time, one action is favored, but many others are not; and it's individually variable, depending on where you stand within this august configuration of stars and planets. To find where you stand, you need a birth chart and astrological analysis; and to find out when it's most auspicious to stand under the wedding canopy, astrological projections from your chart are your best guide. This connotes something startling: in some respects one's seemingly insignificant wedding may implicate all the energies of the cosmos. The actual list of wedding guests may be awesome.

This is not the place to launch a defense and rationalization for the predictive science of astrology. Yet we can observe that the customs of naming the day, consulting the matchmaker, and seeking a moment of high auspiciousness derive from an older, more holistic worldview that tacitly recognized the interconnected universe; or, as the Hermetic axiom, once favored in the ancient Mystery tradition, proclaimed: "As above, so below." Cosmic events have human effects; planetary energies have microcosmic impacts on the human mind-body—in this way did common sense and initiatory wisdom alike once behold the workings of the world.

Unfortunately we have lost much of this understanding though our preoccupation (since the Renaissance) with materialist scientific thought. Instead of an interconnected cosmos we perceive a cold, perhaps Godless human existence on a lone planet in an indifferent universe. From the perspective of traditional folkways and astrology, of course, this reductionist attitude is simple-minded superstition masquerading as empirical science. A contemplation of the origins of the essential marriage customs, regardless of individual culture, reveals a deeply ritualized, metaphysically grounded, and spiritually articulate foundation. The elements of the wedding ceremonial derive from a deep perception of human nature, the dynamics of relationships, and the permeation of both by cosmic influences.

The renewal of this view would greatly enrich our spiritually starved Western customs. As Dennis Elwell notes in *Cosmic Loom: The New Science of Astrology,* "What makes astrology supremely relevant is that it discloses an unsuspected dimension of the world we think we know so well. Its chief claim to consideration lies in the outright challenge it presents to conventional opinion, because if its testimony is valid it means we have mistaken the nature of our reality." Incorporating astrological forecasting and interpersonal analysis into your wedding plans could be the first step toward acknowledging a spiritual dimension in human affairs and an initial gesture toward integrating your life into this transpersonal, primordial, sacramental dimension. Our representative example for this chapter, drawn from Chinese wedding customs, illustrates the depth, subtlety, and value of the astrological nuptial forecast as a legitimate element in the wedding process.

"The Inquiry into the Girl's Name"

Traditional, pre-Communist Chinese culture was a metaphysically rich milieu, with vast bodies of knowledge pertaining to energy, medicine, geomancy, music, and oracular prediction. One would never say of the Chinese that they ignored the data of astrology nor left the determination of dates to serendipity. Ancient China was thoroughly informed by precise star-knowledge. Traditional marriage rites in old China were prescribed in the ancient text called *Book of Ritual and Ceremonies,* which dated back at least twenty-five hundred years. The intercession of the matchmaker was incontestable in Chinese culture, as the *Book of Poetry* made clear: "In taking a wife, how does one proceed? Without a go-between it cannot be done."

The first step in arranging a traditional Chinese marriage between two young people was for the matchmaker, bearing gifts from the groom's family, to visit the parents of the young girl in question. This intermediary was usually a woman; and if she was brokering relations between high-ranking, aristocratic families, she would wear a veil over her head and a purple jacket as a badge of her position. Less prestigious matchmakers wore a cap, carried a yellow handbag, often wore a wide, full skirt, and carried a green umbrella. If the proposed match was acceptable, the girl's parents provided the Four Pillars, their portion of the crucial Eight Characters—personal data, inscribed on a red card, concerning the girl's name, hour, day, month, and year of birth, all of which was necessary for making the crucial astrological computations.

Then the matchmakers—they always went in pairs—collected the red card from the boy's parents, and took both cards, now containing the Eight Characters, to a professional astrologer or diviner for consideration. He produced a horoscope for each, contemplating their details as an augury of their conjugal compatibility. It wasn't unusual for the astrologer to request the personal data for the parents of the bride and groom as well to enrich his computations.

The diviner's job was twofold. First he (or she) must assess the suitability of the match based on a deep understanding of the mechanics and subtleties of Chinese astrology; and he must then project an auspicious or "lucky" date for the betrothal and wedding ceremony. The underlying assumption is that a precise and calculable time exists for every activity. Doing a thing on the right day can maximize benefits and ensure success for the people involved; not doing a thing because it is the wrong day can help you avoid outrageous failure and ill-fortune.

Like any complex philosophical system, Chinese astrology has its own arcane vocabulary.

CHINESE MARRIAGE PROVERBS— A USER'S GUIDE

The Serpent meeting the Hare means supreme happiness.
The Ox and Tiger will always quarrel.
The Ox can battle two Tigers.
The Horse is afraid of the Ox.
When the Pig meets the Monkey, there are always tears.
The Cock and the Snake are always at odds.
When the Tiger meets the Snake, there's always a battle.
The Sheep and Rat are always at war.
When the Dragon meets the Rabbit, good luck is shattered.
Meetings between Cock and Dog always end up in tears.
Never bring a Tigress into the house.
A Sheep as a spouse brings trouble in the house.

Derek Walters, Chinese Astrology— Interpreting the Revelations of the Celestial Messengers

Here the twelve signs of the zodiac, familiar to us in the West, are assigned the symbolic qualities of animals—monkey, tiger, snake, rat, buffalo, rooster, dog, pig, cat, dragon, horse, and goat. These exert their influence for a full twelve-month period; but they also influence two-hour periods during each day. Thus the Chinese astrologer works with a twelve-year zodiacal calendar (unlike his Western counterpart, whose model assigns symbolic qualities to individual months in a twelve-month cycle). For example, if the prospective bride was born in the Year of the Tiger and the groom was born in the Year of the Dog, this portends an "unlucky" or at least boisterous union because in Nature the tiger is likely to eat the dog.

Further, the astrologer analyzes the written names, which are ideogrammic, of the parties for their symbolism within the Chinese Five Element theory (fire, earth, wood, metal, and water). For example, if the young girl's name contains a character for fire, the astrologer says to himself: this will burn the element of wood in the boy's name. Classical Chinese marriage relations, in our perspective, were innately patriarchal, upholding the primacy of the young man's "animal" over the young woman's; so fire burning wood was judged favorable only if it was male fire burning female wood (or male water quenching female fire). If her name has earth or water symbols, however, these are compatible with the boy's wood, and will not unbalance the relationship.

When the astrologer satisfies himself that the destinies under the stars for each individual in the proposed marriage promise a fortunate match, it's time for his next function: "giving the lucky result." He writes out the astrological information on a sheet of red paper and includes the lucky day he divined for the ceremony, all in accordance with the official Chinese calendar of auspicious and unfortunate dates. The Chinese diviner will indicate the precise, lucky time for a variety of prewedding activities: the time to begin cutting out the wedding garments, the time for the groom's family to adjust the bridal bed in its final postnuptial position, the time to finish the curtains for the bridal bed, for the bride to embroider the longevity pillows, for the groom's hair to be plaited, for the bride's hair to be topknotted, and the exact time for the bride to get out of bed and enter the bridal sedan chair and set off for the groom's house on the wedding day.

The Man in the Moon Likes Cake

In Chinese folk custom, Yueh Lao Yeh, the Old Man in the Moon, is a celestial graybeard who presides over all human marriages. Yueh Lao Yeh binds the feet of couples intended by fate for each other, in their earliest childhood, with invisible red cords. The Old Man in the Moon sits up in heaven poring over his grand book of human conjugal destinies, a tome that contains the names of all newborn babies and their future marriage partners. Marriages are made in heaven indeed, and prepared in the moon, say the Chinese. Yueh Lao Yeh's decisions are incontestable. Nobody can successfully contest the marital decisions inscribed in his book, as an old folktale from the T'ang Dynasty makes clear:

Once a young man named Wei Ku encountered an ancient man seated in the moonlight studying a massive book. Wei Ku, in conversation with him, for it was the Old Man in the Moon, discovered the book was the registry of all marriages on earth. Once Wei Ku realized this, Yueh Lao Yeh withdrew his red cord from a sleeve as dramatic proof. One day Wei Ku would marry a woman who had just been born into a poor family, the Old Man told him, showing Wei Ku his future father-in-law, a decrepit old vegetable hawker. This en-

raged the young man, who expected to marry up into the higher, wealthier class; Wei Ku hired a bandit who sought out the infant, tried to kill her, and departed, telling Wei Ku he had succeeded.

Twenty years later Wei Ku had become an important official and wanted to marry. A match was arranged, but when the moment arrived and he lifted the bridal veil to see his wife for the first time, he was terribly disturbed. She had a scar on her forehead, and he was shocked when she provided the history of her wound. Born into a poor family, one day she'd been nearly murdered by a stranger. She was injured but somehow saved, then later adopted by a rich and socially prominent family. And then the matchmaker arranged her marriage with an unknown man. Greatly chastened, our Chinese groom understood that nobody contravenes the decrees of Yueh Lao Yeh because all marriages are made in heaven, or at least the moon.

When the Old Man isn't arranging marriages, he's playing chess with his colleague, the God of Longevity, in a mountain cave. With cosmic detachment these moguls discuss how one man will live for two hundred years, while another will die when he's nineteen. One eavesdropper at this chthonic chess game must have taken away the impression that Yueh Lao Yeh was appeasable, and that cake would do the trick. Every autumn villagers hold their three-day festival of the moon-cakes with midnight feasting and celebration, because that's when the moon's nocturnal influence peaks and presumably Yueh Lao Yeh is more likely to be paying attention to humans. They build an outdoor altar, usually in the courtyard of individual homes, erect the figure of a long-eared "moon hare" in its center, and lay out a dish of thirteen moon-cakes (one for each month in the Chinese lunar year) filled with spices, nuts, and sugar.

Other cultures have recognized the primacy of the moon with regard to weddings and their suitable dates. As one Greek father explained

MOROCCO
EGYPT
GREECE
FINLAND
CAMBODIA
ENGLAND
SUDAN
JAPAN
INDIA
MEXICO
NEPAL
FRANCE
CHINA

when asked what day he would chose for his daughter's wedding, "When the moon is full, for the air must be pure and the sky clear." In Cyprus the first Sunday after the full moon was commonly chosen; Greeks generally avoided weddings during the fourteen-day waning moon cycle. The dread of inaugurating nuptials during the dark of the moon was emphasized by Bishop Burchard of Worms in his eleventh-century castigation against those who were foolhardy enough to begin house-building or hold a wedding at any time other than the new moon. For couples in Borneo, the moment of the

new moon was considered most favorable for a wedding. Cambodians believe that marriages must not be formalized during the "male" (*ko buon*) thirty-day months of their lunar calendar, but only during the "female" (*ko bei*) twenty-nine-day months. Sudanese villagers consult a *fiqi* learned in astrology to determine the lucky date for a wedding according to his knowledge of the "mansions" of the moon. Our wedding, too, was set for the hour of the full moon in the month of the Tiger (Chinese) or Aquarius/Water Carrier (Western).

KARMIC REGISTRARS IN THE MOON

*W*hy does the moon get such high regard when people set their wedding dates? Invariably, when we probe beneath persistent and widespread folk customs, we discover an inner, esoteric truth that makes the outer action deeply meaningful.

In Western astrology the moon signifies receptivity in human nature—the subconscious, the "feminine" water element, emotions, behavioral instincts, collective racial memories, the personality, and the soul. Metaphorically the moon is the eternal Great Mother—Hathor, Isis, Chandra-Devi, Macha Alla, Selene, Mama Quilla, Cerridwen—the fertile, form-giving, nourishing White Goddess. In the zodiac she rules the sign of Cancer; on earth she rules the ocean tides, magnetism, and early childhood; and in human physiology the moon influences the human ovaries, uterus, breasts, stomach, tear ducts, lymphatics, and sympathetic nervous system.

The moon is the planet of fecundation and the "great time-marker of the universe," explains Rosicrucian astrologer Max Heindel in The Message of the Stars. If we liken the sun and planets to the hour-hand on the clock of destiny, showing the year in which each aspect of our destiny is ripe for harvest, says Heindel, then the moon "may be likened to the minute-hand which shows the month when the influences are due to culminate into action."

With respect to the moon, our psyche is a rain barrel. During the growing moon phase, from new to full, the barrel swells with lunar energy and influence, heightening, intensifying, quickening our impulses; in the waning moon phase, the barrel drains and empties out, leaving us in the last few days before the renewal of the new moon with only the dregs. On this basis alone, it's easy to sense why the growing phase of the lunar cycle is generally preferred for affirmative, inaugural acts like weddings.

While the psychological nuances of Western astrology help us understand why fortunetellers always gave attention to the mansions of the moon in their forecasts, Rudolf Steiner illuminates another surprising esoteric aspect. Steiner (1861–1925), Austrian founder of the spiritual science known as Anthroposophy, never fails to provide a shockingly unorthodox view, even if it's a Chinese folktale about the Old Man in the Moon. A clairvoyant, he asserted that within the interior of the moon lives a "spiritual population among whom are very high guiding beings." These etheric, nonmaterial beings once lived on earth as great teachers, educators, and founders of the primordial wisdom tradition. As moon-spirits they are the "registrars of our destiny" and the first spiritual beings we encounter in our soul journey after physical death, claims Steiner. As we journey into the farther reaches of the spiritual solar system (meaning its nonmaterial dimension), says Steiner, a soul must deposit with these moon-beings "everything that during his physical existence was the expression of his propensities, longings, and desires for earthly life." Our personality, our soul, and our karma—the weight, tendency, direction, and aspirations of our accumulated destiny—this we must leave for safekeeping on the moon. We leave our passionate nature— desire being the fuel of our destiny—in the moon. "We carry it with us as an impulse but it remains inscribed in the moon sphere," says Steiner. "The account of the debts, as it were, owing by every person is recorded in the moon sphere."

Steiner's initiatory revelation of lunar arcana vindicates the Chinese tales of Yueh Lao Yeh, and gives us a deeper motivation for factoring the mansions of the moon in our wedding plans. The spirits of the moon—or what another great esotericist, H. P. Blavatsky, called the Lunar Pitris—hold on deposit the passionate residue of our earthly emotional lives, our debts and unfulfilled desires, our karmic signature. That passionate signature is what ties us karmically to other people in a wild permutation of relationships, including conjugal; so Yueh Lao Yeh's red cord is merely the reflection of these supralifetime obligations.

So when the Old Man in the Moon—Steiner's antediluvian moon-beings—inscribes our conjugal destiny in his book and ties our feet with his unseverable red cord, technically he's only reflecting what our karma necessitates. Marriages are made, confirmed, and sealed in heaven, tied up in lovely red ribbon. Our marriage has a spiritual imperative—that's an unconventional view that's both formidable and inspiring. But it also promises something, because as Rabbi Akiva put it (Talmud, Sotah, 17a): "If husband and wife are worthy, the Holy Presence abides with them; if not, fire consumes them."

Reading the Stars in My Palms

Had I been born a Hindu in India, my parents most likely would have commissioned an astrologer to prepare a natal chart for me at birth. It wouldn't have been the trivial predictions of "Your Monthly Stars," which magazine and newspaper editors use as inconsequential filler for the back page. In India astrology has a different reputation; astrologers are as much a part of Hindu family life as the general practitioner is in ours.

Commercial astrologers must possess a university degree in *Jyotish*, usually an eight-year study program of the mathematical and astronomical principles and spiritual implications of the celestial bodies. The Hindu astrologer would have presented my parents with a probable life scenario for me, including a detailed analysis of my character, learning capabilities, possible obstacles and health problems, likely vocation, the qualities of my most suitable marriage partner, and indications of favorable and inauspicious times for making major life decisions and changes, like education, travel, change of residence, career selection—and marriage. My parents would probably contact the astrologer periodically over the years for updated information and projections based on this foundation horoscope.

"Perhaps the astrologer's most significant duty towards his community is sanctioning marriages, still mostly pre-arranged by the parents and one of the most important decisions a woman and man must take," comments Ronnie Gale Dreyer in *Indian Astrology*. For the Hindus matrimony is more than the union of two individuals; it's the joining together of two households, two families, two kinship networks, so it must be undertaken with great care. Hindu parents rely on their family astrologer to assiduously compare horoscopes of

the couple and to talk straightforwardly about the prospects and liabilities of the proposed union. Should he believe the marriage will bring disastrous results, he'll tell you without prevarication. It wouldn't be uncommon to see him adamantly rejecting the match, in a "defiant, commanding tone," expressing his disapproval with much flailing and waving of his arms, as Dreyer notes.

That's the worst-case scenario. If the astrology is favorable, he'll plot out and assign an auspicious date for the wedding. Traditionally he writes it out on paper and dispatches several children to bear the good news to the home of the bridegroom. The formality is appropriate because in this context consulting the astrologer is the first step in the wedding process. In Jain households the child with the astrologer's note stands on a stool until one of the household women gives him a sweet as she takes the document. In the evening the children are feasted and auspicious songs ring out in the homes of the bride and groom.

Of course I wasn't born Hindu, but that doesn't mean I can't consult an expert Hindu astrologer for guidance in making my marriage plans. For many years my soon-to-be wife and I had appreciated astrology's depth of insight and predictive accuracy in the context of our individual horoscopes; we felt it to be an aspect of a larger, comprehensive philosophy of the world that upholds the constant interaction of macrocosm and microcosm.

Astrology's ability to precisely delineate the interpersonal dynamics, with its geometric language of squares, trines, and conjunctions, had given rich meaning and interpretive depth to the concept of compatibility. Not only can an astrological analysis highlight difficulties and opportunities in the present time frame, but it can also outline the probable shape of a couple's future through its technique of progressions and transits. The personal implications of future movements and alignments of the planets are outlined, as well as what effects the changes in star positions might have on an individual marriage. For us, the quality of predictive, interpretive information that astrology offers is indispensable for self-knowledge and marital compatibility. So considering the advice of several astrologers as a key element in our marriage planning was a natural step.

With this in mind, my fiancée and I paid a visit to Ghanshyam Singh Birlaji, director of the National Research Institute for Self-Understanding, in Montreal, Canada. For the last thirty years Birlaji, who holds an honorary Ph.D. in Jyotish from the All India Society of Occult Science in Delhi, has been studying the natal charts and palm prints of Western clients as a basis for life counseling. Palmistry—the interpretive analysis of palm prints called *Samudrik Shastra,* "the science of human morphology," or chiromancy in the West—is one of Birlaji's specialities. Palmistry in its purest form is "a set of investigative principles meant to reveal man's own nature in his continual search for himself," Birlaji informs me. Palm prints and horoscopes in the hands of a competent reader like Birlaji can generate powerful information. Birlaji made several ink prints of our left and right palms, wrote down our birth data, made some calculations, then gave us his sage advice based on the synergistic insights from both sources.

Where Is Mars in Your House?

Marriage and the life of the householder is the first responsibility after one has reached a certain state of maturity, says Birlaji. That responsibility is to encourage the spiritual awakening of your partner. For Hindus the institution of marriage has a spiritual imperative: self-awakening of wife and husband through living together.

Rightly undertaken, marriage is a means to hasten one's evolution, says Birlaji—and even the Buddha wasn't exempt. After he had wandered about India seeking enlightenment as a renunciant practicing austerities, the Buddha, then called Siddhartha, was upbraided by his father for having ignored his wife, Yashodhra, who had also practiced renunciation for seven years. As Birlaji tells the story, Buddha met up with his wife and told her gently: "It was you who in previous lives again and again helped me in my quest for liberation. And in our last life together, my heart melted with your intense concern when you said you would like me to achieve enlightenment. It's you alone who is responsible for my chosen path. So my dear, you, too can become enlightened if you follow this path, which is the cause of my liberation."

The Buddha wasn't trying to squirm out of responsibility for his renunciant's life-style, blaming his wife for his flaws. He was thanking her for reminding him of his deepest life purpose: to become the "awakened one." Marriage can be that powerful a catalyst, says Birlaji. We needn't be Hindus to hold liberation as a high aspiration for married life, Birlaji adds. "The Indian concept of marriage brings forward the fulfillment of *Dharma,* which is one of the four divine tasks and righteous deeds in Hinduism, called *Purusharthas.* The fire ceremony, which takes place at an auspicious time set by the astrologer, promotes harmony in the newly established journey of the two-souls-as-one. They undertake a journey witnessed by cosmic fire invoked with great devotion and reverence through mantra invocations in the wedding ceremony. The husband, from this moment on, is considered Pati Parmeshwar, which means 'the Lord God manifesting as Supreme Soul.' The wife receives the title Dharma Patni, which means 'the Bestower of Wisdom who supports the role of Goddess to help her husband maintain the path of righteousness.' The male takes the oath to regard his wife as a source of Shakti, the cosmic feminine energy, to help him achieve liberation from the delusive cycles of life and death. The woman pledges to see in her husband the source of Shiva, the cosmic masculine energy, to help her achieve liberation and to help them both blend together as one."

One of the cornerstones of Hindu astrological analysis for marriage compatibility, according to Birlaji, has to do with where Mars sits in one's horoscope. Technically this refers to the angular position of Mars in the signs of the zodiac at the time of one's birth. *Mangli Dosha,* the system that describes the positions of Mars, contends that if an individual has Mars occupying the first, fourth, seventh, eighth, or twelfth Houses in their natal chart, he or she is "affected by a Mars-related defect." This individual should only marry a person who also has Mars placed in one of these Houses, otherwise a significant energetic imbalance results. "When I first started to apply this rule, I was skeptical and hesitant," says Birlaji. "But over the last thirty years practicing as a consultant and researcher, I have not found even one happy marriage where this rule of Mangli Dosha was not applied." As things turned out, we didn't have any Mars defects and we won't be mangled by any Mangli Dosha; Mars rests fairly pacifically in the tenth (mine) and eleventh (my partner's) Houses.

Within Indian astrology Mars, called *Kuja,* is an ambivalent energy. It's an aggressive, ambitious, violent, dry, fiery, impulsive, insensitive, even malefic energy; it can harm, cause accidents, incite disputes, and precipitate miseries. But Mars also energizes, imparts courage, drive, and determination, and heightens passion and sexuality. As in Western astrology, Indian astrology characterizes twelve zodiacal Houses, called *Bhavas,* which are states of being, developmental stages, and sequential life conditions within the grand theater of the solar system. The Houses are the same as the twelve standard signs of the Western zodiac; but as Houses the Bhavas take on an added personal significance for each horoscope. The Houses fit into one of four cat-

egories, according to the theory of Purusharthas: Dharma Houses pertain to life purpose and righteous action; *Artha* Houses are about wealth and finances; *Kama* Houses focus on desires; and *Moksha* Houses represent self-realization.

Now let's link the model of Houses with the Mars proscriptions of Mangli Dosha. The First House (a Dharma House) connects with life purpose, character, disposition, health, longevity, will power, and dignity, and defines the mood of the entire horoscope. The soul is born in this house.

The Fourth House (a Moksha House) involves the mother, home, happiness, emotions, the heart, comforts, the level of one's education, and endings. "Here the soul learns to stabilize its purpose through its home environment; it potentially learns how to defy instability, insecurity, and anxiety."

The Seventh House (a Kama House) relates to desires, one's spouse, partners, and married life. "In this House the soul meets its counterpart, in the form of companion, husband/wife, colleague, or business associate. This House lays the foundation for a responsible, committed, selfless, surrendering, sincere, inspired, and flourishing existence."

The Eighth House (a Moksha House) relates to final liberation, the experience of death, joint finances and economic capacity, and sexual vitality. "This House speaks of the transmigration of the soul from one life to another; it's the storehouse of ancient wisdom collected from one's past."

The Twelfth House (another Moksha House) also concerns self-realization, the bedroom, foreign travel, after-death states, solitude, and matters beyond our personal control. "The Twelfth House's renunciation of worldly pleasure halts the soul's evolutionary journey. As Master Shri Yukteshwarji says, 'It's the funeral of all sorrows.'"

"Now you can see how these five Houses play a predominant role in making or shaking the journey of an individual," says Birlaji. "The Mars position in these Houses creates a tremendous impact with its accompanying qualities of excessive activity, fire, passion, greed, anger, jealousy, and even wrathlike characteristics. Two individuals who marry with such a combination, each with Mars in one of these five Houses, neutralize each other; they sublimate each other's passion. They have the strength to cope with each other's flames of wrath, anguish, or fierce determination."

Until the Sun Shines Favorably Upon Your Palms

Besides the Mangli Dosha calculations and the fortunes of Mars, Indian astrologers also use a technical point system of fifty-two *Gunas* to gauge conjugal compatibility, says Birlaji. These points are calculated after a technical assessment of the couple's elemental mixture (how the five elements of fire, air, water, earth, and ether are combined in their psychophysical being). If a couple scores at least eighteen points, the marriage will be "average, good" and the astrologer will condone it; more rarely the compatibility points may be as high as thirty-eight to forty-five, "in which case the marriage is meant to provide a suitable foundation for the evolution of both partners." In one aspect of the Guna system, the Indian astrologer considers the vibratory qualities of each person's name. For example, Richard. My *rashi,* or Zodiac sign based on my given name, is *Tula* (Libra), which reverberates to the constellation sound of *Chitra,* which itself is the sound of *Ri,* which brings us back to *Ri*chard, Birlaji tells me.

The net result of Birlaji's vibrational etymologies is that my partner and I score nineteen and a half Guna points, just over the wire, with "some defects," as Birlaji graciously puts it. "I feel that with due patience and perseverance you can make a healthy adjustment in both your tempera-

ments to allow each other to endure more and advance in your spiritual journey."

But misplaced Mars or low Guna points don't necessarily spell finale for any match. Even seemingly incompatible charts or horoscopes strewn with obstacles are correctable, advises Birlaji. "A good astrologer will always recommend corrective measures, which are used as preventive tools to help mitigate the negative effects of unfriendly planetary aspects." At least at the individual level, the effects of the stars is mutable—the threshold between karma and free will. Corrective tools include gemstones, fasting, color therapy, nutritional and medicinal supplementation, and mantras.

Scoring high in marriageable Gunas isn't what this calculation is all about. The uniform intention is to help each partner become aware of the strengths and weaknesses, both unconscious and recognized, of his or her prospective mate; to get a preview of how each is likely to react and adjust to each other in the light of these psychoemotional influences. "As no two charts are compatible in every area or no marriage filled with heavenly joy all the time, interrupting, intruding, pervasive, and provocative planetary positions exist in each person's chart." The natal chart really becomes a practical marriage guide; similarly, the astute astrologer quickly transforms himself into a couple's counselor for the intimate field that is the husband/wife relationship.

Birlaji's comments are direct and sobering as he moves from palm prints to horoscope to "progressed transits" (a projection of future planetary movements and their ramifications with respect to a birth chart) for us both, sketching out the probable energetics of our conjugal future. Of me Birlaji says: "You are ten months into a serious transformation, a new beginning for a more definite and decisive mode of living and working. Even your hand shows it because it's becoming more spatulate-shaped. Five years ago when I last handprinted you, your hand was much more the square type. You must saturate your sudden promptness

MOROCCO
EGYPT
GREECE
FINLAND
CAMBODIA
ENGLAND
SUDAN
JAPAN
INDIA
MEXICO
NEPAL
FRANCE
CHINA

with patience and tolerance and control any temperamental outbursts which might scare your partner. Your Taurus sun is exalted in your House of marriage, which confirms your partner is of high repute; you must continually admire, appreciate, and bow to her wisdom. Her brilliance will be a constant source of gratification for you. Your sun line is growing quite successfully on your right palm, but it's not 'ripe'; its best period will be in about twenty-eight months."

I ask Birlaji about this sun line—will it burn me? Generally the Sun line refers to likelihood of success in terms of material gains, power, prestige, and popularity, he replies. But it has an esoteric aspect, too. "The line of Sun relates to an ability of the mind to rise above and beyond any limitations or interrupting forces. The individual can form a deep inner conviction and intuitive self-assurance relating to the validity of any of his experiences. This in turn gives him a sense of competence, confidence, and social magnetism and he can work effortlessly without undue self-awareness, gratifying heart, mind, and soul and without any new difficulties swallowing him up. In your case your Sun line needs further deepening because you have an inherent restlessness of thought and expectation. At some time meditation might become necessary to calm these horses of mind."

Of my partner Birlaji says, "Your Saturn and North Node (*Rahu*) conjunct in Scorpio in your seventh House of Marriage. That means you're likely to challenge the happiness of a stable home as strongly as you also cherish it. On some level you'll have to pay a price for changing your personality a great deal to enjoy the best fruits of marriage. Your partner will likely deepen your inner quest without any reticence or competition, inspiring you spiritually to bring out your best in the area of self-transformation. There is a little interference line in your palm whose effect may re-

main with you for the next two years. Regarding marriage it would be wiser to wait six months; then you will be more aware of what is happening to you." The interference line is a blessing in disguise, explains Birlaji. It might arise from family difficulties or "prenatally created karma," but like clouds momentarily eclipsing the Sun, it's an inner challenge of "serious impact" that when overcome, will yield a "lifelong support system of conviction and confidence."

"There are many aspects of your charts that magnify these points in terms of degrees of compatibility," says Birlaji, concluding his recitation of data from his twenty-page astrological report. "Both of you have to judge for yourselves. I'm paving the way for you both to reason and decide to what extent your preference for each other makes sense to both of you. It's a true blessing to prepare one's karmic unfoldment by leading a householder's life. May God bless you both in restructuring a happier life to understand and learn from each other's faults, expectations, and virtues."

It's a chastening, invigorating experience, to hear the truths and secrets of our relationship spelled out so frankly by someone who barely knows us. Birlaji's final counsel is to wait. He recommends we delay the formalization of our happier life until the Sun shines more favorably on our palms—until my Sun line matures and my partner's interference line dissolves. "For you I'm tempted to recommend marriage when your Sun line is in its best period, in two years. Then you'll feel more relaxed and equipped with the capability to view your partner in her true perspective. And for you," Birlaji continues, addressing my mate, "the results of your interference line may persist for eighteen months. If you both marry at that time you will be able to adjust and accommodate each other with added strength, confidence, and conviction."

A Synastry Chart in Our Bridal Registry

As our visit with Indian astrology indicates, a skilled astrologer can draft insightful psychological profiles of the two individuals proposing marriage, and from this analyze the favorable and difficult aspects of this energetic relationship. On the basis of this information, the astrologer may set up friendly warning signals and advisories regarding latent or underexpressed qualities that might cause problems later in the marriage.

Astrology works only with probabilities; it's never a pronouncement of immutable fate. When used intelligently, astrological forecasts can be invaluable as keys to greater self-knowledge and constructive change. As noted astrologer Liz Greene notes in *Astrology for Lovers,* astrology shows us where we are lopsided in our development. "By learning something about your own astrological makeup, you can see pretty quickly just how one-sided your own view of reality is. On any journey we need road maps. Outer road maps are plentiful enough. Inner ones aren't. Astrology is an inner road map." Paradoxically, when two people travel together, if they take advantage of astrology they don't consult two maps but one—a composite natal chart for two people.

In Western astrology the practice of merging and overlapping two individual natal charts to gauge interpersonal energetics is called *synastry,* literally, "a bringing together of" (*syn*) "stars" (*aster*). The methodology is complex, not the kind of plotting an amateur astrologer will feel comfortable with; but a competent astrologer can compile a synastry chart that reveals the interplay, challenges, and development of a human relationship. For a proposed marriage—indeed, for any kind of relationship, whether romantic, familial, or commercial—it's unarguably useful information. A synastric analysis of two natal charts to assess relationship compatibility is "one of the most important and specialized aspects of astrology as a whole," comments Penny Thornton in her excellent guide, *Synastry.* "If the couple are made aware of their own and each other's psychological weaknesses and strengths, then potentially difficult 'energies' can be understood and overcome."

My partner and I posted our birth data to Edgar Winter, Australian proprietor of Get Inspired!, one of Sydney's leading astrology firms, to have him take a synastric look at us. "By comparing and contrasting the interrelationships of two separate birth charts, the astrologer can reveal the many ways and levels in which two people relate to each other," explained Winter, who analyzed our synastry to project a favorable—"lucky"—date for our wedding.

The result is a sophisticated and personally valuable piece of information. First, the individual horoscope presents an interpretive snapshot of the quality, disposition, and tensions of planetary and stellar energies present on our individual birthdays. Second, through synastry, we get an overlay of both snapshots, producing a synergistic composite, a predictive prefiguration of what our relationship is likely to exhibit. And third, through progressing (that is, moving them forward through time) both snapshots (horoscope and synastry) six months into the future, we discover a day whose celestial and planetary energies will prove harmonious and supportive with respect to our snapshots. At least metaphorically it's as if we find a day uniquely, irrevocably slotted by the cosmos for *our* wedding—a day with our signature written all over its hours. For a discerning astrologer like Winter, synastry is a an abstract of our marriage. And for a responsible couple (as we aspire to be) that wants to approach the formalization of their union with respect, understanding,

DAILY MINICYCLES OF ENERGY AND INFLUENCE

Chinese day clock: Oriental Medicine's body clock:

11:00 P.M.–1:00 A.M.	Rat/Gallbladder
1:00 A.M.–3:00 A.M.	Ox/Liver
3:00 A.M.–5:00 A.M.	Tiger/Lung
5:00 A.M.–7:00 A.M.	Rabbit/Large intestine
7:00 A.M.–9:00 A.M.	Dragon/Stomach
9:00 A.M.–11:00 A.M.	Snake/Spleen
11:00 A.M.–1:00 P.M.	Horse/Heart
1:00 P.M.–3:00 P.M.	Sheep/Small intestine
3:00 P.M.–5:00 P.M.	Monkey/Urinary bladder
5:00 P.M.–7:00 P.M.	Rooster/Kidney
7:00 P.M.–9:00 P.M.	Dog/Pericardium
9:00 P.M.–11:00 P.M.	Pig/Triple-Burner

and insight, self-knowledge on this order can be the most valuable wedding present.

The data from our synastry, of course, has only personal value; but a few examples suggest the flavor and range of this interpretive approach: my partner's Mercury in my Tenth House means I will value her for her practical outlook on life and come to depend on her for career advice. Her Mars in my Fourth House means our relationship will have "real emotional overtones, because she has a knack for getting you right in the pit of your stomach." Her Uranus in my Eighth House highlights her directness, which can leave me "feeling exposed and vulnerable." My Sun sesquisquare her Sun means we'll tend to bang our heads together despite an abundance of natural affinity.

From out of his synastric musings, Winter gave us a date—a couple of hours before the full moon on a Tuesday (Mar's day) in February. It was as if for a moment the faces of the celestial bodies were revealed to us, and we could read the face of the cosmic clock. The conventional homily asks the planetary and stellar "Gods" to gaze favorably upon the couple's nuptials. Astrology suggests that your chances of getting a good glance from the stars on your wedding day is really a matter of understanding their predictable mechanism and trying to position yourself at the right time to get the greatest heavenly beatitudes—or at least the minimum of cosmic knocks.

Lawful Hours of the Day

We learn from astrology that there are schedules within schedules, systems within systems. Time is cosmically meaningful in a calendar of months, days, and even the twenty-four hours of the individual day. Consider these different clockwork mechanisms: (1) Oriental medicine charts a twenty-four-hour cycle for ch'i circulation throughout the body's twelve "organ" systems. (2) Chinese astrology says the twelve personality profiles (animals) each influence a two-hour daily period. (3) Western astrology's diurnal cycle plots the two-hour periods of influence of each zodiacal House on the ascendant (horizon) during a single day. So practically, if we want to maximize certain energetic qualities, we can schedule our wedding (or engagement ritual, bridal shower, and honeymoon) with respect to the exact hour within these minute cycles of influence.

We find traces of this awareness in a sampling of folkways regarding suitable times of day for weddings. For the Moors of West Barbary, articles of marriage were most auspiciously signed in the afternoon or evening, but never during Ramadan (the ninth month of "great heat" and fasting in the Muslim calendar), Lent, or on Tuesday, Wednesday, or Friday. Some Orkney seacoast couples also sought to time their weddings with the high tide, which could put the wedding at any of four six-hour intervals during the day or night.

In Shakespeare's day church wedding ceremonies often began at 5:00 A.M., which gets in under the wire for the praise of this standard proverb: "Happy is the bride on whom the sun shines." But in *Romeo and Juliet,* old Capulet is greeted at his doorstep at 3:00 A.M. by Count Paris, the eager groom, with musicians in tow; and in *The Merry Wives of Windsor,* the hour "to give our hearts uniting ceremony" was pushed so far back it was performed between midnight and 1:00 A.M. The importance of an early nuptial is captured in this old English folksaying: a woman on her wedding-morning is "The bridal flower, That must be made a wife ere noon." In the early 1600s, the church formalized this through instituting its daily canonical hours: for weddings to be valid, they must be performed between eight and twelve noon.

The Tibetans also favor an early morning nuptial, regarding the predawn hours as especially auspicious. Yogic tradition has always maintained that in the two hours before dawn we find the maximum amount of vitalizing ch'i, which is generally understood to mean life force, *prana,* or subtle cosmic energy. As any Buddhist monk or nun will tell you, it's also *the* preferred time to be up and meditating. Tibetan brides braced themselves for a 4:00 A.M. wedding ceremony—and a much earlier rise from bed—up there on the roof of the world. Shakespeare's Elizabethan early risers and the Tibetan predawners were pushing their way back into the same species of after-sunset and mid-evening wedding ceremonies observed by the Santals, some Moroccan tribes, the people of the Babar Islands, and New Zealand's Maoris.

The preference in the Lubavitcher Hasidic tradition is to marry under the stars in the early evening. In the case of a mid-1985 Lubavitcher Hasidic wedding in Crown Heights, New York City, the fact that it was winter in a giant city made no difference, because the reason for starlight weddings is unassailable. Stars are associated with God's promise to the patriarch Abraham to bless his lineage with fertility: "Thus shall thy children be, as the stars of the heaven." The bride's female attendants reiterate this link of stars and matrimonial fertility when they intone: "O sister, be thou a mother of tens of thousands!" The *chuppah,* or wedding canopy, made of four stout poles topped with a gold-fringed blue velvet canopy, was erected outside, in front of the synagogue. The groom's male assistants carried candles in the bridal procession in symbolic recognition of the profound event when lightning appeared as Israel, the bride, accepted God, the bridegroom, at Mount Sinai, in a holy marriage that wed the Jewish people with divinity.

MOROCCO
EGYPT
GREECE
FINLAND
CAMBODIA
ENGLAND
SUDAN
JAPAN
INDIA
MEXICO
NEPAL
FRANCE
CHINA

Marriage as a Path to Awakening

Some knowledge of astrology, whether it's Chinese, Hindu, or Western, helps us understand what was once a prominent element in the perennial wisdom tradition. Naming the day through astrological counsel can be an effective means for gaining a deeper knowledge of ourself and our partner, and even the mysteries of the world itself. Honoring the competency of an astrological analysis can give the partners in a relationship the lifelong habit of striving for clarity and resolution of all interpersonal issues, so that instead of stumbling from crisis to disaster, we are equipped to use the conflicts in the relationship as tools for greater understanding and growth.

Compatibility need not mean perfect harmony and domestic tranquility, which would actually be boring and could lead to stagnation. A few sparks can be valuable probes. Many psychologists now contend that some degree of tension is constructive for a healthy relationship. Responsible attention to the personality issues highlighted in both the individual birth chart and the joint synastry chart can deepen our self-knowledge and generate greater maturity and sensitivity within the relationship. Our marriage can act as a work-

shop for self-growth, should we choose to take advantage of the opportunity. Astrology is not a license to blame one's difficult moments on the stars, and from this seek exemption from responsibility. It does, however, provide the context necessary for some detachment as we struggle to understand the varying emotional pressures and psychological turmoils we experience at various times in our life.

In the larger sense, astrology teaches us that time has a sacred, sacramental dimension, as indicated by liturgical calendars and the yearly round of festivals, and that these yearly nodal points may correspond to activities and energies of the cosmos and spiritual worlds. Astrology shows us how, in the twentieth century, we can assure that our major life transition rituals can occur gracefully and powerfully in their rightful times.

When we understand the import of "naming the day," we begin to reanimate this element of the world culture wedding. At the same time, we enter a worldview brand new to us, but timeless in essence: what the ancients called the macrocosm as the greater context into which our human events, as microcosm, properly fit. We can now move on to the next phase in the eightfold wedding process—betrothal, the formalizing of the relationship and the avowal of its goals in the context of witnesses.

3

THE

YUINO

REANIMATING BETROTHAL AND ENGAGEMENT

A contract of eternal bond of love,
Confirm'd by mutual joinder of your hands,
Attested by the holy close of lips,
Strengthened by interchangement of your rings;
And all the ceremony of this compact
Sealed in my function by my testimony.
                    —*William Shakespeare*, Twelfth Night

Now that we're in love, how can we formalize the relationship? Creative options for the iconoclastic betrothal are numerous, as these examples from recent engagements highlight.

Michael, forty-one, proposed to Linda, thirty-three, at the finish line of the New York City Marathon on live television. Volunteers for the New York Road Runners Club, their job was to congratulate runners as they finished the course; during a live TV interview at the finish line, Michael fished a diamond ring from his pocket, slipped it on Linda's finger, announced to her and to the viewing audience, "This is the day we've been waiting for."

A Connecticut groom named Allan, twenty-five, devoted a full day to making his proposal to Melissa, twenty-four; at breakfast he sent her a silk handkerchief embroidered with champagne bottles; at noon she received opera tickets in the mail; in the evening he took her out to a swank Upper West Side (Manhattan) restaurant, and the waiter brought Melissa a diamond ring on the dessert tray. "The proposal is the start of the process, and it should be the most exciting time because after that you're burdened with a lot of preparation and decision-making," Allan reflected afterward.

Another groom made his case quite persuasively. He sent his intended bride gifts of poems, chocolates, flowers, stuffed animals, photographs of his palms, singing telegrams, and three engagement rings.

And then, of course, there is simplicity. A Hasidic groom, who had not kissed his partner but had dated her eight times, sent her a bouquet of roses and a handwritten card that read, "Will you marry me?"

Troth-Plight and Espousals

Yes, clearly we are in love; but why should we formalize our relationship by the *bonds* of marriage? This is the implicit question resolved in the betrothal stage. Bonds carry responsibility; they require commitments to be honored, vows to be upheld. Betrothal has lost its ritual significance in our largely secular society. We ask our partners, usually in private, if they will marry us; and the results of the proposal are then presented to the public as a fait accompli. But in an earlier time, making a marriage proposal was tantamount to explaining, even justifying, why one was a suitable, desirable mate, and was virtually the same as making one's nuptial vows.

A man would say: Marry me because, not only do I love you, but I promise to act in *this way* with regard to you. He then articulated what "this way" would entail through saying his vows. In addition to position, family, income, property, physical appearance, or other material blandishments that were once considerable factors comprising the arguments for a match, a man proposing to a woman made his case by avowing his commitment and marital intentions. The marriage proposition was the occasion for the first formulation and expression of matrimonial vows—the ways in which the bride and groom promise to act after marriage. The exchange of vows required witnesses to ratify the goals, and later to testify to the couple's original intent when perhaps the exigencies of the relationship obscure them.

For many couples today, the public dimension of the wedding process begins with bridal showers and registry lists, then proceeds dizzyingly through to the marriage ritual. The betrothal stage and first articulation of vows is private and thus peripheral to the public show. Impassioned proposals only happen in the movies—the old black-and-white romances from the 1940s. Typically engagement means a man proposes to his partner in privacy, and if she accepts he gets her an engagement ring—diamond, if he's flush—as a memorial of their joint commitment. Engagement as a crucial, ritualized stage isn't included too often in the grand progression of contemporary wedding plans and complex arrangements; it's personal to the couple, a formality, and sometimes a business negotiation if both people are propertied. Its timing is often serendipitous, even whimsical, as the examples above illustrate; as a result, its import diminished, it's a brief preface to the main text.

In Old English this important stage in the wedding process was called "troth-plight" (later, betrothal) and later, "espousal." Troth-plight—the words still carry an inspiring vision of conjugal responsibility and intention. *Plight* means to pledge, warrant, assure, or bind; *troth* means one's word, oath, promise, in effect, one's personal truth and verity. In practice, then, troth-plight means to make, out of good faith, fidelity, and loyalty, a solemn promise and covenant to marry—in other words, to be-troth. Troth-plight means more than a couple agreeing to marry on a certain future date; it establishes the meaning of marriage at a far deeper level of intimacy and bonding between the woman and man. Betrothal, in this strict and pure sense, is really the antecedent and underpinning of all subsequent marriage vows. The betrothal stage, then, is far more significant than the later formal joining ritual, which is more of a public confirmation of the pledged intentions engaged at this foundational stage.

In Elizabethan times plighting one's troth was virtually the wedding ceremony itself, as Richard Whitforde noted in *A Werke for House-holders* in 1530: "Here I take thee Margery unto my wyfe & thereto I plyght thee my trouth. And she agayne unto him in lyke manner." Shakespeare's *Twelfth Night* provides a cogent description of the formalities of the Elizabethan betrothal ceremony—the hand-joining, the kiss, the exchange of rings, all of which are offered as confirmations of the "eternal bond of love" thereby pledged. As Shakespeare recounted, the two individuals plighted their good faith to each other, usually before witnesses; thereafter they considered themselves as if already united in wedlock.

The proverbial "Scottish marriage" was an act of free union ratified by *handfasting* (the couple clasping hands) before witnesses, while declaring forthright that they were by this act husband and wife; this was once considered legally binding in Scotland. In the classic Catholic espousal ceremony, the man and woman pledged their fidelity in the church before the bishop and several witnesses, thus ratifying the nuptial contract, or *sponsalia;* as St. Augustine formulated it in the fifth century, the articles of agreement of marriage (*tablulae matrimoniales*) were read aloud and signed and then the man presented the woman with the *arrha,* usually a ring or other present (literally, "earnest money," a formal gift-giving gesture called *subarrhation,* a token derivative of the earlier practice of paying a bride-price).

When we understand troth-plight's intention and review its ceremonies through a survey of ethnographic examples, we'll see why the betrothal phase could usefully be brought back, reanimated, and creatively reconstructed and ritualized as a key aspect in the world culture wedding. In essence the betrothal stage involves presenting vows (espousal) between partners in the context of a ratifying community of witnesses. Betrothal affirms and defines the relationship in an act that requires witnesses for confirmation. Traditionally, as in this chapter's representative example, the *yuino* from Japan, those witnesses are parents, who act as chief negotiators and chaperones; but there's no reason why we can't copy the form but substitute a circle of peers in place of exclusively the parents. Parents,

relatives, and family members can participate, of course, but as coequals to a larger community assembly of friends, colleagues, and gender peers. This community witnesses, testifies to, blesses, and ratifies the couple's public avowal, or espousals, and symbolically seals the betrothal agreement and commemorates the occasion with a variety of means, including a ceremonial meal, engagement rings, religious blessings, the exchange of drinks, foods, gifts, household goods, and entertainments and symbolic gestures.

Before "espouse" came to mean "to wed," it actually referred to the stage at which the parties made their contract to get married. Espousal meant the "assured pledge of a perfect promise, *i.e.,* the ring of engagement," as John Cordy Jeaffreson remarks in *Brides and Bridals.* Spouses were acknowledged to be regularly engaged, or betrothed, lovers, but not yet legal husband and wife. For example, the man became a spouse when he declared his intention to his partner: "I *will* take thee for my wedded wife," meaning, he hereby plights his troth; later, at the marrying-service, his verb tense shifts to the present, when the vows and promises are formally stated: "I take thee for my wedded wife."

Various tokens were always exchanged as a mark of a couple's troth-plight. The groom might present his future bride with a pair of gloves, two oranges, two handkerchiefs, and a red silk girdle; wealthier couples exchanged gifts of lace, kerchiefs, ribbons, and locks of their hair made into true-lovers' knots. Or they might break a "ring of pure gold" (or silver) in two pieces, each keeping one half to commemorate their verbal pledge; a more pecuniary couple might break a ninepence silver coin, breathing and casting their oaths and prayers upon both halves, then each keeping one half, to rejoin them again upon their marriage. It was customary to wear the broken piece of money or bent metal on a neck-string so that it rested over the heart as a constant reminder and quiet benediction. They believed that the halved coins

JAPAN
PALESTINE
CHINA
GREECE
ICELAND
TURKEY
MOROCCO
RUSSIA
BELGIUM
HUNGARY
NETHERLANDS
TIBET
GUATEMALA
ITALY
POLAND

became virtuous amulets imbued with sanctity and curative properties, and were safeguards to ward off evil influences. Couples could also wear a flower as a conspicuous emblem of engagement.

In Roman times the groom sent his bride an iron ring called *annulus pronubus,* the antecedent of the engagement ring, initially worn on the woman's left hand. If the groom was indigent, his kiss could serve as a pledge. We take kisses for granted, but in an earlier, more chaste age, the virginal espousal kiss had nearly mystical significance. "By the joining of their lips, spouses were thought to commingle their spirits, and to be made one human life," explains Jeaffreson. The kiss "ratified the exchange of hearts" and signified their complete spiritual union. The betrothal was "attested by the holy close of lips," said the priest in Shakespeare's *Twelfth Night.* "Wet bargains" were considered more binding than "dry" ones, too. When it was learned that with respect to the details of her engagement, an Elizabethan woman admitted she and her groom "broke no gold between" them nor "drank to each other," their marriage contract, it was judged, "cannot stand good in law." The espousal contract must be solemnized with drinking, as the seventeenth-century dramatist Thomas Middleton noted in *No Wit Like a Woman's:* "Ev'n when my lip touched the contracting cup."

The "Main Tea" of Yuino

The yuino, a Japanese betrothal ceremony, involves family members in a scripted, hierarchical scenario that the world culture wedding can emulate—at least in its spirit and ritualized drama. In the traditional Japanese ceremony of yuino we find preserved a complete ritual for betrothal, involving the families of the couple, gift-giving, drinking, and vow-making. Originally yuino marked the transfer of gifts from the groom's household to the bride's by the *nakodo,* or intermediary matchmaker, but without any face-to-face meeting between the couple. Later the yuino ceremony included all parties to the marriage but remained a close-knit family affair. In its purest sense, the ritual had two parts: the first was called *saketate* ("offering sake wine"), in which the two sets of parents negotiated the dowry and terms of the marriage; the second was yuino (from *yuimono,* meaning "gifts of betrothal"), with the formal "main tea" ritual of *honja.*

The classical Japanese yuino was paternalistic. The parents held the negotiations and made the arrangements, presenting it to the marriageable "children" as a beneficent fait accompli. The goals behind yuino are threefold: to establish a mutual, cordial relationship between both families; to assure the continuity of the family line; and to gain social approval for the proposed match. While the yuino's implicit paternalism is unsuitable for most Westerners, the idea of including the parents (and extended family, even children, if it's a second marriage) of both couples in an egalitarian betrothal ritual is a useful, possibly fruitful one. In place of the parents as the dominant actors, as suggested above, we can substitute our gender peers, professional colleagues, teachers, mentors, or counselors, and other couples.

The initial saketate stage is also called *kimeja,* meaning "decision tea," and *kugicha,* meaning "nail tea," to signify the binding nature of the meeting between parents. Here the groom's family present gifts of tea, sea bream (a favorite Japanese fish), and sake wine to the bride's parents. Members of both families dress formally in black, the women wearing the traditional black kimono inscribed with family crest, the men in black suit and tie. The ceremony itself, though simple, must be conducted with scrupulous precision. The groom's father kneels, like everyone else present, on the soft tatami floor mat, and presents his gifts to the bride's family, saying: "*Kochira no ojosan o kudasai,*" which means, "Please give this to your daughter." The gifts are accepted, a meal is served, and details of the forthcoming yuino are discussed.

The saketate gifts each have symbolic significance. The sea bream (called *tai,* and phonetically linked with *omedetai,* meaning "congratulations") are presented on a platter, with their stomachs pressed together as an explicit reference to the fruitfulness of the union. The tai have labels with the Japanese character *shimeru,* which means "to tie up," implying the binding together of two families into one joint destiny. Depictions of the crane and turtle, both symbolizing longevity, are found on the rim of the red lacquer platter, whose color signifies a celebration.

A few weeks later, a more elaborate yuino ceremony initiates the contract of matrimony. Again the groom's family offers gifts, but this time they are more impressive, costly, numerous, and symbolically important. There are ten gifts in all, which include money, materials for the bride's kimono, and symbolic objects; but as the Japanese prefer odd numbers (because an odd number can't be evenly divided or cut up), the gifts are often amalgamated into nine or eleven items. Usually the gifts are wrapped in open hexagonal envelopes, white outside, red inside, tied with gold thread in ornate designs, and decorated with images of the turtle and crane; gifts are commonly tied with *noshi,* or dried abalone.

The first gift is actually the list of contents (called *mokuroku*) for the whole presentation; the second is the *naga noshi,* the "long" dried-abalone binding of the gifts itself. *Tomoshiraga,* or "white hair together," is the third gift, which signifies, usually through a length of hemp used to bind wooden clogs, the unseverable conjugal bond. Next the bride receives two white fans (called *suehiro*), to symbolize prosperity and happiness;

again, the intention of presenting two gifts at once is to skip over the even number four, considered unlucky, and move directly to the fifth gift. The next two gifts are dried cuttlefish (*surume*) and dried kelp (*konbu*), accompanied by two pieces of dried, flaked fish called *katsuobushi,* used as a seasoning. The main reason for cuttlefish and kelp being gifts is etymological: the Japanese characters in their names are similar to those in characters translated as "female longevity" (cuttlefish) and "child-bearing woman" (kelp).

You couldn't have a yuino without something to drink, which is why the next gift is a *yanagidaru,* or "willow-wood barrel," of sake (about 3.6 liters), traditionally in the form of a relacquered bucket with long wooden handles. In recent decades the Japanese have included the Western-style engagement ring called *yubiwa* to the yuino gift package. The characters for the word *yubiwa* mean "finger" and "circle"; but in the context of the yuino, they take on the additional nuances of "bind, beauty, and peace." Sometimes the bride will also receive a black kimono, called *tomosode,* as a generous coda to the groom's family's gift-giving.

The yuino ceremony takes place in the bride's family home in a decorative alcove called the *tokonoma* within a specially provisioned room. Here the groom's family set out their gifts as they exchange formal, ritualized greetings with the bride's family. Often the nakodo is present as an officiator, and makes a brief formal statement noting the day's auspiciousness and expressing his anticipation that the nascent relationship will prove enduring, carefully selecting words such as "forever" and "everlastingly." (Here Western couples might substitute the nakodo for their marriage's spiritual godparent, benefactor, or mentor; or justice of the peace, minister, priest, or rabbi.)

The groom's father says: "This is the yuino from this family; please accept it eternally." The bride's father graciously accepts the yuino, then inspects the gifts on behalf of his daughter; sometimes he writes out a receipt, which marks the formal conclusion of the ceremony, followed by a meal and drinks. In contemporary Japan the bride often gives the groom simple gifts, such as a watch, tie pin, or cufflinks. "The formal ceremonial content, therefore is minimal, a simple exchange handled in polite language," note Michael Jeremy and M. E. Robinson, in their firsthand sociological study, *Ceremony and Symbolism in the Japanese Home*. "As is often the case, however, it is in the preparation and arrangement that people show their awareness and concern."

Kiddushin—*Establishing the Marriage Bond*

In the orthodox Jewish marriage ceremony—*Ke'dat Moshe Ve' Yisrael*—betrothal, or *kiddushin* (the act of acquisition), was originally the first event, followed weeks later by the nuptials, or *nissuin* (the act of union). Kiddushin is an implicitly sacred ritual, as its name itself indicates, derived from the Hebrew root KDS, meaning "to be holy." Kiddushin avows that through marriage we sanctify our existence. But beginning in the twelfth century in Germany and France, the two components, formerly separated in time, were fused into one ceremony performed on the same day and including the marriage proposal and contract, the exchange of rings, and benedictions as its central elements. However, among the Samaritans, an ancient Hebrew sect formerly occupying central Palestine, the betrothal ceremony remained an event performed separately from the formal wedding ritual; as such it contains elements useful for the world culture wedding.

For the Samaritans the act of engagement (kiddushin) involves parental supervision of both the young woman and her chosen groom. When the parents are notified of the son's marital choice, they visit the young woman's family, who tells them, "We will call the damsel and inquire at her mouth." The engagement is ratified at the prospective bride's family home and may be sanctified by the recitation of the *Shema,* or verses from the Pentateuch by a Samaritan priest.

The next stage, *erusin,* technically marks the betrothal. The young woman may not be present, but a representative, usually her father, uncle, or guardian, acts as her proxy in the meeting with the future groom. The groom and the bride's proxy clasp right hands as a sign of the bond; the priest places his right hand over this handclasp and pronounces blessings. Then the young man hands the priest a tied handkerchief with six silver coins, which he transfers to the bride's representative as a symbolic bride-price, in recognition of more ancient customs when brides were purchased. The priest reads aloud from the scriptures: "It is not good that the man should be alone; I will make a helpmeet for him." The groom kisses the hands of the priest and other notables present and, strictly speaking, he is now married.

Among the Jews of medieval central Europe, at a time when the betrothal and joining rituals were still separate, activities after the conclusion of the initial marriage arrangement (known as the *te'nai shidukhin,* "first conditional agreements") were usually supervised by an intermediary. It was customary to next draw up a legal contract (called *ketubah,* and representing the "last conditional agreements") between families, stipulating the date for the wedding, the bride's dowry, and the monetary penalty for breach of contract or subsequent divorce. Important familial business deals such as these were accompanied by a banquet, called *Knas-Mahl* (a German-Hebrew hybrid

KETUBAH—THE MARRIAGE CONTRACT

*I*n our highly litigious society, wedding bells can easily signal the need for a prenuptial agreement. The trend in the 1990s is for these to become complex financial documents, often running to forty pages, and costing on average $2,000. In this economically charged context, it's more often balance sheets and bottom lines the couples negotiate rather than marital obligations and relationship vows. Where once both sets of parents officiated at the betrothal, now it's two lawyers who hammer out the "relinquishment" details (in the "hypothetical" event of a divorce) of estate and support rights, property ownership, and disposition percentages—an arduous, protracted experience in which couples expose their financial souls. Some couples now include a "sunset clause" calling for contract renegotiation in three years or after the birth of their first child.

On the positive side, the marriage contract can also include an affirmation of the marriage goals, aspirations, and commitments of both parties, and to carry that intention forward in time, even reminding them in times of stress and dissension of what they pledged in good faith. While such a contract is a relatively new innovation in American Christian marriages, it has a long history among the Jews, where it's known as the ketubah.

The ketubah is the formal, written Hebrew marriage contract drawn up in the presence of witnesses and stipulating the husband's obligations to his wife. He presents his bride with the ketubah during the wedding ceremony, after its contents have been read out loud to the congregation. Although the flavor and tone of Orthodox Hebrew customs have been criticized as being too patriarchal, the ketubah's sole intent actually is to honor the woman's independence and protect her financial well-being in the event of divorce. The groom may woo and propose to her, promise to support her financially, and generally initiate the entire process, but it's the bride's inalienable right to give positive, willing consent (called daat) to the union; without this, the marriage cannot be legal. In exchange for her consent, which she acknowledges by accepting his ring during the wedding ceremony, the husband presents her with the ketubah, which declares his binding obligations.

The husband declares: "I shall work for thee, honor, support, and maintain thee in accordance with the custom of Jewish husbands who work for their wives and honor, support, and maintain them in truth, and I shall go with thee according to the ways of the world." The ketubah also accords remunerative rights to the husband; if his partner "transgresses the Mosaic Law or womanly etiquette" such that this precipitates divorce, she may forfeit some or all her ketubah protections. At the conclusion of the te'naim negotiations, and the acceptance of its terms (called kinyan), the two mothers involved wrap a plate in a cloth napkin and together break it over a chair. The shattered pieces of the plate remind the bride and groom of the moral severity of breaking their te'naim: once it's broken, it cannot be mended and must be discarded.

expression meaning "penalty-feast"), sponsored by the bridegroom.

The engaged couple exchanged gifts at the Knas-Mahl and themselves received gifts such as rings, garments, prayer books (an illuminated Haggadah for Passover eve rituals, for example), sweets, confections, girdles, hair ornaments, and money from their friends. In Germany the bride's father presented the groom with a gold engagement ring, while the bride didn't get a ring until her wedding morning. But for Jewish women in Greece, Turkey, and Italy, engagement rings—often several, if they could arrange it—were bestowed at the time of betrothal. These engagement rings weren't actually wearable: they tended to be stunningly large metal hoops with ambitious designs worked in gold, such as a miniature turreted building (typically the Temple of Jerusalem) with movable weather cock at its apex. Folk tradition asserts that a sprig of myrtle was often inserted within the ring, which also bore the Hebrew good luck inscription, *Mazel tov!*

The Ceremony of the Cups

The Chinese family-based betrothal ceremony is similar in spirit to the Hebrew kiddushin and Japanese yuino rituals. In China, after the astrologer had confirmed the suitability of the proposed match and determined the most auspicious date for the wedding, the two families proceeded to an exchange of red cards as the opening act in the betrothal ritual. The day for this card exchange was set according to astrological counsel. The groom's card contained vital biographical, familial, historical, and professional information, listing, for example, the official functions of family members for three generations, his birth data, and his

inheritable property. The bride's family next sent their own card, which contained the young woman's birth data, status in the family, prospective dowry, and list of inheritable, transferable property. Both cards were delivered in dishes decorated with colorful cloths. When the card exchange was completed, the bride's family chose another day of lucky augury for the "ceremony of the cups," the next key element in the Chinese traditional betrothal.

The bride's parents visited the groom's family at their house, unless they had made arrangements to meet in a separate garden or on a boat. Bride and groom exchanged marital promises in each other's presence while exchanging cups of rice wine in a precise manner: the man drank four cups, then the woman drank two. Next the man stuck two hairpins into his partner's topknot (or, alternatively, two strips of brightly colored satin were dispatched to her home). Afterward came a flurry of gift giving. The groom's family sent her a bevy of presents, including head ornaments, gold vases, brocade skirts, rice wine, and culinary delicacies; and her family reciprocated by sending the groom's family presents of cloth, rings, two sticks, two onions, and two bowls with four live red fish swimming in them, a rite known as the "sending in return of sticks and fishes."

For the Chinese marriage is a gradual process with many carefully orchestrated stages, as Francis L. K. Hsu observed in 1943 in her observations of Chinese culture and personality, *Under the Ancestor's Shadow.* For example, in the community she studied, the first stage in the betrothal process marks "the beginning of the formal admission of the relationship"—which means that a lot of presents wrapped in red paper are exchanged. Here, incidentally, is a lucid expression of the hidden agenda of the betrothal stage: the *formal admission* in the company of witnesses of the relationship and its intentions. Regarding presents, specifically, the groom's mother presents the bride's family with six or more pairs of sugar lumps (one pair weighs two pounds); two or more packets of water-pipe tobacco (about a pound and a half); two bottles of white wine; several pounds of sweetmeats (walnuts, pine nuts); and cash (in 1943, $1,000). This bounty was followed by a banquet, yet it marked only the first of three gift-giving gestures by the groom's family—the *Hsiao Ting*, or minor betrothal. Later the young man's family will send such presents as jade bracelets, silver hairpins, and earrings, plus, on average, up to $10,000 in cash. Almost unbelievably, the third cash award is yet larger: close to $40,000 (in 1943 dollars), accompanied by half a cured pig, four other kinds of food, and materials for dressmaking. Truly the Chinese bride is materially blessed, one would naturally think, but we must remember that even in the 1940s early betrothals—beginning at age seven—were preferred among families described by Hsu.

The groom's family makes two further gifts during the months after betrothal and before the wedding. At the time of the autumn festival (the fifteenth of the Eighth Moon), the young man's family sends a large, round wheaten cake; made from white flour, it's very sweet, decorated in red with floral designs, three feet in diameter, and weighs twenty pounds. Then, on the seventh of the Ninth Moon, the boy's parents send another twenty-pound cake topped with flowers, this time mixed with sorghum to turn it yellow. The family and relatives of the young bride are free to enjoy the culinary spoils of betrothal. In the Ting Hsien rural community in northern China, it was customary as recently as the 1950s for the groom's family to dispatch the matchmaker with literally a cartload of presents a few days before the wedding. These presents typically included twenty-four loaves of bread, a box of noodles, salt, rice, and half a pig. The bride's family kept everything except one half of the pig (that is, one quarter), which they returned to the groom's family along with the traditional red boxes containing the bride's dowry.

According to a more recent account (1971), this is what the groom sends, all born on a red tray by the matchmaker: a leg of roast pork, money, two bottles of brandy, two ducks, two fowls, two candles ornamented with colored paper, and a small box containing the astrologer's recommendations. The bride accepts one fowl, one duck, one slice of pork, all the money, and both candles, which will be lit at the birth of their first son, and sends the rest back. Next, both families pay obeisance to their household deity, the *Tokong*, which might be an idol or picture of a "sainted" countryman or woman. The completion of this genteel ritual of cups, gifts, and trays marks the betrothal, after which the astrologer determines a favorable date for the wedding.

The Gimmal-Ring

The betrothal ring succinctly and tangibly summarizes the entire betrothal process and its espousal of vows in the presence of witnesses. As a public matrimonial document, the engagement ring continually testifies to the couple's intention to enter the bonds of marriage. A common practice, and one anciently observed in the Anglo-Saxon *trowhplyht* (troth-plight) process, was for the couple to break a piece of gold or silver in two, each one keeping a half as a betrothal memorial; after breaking the gold, they drank to each other. As Doggett noted wryly in his *Country Wake* memoirs (1696) with respect to his betrothed wife: "I ask't her the question last Lammas, and at Allhollow's-tide we broke a piece of money, and if I had liv'd till last Sunday, we had been ask'd in the church." Couples made their vows to heaven and ratified them on earth by pledging a piece of gold broken jointly to tie and seal the matrimonial knot. An added measure of good luck was believed to accrue to those who broke a crooked coin.

In an attempt to replace the laborious breaking of coins, the gimmal-ring was introduced. The gimmal-ring (from the Old French *gemel,* meaning "twins," or things associated in pairs, and *gimmes,* meaning linked fastenings) was a jointed finger ring that could easily be pulled apart or rejoined, forming two halves or a single ring, as the occasion demanded. During betrothal the man and woman each inserted a single finger through one of the gimmal-ring's hoops, symbolically "yoking" themselves together; often they did this in the presence of witnesses and with their hands held over a Bible.

In its simplest form, the gimmal-ring comprised two circlets (sometimes one gold, one silver), although if they were contrived by a jeweler, they might bear the inscriptions of their partner's name. A more complicated gimmal-ring might have five or eight connected parts, on which the words of a concise posy on the qualities of chivalric love were inscribed. For example, the five-hooped golden gimmal-ring presented by Edward Seymour to Lady Katherine Grey bore this poetic inscription within its polished surfaces:

> As circles five by art compact show but one ring in sight,
> So trust uniteth faithfull mindes with knot of secret might;
> Whose force to breake but greedie Death no wight possesseth power,
> As times and sequels well shall prove; my ring can say no more!

In the case of a gimmal-ring with more than two circlets, the supernumerary portions were given to witnesses of the betrothal contract; they would return the hoops at the altar when the ring was made whole again. The fancier gimmal-rings were so crafted that each of the hoops had upon it a miniature hand (sometimes bearing a heart) issuing from a sleeve; when these were united, as the gimmal-ring's hinges closed upon themselves, this caused the hands to join in a clasp, suggesting love, fidelity, and union. As a variation the one-jointed gimmal rings of the early Christians often had representations of pigeons or fish, as well as the dual clasped hands. Italian espousal rings of the sixteenth century were typically in silver inlaid with niello; the shoulders of both hoops formed sleeves from which issued a right hand; both right hands were joined. But the medieval Italians also fashioned betrothal rings from diamond, calling it the *Pietra della Reconciliazione,* because they believed diamonds emanated a virtue that enabled husband and wife to maintain concord. A fifteenth-century Yorkshire betrothal ring depicted two orpine plants (a perennial herb with purple flowers) joined by a true-love knot under the motto, "My sweetheart wills."

Sometimes the groom got a more tangible true-love knot when his betrothed wove some of her hair—"a snip of woven hair, in posied lockets" as one poet said—into this traditional form. As a woman admits in *Cupid's Revenge,* a play by Beaumont and Fletcher: "Given earrings we will wear / Bracelets of our lover's hair / Which they on our arms shall twist / With their names carv'd on our wrist." The Irish bride would weave a pair of hand bracelets from her tresses. Other seventeenth-century testaments to betrothal ardor included pink flower "sops-in-wine," "rush-rings and myrtleberry chains," ribbons, handkerchiefs, garters, gloves, scarves, and fans "worn of paramours" and displayed publicly and proudly. Among medieval Genoese suitors, it was obligatory to present his *sponsina,* or betrothed, once she had formally accepted his hand, with a fresh bouquet of flowers—the bigger, the more ardently committed the suitor, it was believed—every day, which she displayed publicly as her mark of distinction.

The Family's "Half-Wedding"

Among contemporary Greeks the betrothal ritual is a highly festive event involving all the members of both families. Traditionally the father or eldest brother of the groom visited the household of the bride, which offered him Turkish delight (an intensely sweet, rich confection) and ouzo (a licorice-based spirit). The heads of the two families exchanged rings to formally seal the marriage contract. The representative of the young woman handed over her wedding ring, which was tied up with rice, red and white wool, and a gold coin in a white handkerchief, to the groom's party; they received in exchange the groom's wedding ring. Thereafter bride and groom maintained their partner's ring by their side until their wedding day, as a pledge that their betrothal would be honored by nuptials.

In recent decades much more of the Greek family has started to participate in the exchange of rings ceremony. They arrive at the bride's home on Sunday, where they are regally entertained with dancing and feasting well into Monday morning. Musicians with *daouli* (large drums) and bagpipes keep the air lively with dance songs, while family members—and often nonfamily villagers—enjoy fried octopus and great quantities of brandy and special liqueurs. On account of this prodigy of partying, the Sarakatsani of Greece refer to this phase of the marriage service as the "half-wedding," considering it the sacramental equal to the later joining ritual of Crowning.

About one hour before the reveling groom's party is about to leave—around five o'clock in the morning—the bride appears in the doorway bearing a tray of Turkish delight and small glasses of ouzo, which she offers to everyone present, including her future husband. Fifteen minutes later she reappears with cups of coffee, which she offers to the groom and his family. As a variant the couple might plight their troth by exchanging glasses of sweet liqueur and heavy rings.

The bride receives a series of symbolic gifts from the groom's family: a pair of new shoes, with a gold coin in the right one, which indicates prosperity on her new path in life. The brother of the groom places the shoes at her feet and greets her, taking her right hand in his. She returns the greeting, carrying his outstretched hand to her lips, to her forehead, and back to her lips, as a sign of respect and welcome to her new family. Other gifts are presented to the bride, including pieces of gold and silver, jewelry, earrings, bracelets, and necklaces with pendant crosses. The women of the groom's family formally greet the prospective bride by kissing her on the right cheek, then the left; she responds with the same hand-blessing she gave her new brother-in-law. Finally she kisses the hands of her parents and leaves the room.

"The Gods Bring Luck! I Betroth Her"

In the classical Roman betrothal sequence, first the *dos* (dowry) and *donatio* (a substantial marriage gift) were paid by the groom's family to the bride. Then the future groom and the bride's father exchanged words. "Do you promise to give your daughter to me to be my wedded wife?" the suitor demanded. "The gods bring luck! I betroth her," replied the father. The couple kissed and the groom slipped an iron ring on the fourth finger of his fiancée's left hand, because the Romans contended that a vein ran from this finger straight to the heart. The Roman paterfamilias may have conducted most of the betrothal business, but his

daughter's freely given consent was indispensable according to Roman law: *Nuptias consensus non concubitus facit*, meaning, "Consent, not intercourse, makes marriage."

vows in front of witnesses and sealing the commitment, again in the presence of witnesses, with a ring. The ring and the word of the witnesses would then bear public testimony to the couple's espousal until the time of the wedding.

A *Viking* Festar *Ends in a Handshake*

In the Scandinavian betrothal rituals (the *festar*) of the Viking age, the tie between the *festarmadr* (betrothed man) and *festarkona* (betrothed woman) were considered legal and essentially unbreakable. The woman's father, guardian, or kinsman—the *giptingar-men*—conducted the betrothal, which he sealed with the festarmadr with a *handsal*, or formal handshaking; meanwhile both parties named specific witnesses to their betrothal. The newly betrothed man declares on behalf of his kinsmen: "We name witnesses that thou (name) bethrothest thyself to me (name) with a lawful betrothal, and givest me the *heimanfylgja* (the "home-following," or dowry) with hand-shaking, as the fulfillment and performance of the whole agreement which was a while ago recited between us without fraud and tricks."

In Iceland a very large ring, variously made of silver, gold, jet, stone, or bone, was used at this point to ratify the agreement; it was so wide that the palm of the groom's hand could fit through it. As part of the solemnization of the betrothal agreement, the bridegroom passes four fingers and his palm through the ring to receive the bride's hand on the other side. Unless there were technical obstacles or faults with either party, this oral statement secured the lawfulness of the betrothal, which typically would last no longer than twelve months. In this vivid example, we see combined the central betrothal elements of making marriage

The Canonical Engagement

The betrothal ceremony assumes a spiritual dimension when it's undertaken as a blessing, with religious intermediaries as witnesses. The canonical engagement is a formal betrothal ceremony conducted in a Christian church before the altar of the Blessed Mother Mary and under the spiritual aegis of a priest. As such it has deep roots in the Catholic ecclesiastical past and has enjoyed a renewal since the 1960s.

According to Kay Toy Fenner in *American Catholic Etiquette*, both laypeople and clergy are attracted to it because it weaves "the beauty and symbolism of our liturgy into our practice of our Faith" and invests "all the important occasions of our life with a religious or sacramental character." Further, the act of solemnizing one's betrothal in a canonical context establishes the proper mood of engagement, namely, as "a time of serious and thoughtful preparation for the responsibilities and joys of marriage." Here the witness, as a religious intermediary between the couple and divinity, adds a spiritual dimension to the betrothal experience. This quality of spiritual ratification can serve the couple well later on in the marriage as a touchstone for the purity of their vows.

Fenner suggests the following format for a canonical engagement. A week before the ritual, the couple meets in the rectory office for pastoral counseling, where the priest outlines the documentary promises of Catholic married life: namely, frequent reception of prayer and holy sacraments, attitudes of charity and mutual respect, and the habit of marital "chastity" (fidelity). On the day of the engagement, the couple stands before the pastor at the altar and read aloud then sign their marital promises (which are in effect an engagement contract), which the pastor then signs, too. After he blesses the engagement ring, sprinkling it with holy water, the groom places it on the bride's finger and says: "In the name of the Father, and of the Son, and of the Holy Spirit, Amen." The pastor gives them words of encouragement, then they kneel and pray to the Blessed Mother, asking for her blessing, help, and protection in their marriage. Finally the pastor congratulates the couple and suggests they begin a "Family History Book," with their canonical engagement as the first entry.

The Testament in the House of the Bride

The late medieval Eastern Orthodox Christian rites of betrothal contain many elements emulable by the world culture wedding. The following examples illustrate the sacramental dimension possible in the betrothal when it's conducted as a ritual. Again, the essential quality added here is the spiritual blessing for the couple imparted by the priest and the ratification of their espousal "in the eyes of God." They exhibit a rich mixture of folklore and Christian ceremony, prayer forms, and symbolism, according to Kenneth Stevenson in his *Nuptial Blessing: A Study of Christian Marriage Rites.* In the rites of the various sects—Byzantine, Armenian, Coptic, Syrian-Jacobite, Maronite, Chaldean—the marriage service is a two-stage process of betrothal and joining.

An eighth-century Byzantine betrothal ceremony consists of two priestly blessing-prayers. The first prayer recounts the legendary biblical betrothal of Isaac and Rebecca, which is invoked by way of mentoring example and for requesting God's blessing on the couple in their coming married life. The deacon asks the congregation to bow for another blessing and prayer.

In a related rite from Constantinople, the priest offers a short litany with special relevance for the couple, which is followed by prayers and, beginning with the eleventh century, the presentation of the rings—gold for the man, silver for the woman. A betrothal ritual conducted under these auspices initiates bride and groom into the sacramental dimension of the marriage process, enhancing the solemnity of the vows and instilling an awareness of the responsibility of the matrimonial bonds. The betrothal rite concluded with a blessing, an invocation of hoary biblical characters, and as Stevenson puts it, "a catena of allusions to the use of the ring as a pledge." Around this time it was common for the betrothal ceremony to segue smoothly into the full wedding service, if not in the same hour, then the same day.

Armenian marriage rites of the ninth to twelfth centuries consisted of a three-stage process, beginning with betrothal, then marriage by crowning, and concluding with the removal of the crowns a week later. The betrothal segment began with the presentation and blessing of gifts, which included rings, a necklace, earrings, and veil; it continued with the "blessing of robes" through liturgical readings, hymns, and blessing-prayers; then culminated with the "joining of hands," in which the couple stretched forth their hands for a blessing by the priest, then a prayer that quotes Basil of Caesarea's famous definition of marriage as "the uniting of those who are separate"; after this came confessions from both bride and groom, and a final expression of consent.

JAPAN
PALESTINE
CHINA
GREECE
ICELAND
TURKEY
MOROCCO
RUSSIA
BELGIUM
HUNGARY
NETHERLANDS
TIBET
GUATEMALA
ITALY
POLAND

In the eleventh-century Coptic betrothal rite, the bride and her family proceed to the church early in the morning. There they are met by the priest, who carries candles and musical instruments. The bride stands in a particular section of the nave (specifically at the head of the women's division of the architectural space), while the groom stands in an opposite, "male" section of the nave. After a thanksgiving prayer, a rite of incense, two readings, and the recitation of the Creed, the priest offers three betrothal prayers, followed by a blessing of the wedding attire—a multihued tunic, a cincture (belt or girdle), and a white veil. Next the groom's party visits the bride's contingent in the nave; the now blessed wedding attire is put on, the groom presents the bride with a cross, the priest gives him the ring, and he slips it onto the bride's outstretched finger. Finally the priest covers them both with the veil.

The Syrian-Jacobite betrothal ritual took place on the eve of the wedding. Then the priest visits the groom's household, asking, in the presence of witnesses, if he willingly takes the woman as his wife. After an affirmative answer, the priest visits the bride's house, asking her if she willingly consents to the groom. When she affirms her consent, he blesses the engagement ring, puts it on her finger, and offers a blessing-prayer.

The Maronite service divides the marriage process into two parts—the testament (betrothal) and the crowning (the joining ritual). The entire wedding party gathers in the house of the bride for the Testament. The priest inquires if the couple truly desires to marry; they join hands and the priest invokes the Holy Spirit in prayer. The two rings, cincture, robe, and bridal jewelry are blessed, and according to much older texts, the feet of the couple (or groom alone) are anointed with oil in commemoration of the anointing of Jesus' feet by a woman who sought absolution of her faults.

The Chaldean rite, supposedly based on dictates of the Synod of Catar in 676, ushered the couple into formal, sanctified marriage in six stages. First came "consent, in which the priest sends a woman as intermediary to the bride, offering her a ring if she consents to the marriage. The "joining of right hands" came next; here the right hands of the couple are joined, then blessed by the priest who cites ancient biblical couples, invokes the Virgin Mary, and makes the sign of the cross above their hands. The third stage—betrothal— begins with a long chant followed by lengthy, lavish blessings that contain powerful symbolic images: "Embrace, Lord, the bridegroom and bride with the fire of love and mercy." The priest blesses the couple with a chalice, with water; he blesses the ring by placing it in the chalice; he deposits sacred ash in the water (a mixture called the *Henana*), and offers it to each. The complex rite concludes with the blessing of the robes, the crowning, and "the making of the bedchamber."

Milk, Dates, and Coins on the Forehead

In Moslem Fez in Morocco, the betrothal blessing is accomplished by prayers made by the fathers and their male peers, and often a spiritual figure. A few days after the marriage proposal has been accepted and the preliminary negotiating phase—"the giving away"—has been completed, women of the groom's family visit the bride's household. In this stage, called *kèmlet l-àtîya*, their intention is to make their daughter-in-law (the *mmèllka*) "sweet" with respect to her new family, so that there should be no quarrels; the bride's mother receives them graciously with tea, food, and honey (construed as a prewedding good luck charm).

On the next Friday, the fathers of the couple and other friends meet for midday prayers at a shrine; when these are finished, they conduct their own ceremony, called *fâtha,* in which they recite prayers with their hands stretched out, their palms turned upward. A man from the *mmèllek's* (the groom's) party (but not the father) stands in the center of a ring formed by all the other men present. They request another *baraka* (a saintly man with religious inspiration) to complete their ritual. He moves his hands over his face and chest, kissing them as they pass his mouth; everyone in the ring copies this gesture. Then the man in the center of the ring says, "Thanks be to God, Lord of the worlds." Men of both parties congratulate the groom's father, extending their right hands to him, saying, "Be blessed and lucky," to which he answers, "May God bless you." Then they repeat the felicitations to the father of the bride, after which the party disperses.

In the afternoon of this same Friday, the groom sends new clothing to his partner; at sunset she sends him small tables piled with sugar, fresh butter, milk, mint, *kàb gzel* (a crescent-shaped confection with an icing made of pounded almonds, sugar, and cinnamon laid over a thin pastry), and *grîba* (buns made of butter, sugar, and flour). The young man sends the tables back, this time bearing a handsome garment. In the evening his father presents a feast, called "the evening of fâtha," in their home with musicians and lots of invited guests. Then women attendants (called *ngâgef*) dress the man in woman's garments so that he looks like the bride, after which he sits demurely on a floor cushion with his eyes closed. One of the ngâgef sings: "Where are you, O friends of the bridegroom?" This is the cue for his male companions to enter the room. Next, a *nggâfa* gives the groom milk (to make his life "white") and puts a date (signifying wealth)

in his mouth; dates and milk are offered to his friends ("May God give dates and plenty," says the common blessing), and they in turn affix coins to his forehead.

The same ritual is observed on the same day in the house of the bride, after visiting the hot baths in the afternoon. Present at this fâtha are female musicians, ngâgef, and various women guests. The young woman is dressed in a fine costume, and like her partner in his father's house, she sits on a cushion opposite the door. A nggâfa gives her milk to drink, then puts a date in her mouth; then dates are offered to the musicians, who decorate the bride's forehead with silver coins.

Announcing the Obrazovanie *with Bells on Horses*

A key aspect of the Russian urban wedding ritual in the late nineteenth century was the "blessing" or "formation," otherwise known as betrothal, which followed the "bride showing," "bride testing," and general negotiations about matchmaking and dowry. Among the prosperous city dwellers, both sets of parents officially met for the ritual of betrothal blessing performed by a priest. During the "formation" ritual (the *obrazovanie*), the parents added their blessings to the couple and exchanged bread and salt, a traditional custom; this was often followed by a drink in honor of the bride—or several drinks, in fact. The betrothal drinking bouts (called *zapoiny*) could last, intermittently, as long as two weeks. Often, directly following the parental blessing, the bride would step out onto the porch and publicly announce her engagement. That evening, the young people of the community would gather on

JAPAN
PALESTINE
CHINA
GREECE
ICELAND
TURKEY
MOROCCO
RUSSIA
BELGIUM
HUNGARY
NETHERLANDS
TIBET
GUATEMALA
ITALY
POLAND

the common pasture for games and honey-cake, provided by the groom. The betrothal celebrations concluded with the betrothed couple riding around the pasture on horses decorated with bells.

Dancing in the Embers of the Great Fire

The canonical engagement and its variants is a way of invoking spiritual fire to bless the betrothed couple. But fire, whether it's divine or material, is a purifying energy. In this example the couple's espousal is confirmed by a literal fire. Unlike other cultures, for whom the betrothal ritual was a virtual seal of matrimony, among the Condrusian peasants of Belgium betrothal was a period of persistent uncertainty and instability. Their engagement announcement and its specific details (called banns) is posted and read aloud in church service by the village curé as they sit nervously in the pews; but what most unnerves them is the ceremony of the "Great Fire," a marriage fire (called *fouwas d'marièdje*), both a mark of unification and a rite of passage.

Each young man must accompany his betrothed and dance with her in the embers of a great bonfire. No couple was exempt from this requirement, and failure to participate was tantamount to nullifying the engagement. Neighbors constructed the marriage bonfire before the house of the couple on their wedding night. Their popularity among villagers was evidenced by how much straw and branches each neighbor brought to heap upon the flames. The bridegroom emerged from the house to toss copper coins into the fire for the children to collect later; meanwhile the young folk tossed withes of straw into the bonfire, exclaiming

"po nosse fouwa" ("for our fire"). The betrothed couple symbolically tossed their past life, childhood, adolescence, virginity, and patterns of family dependence into the purifying flames in a public expression of their changed status.

Other ritual acts were specified for both bride and groom. The bride must also cook three specially dyed eggs in the marriage fire's embers for presentation to her partner on Easter morning. The groom had to provide two white gloves, both for the left hand, painted in crude images of saints, bleeding hearts, and other sentimental images, and inscribed with affectionate remarks. The village curé blesses these gloves when he reads the banns; on the wedding day, the bride and groom each wear one left-handed white glove, after which they become family heirlooms.

Burning the Flax-Spindle

In the betrothal ritual among pre-Revolution Central Russian peasants, family members and relatives of both bride and groom would first meet in a party atmosphere to discuss the timing and conditions of the marriage. The groom's family provided a certain sum of money toward expenses, while the bride's family would decide upon the extent of her *pridaneo,* or extended trousseau; she was expected to provide sufficient clothes for herself and her (presumed) forthcoming children, as well as household ornaments. If the groom wasn't local, everybody in this betrothal made an inspection tour of his premises to make sure it was commensurate with the quality and station of the young woman. When these matters were resolved, the bride's family hosted a formal betrothal party at their home. At this time the groom burned the woman's flax-spindle (the tapered round stick that

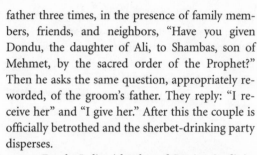

holds the yarn in hand-spinning) as a sign that she was to be a spinster no more.

I Can't Keep You Out of My Sight

The betrothal ritual among the Dobu islanders of Polynesia in the Western Pacific consisted simply of staring. Villagers, gathered in a circle before a platform on which the intended bride and groom are seated, stare silently and aggressively for thirty minutes at the mute couple. The staring ceremony deliberately reverses the couple's previous reclusive privacy, thereby turning their relationship public and making the engagement. Presumably the couple is purified by the fiery and surely intimidating gaze of the assembled witnesses. When the starers finally disperse, the bride's mother, who has been in charge of these matters, hands the groom a digging-stick and commands him to "Go, make a garden."

Drinking Sherbet

In some countries the sharing of a single beverage—sherbet, beer, gin, coffee—carries the symbolic weight of the betrothal ritual. Among the Muslim Turks of Anatolia, the betrothal ritual is marked by a formal ceremony of drinking sherbet (from the Turkish *sharbat*, meaning a refreshing drink made of diluted fruit juice) out of a copper vessel. So closely identified is this custom with the act of betrothal that for the Anatolian Turks, the term "drinking sherbet" is considered synonymous with the public acknowledgment of engagement. The local imam (prayer leader) asks the bride's

father three times, in the presence of family members, friends, and neighbors, "Have you given Dondu, the daughter of Ali, to Shambas, son of Mehmet, by the sacred order of the Prophet?" Then he asks the same question, appropriately reworded, of the groom's father. They reply: "I receive her" and "I give her." After this the couple is officially betrothed and the sherbet-drinking party disperses.

For the Italian islanders of Corsica, Sardinia, and the Balearic Isles, the *abraccio* (betrothal) ceremony generally takes place in winter. In the evening the nearest relatives of the bride bring the young groom to their home. The couple kisses formally, and sits down side by side, as the other family members, over a repast of cake and wine, arrange the details of the wedding. It's customary for the groom to spend this night with his new partner, so ritually binding is the abraccio; nor would it be unusual for the young bride to be pregnant (if not delivered of her first child) by the time of the actual wedding ceremony many months later.

The Begging Beer

In the preinvasion Tibetan betrothal ritual, if the horoscopes for the woman and man who propose marriage are judged auspicious, the groom's parents present the bride with a *ka-ta*, a ceremonial scarf, and other presents. Both families cooperate in fixing a date on which the groom's party will formally visit the bride's home for the *long-chang*, or "begging beer," which is the beer they offer when asking the family for their daughter in marriage. On this day the groom's parents also make the bride's mother a gift of an apron and two thousand *gnu-sang* (in 1928, when this account was published, that was about $1,000) as the *nu-ring*, "the price of the breast." Then both sets of parents, with their relatives as witnesses, draw up and seal a nuptial contract outlining the intended conduct of the couple. After the groom's family presents more gifts, such as a suit of clothes accompanied by another ka-ta, to each member of the bride's family, and a scarf and some money to the family's senior servants, the begging beer is completed.

The Betrothal Is Proved by Strong Gin

For the Walloon villagers of Château-Gérard, a former monastic manor in Belgium, the traditional betrothal ritual got underway on Sunday afternoon with a strong shot of gin—120 proof. The suitor gathers his male friends, dressed in their Sunday finest, to pay a call at the bride's family home. They knock loudly on the front door and are received in a formal, brusque manner by her parents; the father asks them why they have arrived. "You have a pretty girl in there and we want something to drink," the young men respond in classic male bravado. The father invites them in for several rounds of potent, tongue-loosening gin.

While the parents and bachelor callers wax loquacious and merry, the bride and groom must remain silent, sitting on opposite sides of the room. When the family and visitors dive into a card game, which can easily last from late afternoon into mid-evening, again the couple must remain aloof and quiet. If the proposed match is to be ratified, the bride's mother indicates this by offering the groom's male companions a strong cup of coffee in token of their good behavior. Fifteen days later the suitor returns, the procedure is repeated, and the match agreed upon—or rejected.

GIVING AWAY THE BRIDE REVISITED: LESBIAN UNIONS

Probably the most dynamic, creative, and culturally courageous expression of the principles of the world culture wedding are exemplified in the innovations of lesbian joining ceremonies and weddings, which have slowly gained prominence since the 1970s. The lack of formal, legal, or religious sanctions—not to mention widespread public disapproval—for lesbian unions has challenged women to rethink and resacralize the wedding process. The lesbian nuptial solution is often stunningly creative, reframed in the context of Wicca, Quaker, Catholic, Native American, Jewish, or Buddhist spiritualities, as well as a variety of free-ranging original ceremonies. As poet Adrienne Rich observed: "The rules break like a thermometer / quicksilver spills across the charted systems . . . whatever we do together is pure invention / the maps they gave us were out of date by years."

Becky Butler and her partner, Patty Bralley, worked with the quicksilver of pure invention a few years ago when they developed their own lesbian commitment ceremony. Butler found no books to guide her in the daring protocols of lesbian marriage, so in 1990 she published a valuable reference work, Ceremonies of the Heart: Celebrating Lesbian Unions, in which she presented the rites and commentary of twenty-seven wedded lesbian couples. "It was so profoundly liberating," Butler remarks. "It is extraordi-

narily freeing to be outside of the heterosexual tradition of weddings and marriage. There is something at once so heady and so sacred about the process of creating an event to celebrate and honor a lesbian relationship."

One of the first heady issues Butler and fellow lesbians invariably face is the foundational, "astounding" question, What does a ceremony mean in the context of creating new forms and new bonding traditions? Many lesbians have found this stage of inquiry, self-reflection, and shared vision to be the most valuable aspect of the whole process. "In many ways the ceremony itself begins here, with answering the question of exactly what the ceremony means," says Butler. The lesbian ceremony can express a couple's gratitude for what their relationship has yielded them; it can dramatize their commitment to sustain the bond; it can be an implicit request for public support for their unorthodox union; and it can be an unmistakable way of "being profoundly visible." The ceremony can be "deeply transformative," for participants and witnesses alike, as the carefully chosen rituals, consciously chosen symbols, and same-sex liturgies facilitate the intermingling of matter and spirit, says Butler.

"There are no scripts, no rules, no assumed models, no checklists for the mother-of-the-bride. Each ceremony arises directly from the experience of the couple" and represents an interweaving of personally meaningful elements from established traditions with "words and images from their own imaginings," Butler observes. "Lesbians are manifesting their own loving and powerful visions of relationships, and creating out of their own hearts and minds the ceremonies to acknowledge and celebrate those relationships."

There is one rule lesbian couples are likely to confront, however. That's the political-juridical issue of whether their union is legally binding: marriage laws and sanctions originated in a strongly heterosexual context. The legal right of same-sex couples to marry, and the securing of this right is a social process still underway.

That movement began on June 12, 1970, when the first marriage to "legally" unite two women, complete with the exchange of rings and vows, was performed in Los Angeles. The legality of the ceremony was qualified and then rejected by a subsequent technical reading of the California statutes. Meanwhile, in Kentucky, a lesbian couple was pushing the heterosexual juridical paradigm by taking their contested "legal" union to court. They lost, but the case inspired strongly supportive words from the San Francisco Chronicle in July 1970: "Marriage is the public announcement of a civil contract between two people showing binding intent to share their lives." Marriage represents a "personal contract" to share emotional and mental resources and a "rendering public" of an honest social commitment. "It would seem only in keeping with the times that consideration be given to allowing the homosexual minority the same rights to this sense of fulfillment."

As of 1989, Denmark is the only country that legally recognizes same-sex marriage, but "individual efforts to achieve legal sanction of lesbian partnerships" is continuing in America and elsewhere, says Butler. Acceptance for lesbian wedding ceremonies is gradually building among traditional religions, too. In 1968 the Reverend Troy Perry founded the Universal Fellowship of Metropolitan Community Churches, an effort that grew rapidly; by 1972 MCC had 43 congregations, an international membership of 15,000, while Perry had performed 250 "services of holy union for same-sex couples," says Butler. More recently lesbian holy unions have been sanctioned by selected clergy from United Methodist, Unitarian, Episcopal denominations, Reform and Reconstructionist Judaism, and Quaker Meetings.

The Engagement Procession Laden with Feast Foods

In other traditions the betrothal may be sealed and celebrated with the exchange of special foods—fruit, cornmeal, condiments, sauces, bread—usually in large quantities. When a contemporary Aztec Indian man of Mexico's Milpa Alta becomes engaged, his parents ask his baptismal godparents to also serve as his marriage godparents. This is more than an honorific post, however, because marriage godparents are expected to cover all the wedding costs. All the family members, relatives, and godparents make an engagement procession, accompanying the groom, as they bear gifts of fruit, candy, and cakes, en route to the bride's home. They stop at every corner to dance to live band music provided by the groom's family. Once arrived at the bride's home, the couple exchanges "love tokens": he gives her one of his handkerchiefs, while she gives him her scarf, earrings, hair ribbon, or photograph. During the evening feast, they announce their wedding date.

When a Hopi Indian woman wanted to wed, she took the initiative by sending the young man of her choice thin cornmeal biscuits called *piki*. If he eats them, that signifies his acceptance of her proposal; then if she is seen combing his hair in public, this represents an announcement of their engagement.

Bride Gifts and "Performing Ceremonies"

A ritualized schedule of bride gifts marks the betrothal process for families in the Guatemalan village of Chichicastenango. The bride's first gift, when tentative inquiries and proposals are made, is twenty-five to thirty seeds of cacao, the sacred seed of the Quiches, and *sapuyul,* a condiment used in ceremonial drinks. Her acceptance of the cacao and sapuyul seals the betrothal; more gifts follow, such as a jar of *atole* (a beverage made of toasted cornmeal mixed with cocoa butter), a jar of *puliq* (a spiced sauce used in festive dishes), a basket of foods to be cooked in the puliq, a chicken, bread, and chocolate—all presented by the groom's mother. The gift presentation, called *hacer costumbre*, which means "performing ceremonies," is repeated six times at two-month intervals. With each gift presentation, the bride's family welcomes the gift-givers to a party and a feast.

At the end of this cycle, representatives from the groom's family arrive with six large jars of atole, one of which is consumed on the spot, the rest left as gifts. This signals that it's time for the groom's party to collect the bride in preparation for the wedding. The groom presents her family with a load of firewood and aromatic leaves for use in their medicinal sweat-bath, necessary to dispel their loneliness after their daughter leaves the home.

Delivering the Pitchers and Bread

For the Andi villagers of nineteenth-century Russia, once the betrothal terms were concluded by the couple's parents, the next step was the *kh'aba-g"an bik"g"ol"ir,* the "delivery of pitchers and bread." Members of the groom's family and their friends conveyed refreshments to the bride's home; these might include a pitcher of meat bouillon, a pail of sweetmeats, or a *chongol* (large enameled dish) filled with a mixture of flour, butter, and honey. With the presentation of these refreshments, the young woman was now tacitly considered *khodib*, "requested," which was another stage in the prewedding formalization of ties. On the following day, the groom's family feasted the bride's family again, this time in the former's household. During the interval between betrothal and marriage, which typically was up to one year, the groom's parents gave the bride's parents *k"ali bokhoson*, approximately fifteen kilograms of grain (often much more), a large quantity of dried meat, and clothing; in addition his parent's made gifts to her family on folk and religious holidays.

Secret Engagement Aprons and Shirts

Instead of ritually presented beverages or foods, other betrothal ceremonies turn on the exchange of personal or household gifts, such as clothing, saucepans, sandals, dinner plates, or shoes. The young Hungarian groom among the Matyo people receives a special black apron, embroidered chromatically at its hem, from his future wife. The apron is meant as a betrothal token of affection, as the couple is otherwise enjoined against physical displays of fondness. The bride also presents her groom with a shirt, meticulously embroidered in red and blue threads. The couple agrees upon a date, usually midnight, at which time the groom will surreptitiously wear his betrothal apron and shirt on his walk home, unseen by anybody, to avoid what the Matyo regard as a disgrace. Further, the groom gets two plates loaded with foods—a fattened duck, a stuffed chicken, a tart, apples, nuts, gingerbread, and various old-fashioned Hungarian confections—cigarettes, some "apron money" (small coinage), and a bridegroom's bouquet made of rosemary sprinkled in gold dust. All

of this bounty comes into the groom's hands on a Saturday. Later he announces his good fortune—and her name—to his bachelor friends, treating them to drinks with his apron money, and they all pay his fiancée an introductory visit, at which she serves them apples and nuts.

Saucepans and Fire Irons Protect the Betrothal

The traditional seventeenth-century Dutch betrothal sequence has equal amounts of license and chastity in an amusing combination. When the young man had cast his eye longingly upon a marriageable woman, he announced his intentions to court by attaching a flowery wreath to her family's front door. It was improper for the woman to respond affirmatively—at least not too soon—so the wreath was taken down, placed on the threshold, and allowed to wither unattended. Undeterred, the potential groom fixed a fresh wreath on her door every day until at last she allowed it to remain; as a further modest confirmation of her change of heart, she placed a small basket of sweetmeats conspicuously on the inside windowsill.

The new status of the wreath and the appearance of the sweetmeat basket signaled to the young man that it was time to move into the second phase of the wooing ritual. He began paying formal visits to her home, speaking briefly with her parents, who accepted him as their daughter's official suitor. Later each night he climbed in through her bedroom window and slipped under the eiderdown with her in bed; this cheeky move was also officially sanctioned by the parents because they knew he'd never precipitate any indecorous behavior— the woman had a supply of metal saucepans in bed with her, and fire irons were

JAPAN
PALESTINE
CHINA
GREECE
ICELAND
TURKEY
MOROCCO
RUSSIA
BELGIUM
HUNGARY
NETHERLANDS
TIBET
GUATEMALA
ITALY
POLAND

nearby. Should the man wax overamorous, she had sufficient noisemakers to alert her parents to the imminent breach of nuptial trust. This was the theory. It seems, however, that a fair number of Dutch brides took their marriage vows secreting their babies under their wedding cloaks, leaving one to speculate that perhaps the parents were hard of hearing or the fire irons too heavy to lift.

Whatever the public or private outcome of the eiderdown visitations, the final stage in the betrothal process was the act of formal engagement. Here the couple exchanged rings with both their families as witnesses, and they kissed publicly for the first time. In some instances the young couple cut their fingers and swallowed each other's blood as a pact of conjugal intimacy and fidelity.

With This White-Wool Sandal, I Do Thee Wed

Once a year all the marriageable young Incan men living near Lake Titicaca on the border of Bolivia and Peru were summoned by the *curaca*, their local administrator. The curaca and a member of the Incan nobility would then take couples from their respective classes (the curaca handled men and women of "ordinary" lineage) and join the partners in a handclasp, thereby formalizing their betrothal and bestowing official permission to wed.

The next day the groom and his parents visited the bride at her home, where he bound himself to his partner by slipping a sandal onto her foot. If she was a virgin, the sandal would be of white wool; if she was sexually experienced, it would be made of *ichu* grass. The two journeyed back to his family home, where the bride gave him a gift of a woolen shirt and jewelry, which he started wearing at once. They sat together until nightfall, as family members gave them friendly marital advice, and the day ended with an elaborate feast. According to Incan law and custom, the young man's marriage marked his transition to adulthood, a rite of passage handsomely acknowledged by the state, which exempted him from one year of taxes.

The Amatorii *Collection*

Medieval Italian couples of Genoa exchanged decorated earthen plates, and other items of Majolica ware, as a mark of their betrothal. Popular among these was the *amatorii*, kitchenware including plates, deep saucers, and jugs upon which the cavalier suitor had painted the image of his partner above her name and the additional word-gift, *bella* (alternatively, if not her portrait, then an image of two hands united and two hearts in flame). These plate-pledges of affection were usually filled with a variety of sweetmeats at presentation.

Back in the sixth century, St. Leobard of Tours gave his partner a ring, a kiss, and a pair of shoes as betrothal gifts. The shoes symbolized his subservience to her: as the ring bound his hand, so the shoes bound his feet—which in our time we might understand to mean he wasn't planning to walk away from the match.

The Ordeal *of* Fidanzamento

Still another variant in the rites of betrothals is the presentation of special entertainments or symbolic public gestures. For Italian hill-towners,

the period of formal engagement, called *fidanza-mento,* and often lasting several years, can be both stressful and "the best time of life." The bride's obligation during this perilous time is to assemble the *corredo,* her trousseau of household and personal linen, which is somewhere between twelve and forty-eight sheets, depending in her family's affluence. She's also responsible for providing a share of the bedroom furniture, such as mattress, dresser, and mirror, for their new home. The young man, meanwhile, must establish his livelihood and contribute two-thirds of the bedroom furniture, including the bed, a large wardrobe, two end tables, a dressing table, and a chair.

During the time of fidanzamento, a series of betrothal gifts must be successfully exchanged before further plans are laid for the wedding. At the time of engagement, the groom offers his partner a wide, engraved gold ring (a diamond ring or watch may be substituted); she gives him a ring or gold chain in return. Clothing changes hands, too: the young man (the *fidanzato*) gets shirts, the young woman, dresses. Next the fidanzato provides the wedding dress and bridal jewelry, typically coral beads; his future spouse reciprocates by supplying his wedding ring and minor clothing items for his nuptial attire.

Flowers and Flowery Words for Your Hand

In northern Sardinia couples provisionally interested in each other are permitted to dance publicly together, but the custom that's most auspicious (and richly poetic) for proferring an engagement offer is a wool-carding party. Musicians and the house-poet (or village bard) are surrounded in a hall by young female friends of the prospective bride, who sit along the wall carding wool. The young men stand before them, helping with the work; often each of them is given a flower by the hostess upon entering the hall. Should any man wish to further his desires to marry a particular woman, he must publicly avow his intentions. He presents the young woman in question with his flower and declares his romantic interests and prospects in extemporaneous poetic verse; her acceptance or rejection must also be presented in acceptable verse. If either fail to hear the Muse speaking sweet poetry in their ears, they may prevail upon the house-poet for assistance. The more eloquent candidates for betrothal may compete among themselves to generate the most accomplished spontaneous verse; refreshments and dancing follow.

As an alternative the young people may pledge their troth with a formal handclasp or through the exchange of a flower or handkerchief. Afterward the families stage an intimate engagement party, performing charming little comedies—*l'abbracciu,* meaning "the embrace"—followed by feasting. Each family invites friends to visit them at their homes.

Meanwhile the young man, with his father, the house-poet, and a squadron of frisky male companions, gallop off on horseback to the bride's house, dramatically firing off pistols as if defending against an attack. Then the acting begins. The bride's father inquires as to why this sudden display of shooting and horsemanship should be staged at his front door. The groom's party, dissembling, replies that they were looking for a dove (or lamb), without which the groom could not possibly survive; using poetic speech—if not excess—they extol the physical beauty and virtues of this errant dove, still maintaining the comic feint. Finally they enter the bride's house, as if expecting to find their wondrous dove within. Introductions are made and eventually the bride-to-be appears. The pretense is suddenly dropped as the groom jumps to his "dove's" side; the abbracciu begins with joyous shouts and more pistol shots from companions outside.

A Groom's Pledge of Servitude

In Cambodia the groom makes an extraordinary gesture that is both symbolically and tangibly impressive. The engagement ceremony, which involves a regular exchange of gifts, is sealed when the woman accepts a box of betel nuts. The gift-giving continues with exchanges of more betel nuts, sampots (a kind of sarong), and scarves, which have a symbolic value: they "fix the words and tie the hearts" of the engaged couple.

Once engaged, the groom accepts his responsibilities to his new family by taking a vow of servitude, called *thvo bamro:* in the intervening period of one to twenty-four months before the wedding, he helps them with their daily household and agricultural tasks. This "servitude" is a kind of husband-testing, in which future in-laws can assess his character, integrity, and commitment, which is to say his ultimate suitability to be husband of their daughter. If he shows disrespect, complains, or fails to impress them during the time of his thvo bamro, they can summarily cancel the engagement.

A Sprig of Sweet Basil
at the Doorstep

Among Greek families living in Turkey one hundred years ago, it was customary for the mother of the prospective bride and her matrimonial agent, the matchmaker called *proxenetes,* to eat a cinnamon stick together after the terms of the betrothal had been agreed upon and witnessed.

After the news is publicized, the *arravoniasticos* (groom), accompanied by his relatives, visits his partner's family home, where they are received with great formality. Meanwhile the *arravoniastike* (bride) affects a standing posture of humility and modesty, her hands crossed on her chest, her eyes cast down, as she receives the greetings of the groom's party—"affected as a bride," as the Greek saying has it. Compliments on the imminent matrimony are exchanged, followed by coffee and cigarettes, and then the groom's party departs. But as they're leaving the betrothed young man kisses the hands of his future spouse and her relatives, while they present her with gold coins and sprigs of sweet basil.

Tangled Silk and a Larder
Wrapped in Rosemary

In eighteenth-century Polish betrothal ceremonies, the young woman was given a skein of tangled silk to unravel. Unraveling the silk was probably a demonstration by the bride-to-be that she would "undo the knots" of adolescence and life with her family in preparation for married life. The gesture carries the sense of smoothing out the complexities of the past and starting fresh, without encumbrance or restriction. She also received a ring from her fiancé. Her friends immediately set off on a hunt to bring good luck and material bounty to the couple; she dispatched them in good cheer by momentarily revealing her ankles. Later, at the wedding, she carried a bouquet of rosemary in whose leaves were secreted a piece of money, bread, salt, and sugar, to signify that the couple would never want for funds or food and that the relationship would be palatable and sweet to the end of their lives.

An Ardent Pledge of Nettles

"The longer you court, the shorter you'll live together," cautioned the Welsh. The English expressed a similar sentiment this way: "Happy is the wooing that's not long in adoing." But if you happened to be living in sixteenth-century England, you'd better watch out for the water pitchers.

In the north of England, friends of the betrothed expressed their approval of the engagement by "pitchering," a form of benign hazing in which a jug of water was held over the heads of the engaged man and woman; they would empty its contents all over them unless they paid a "pitchering brass." If you were a suitor on the job in Cornwall, you might find your friends collecting you in a wheelbarrow and dumping you in the nearest farm pond. And if you were ardent but impecunious, like a determined woman named Bridget Rose, you could plight your troth with something as dauntingly humble as sixpence and a cluster of nettles, knowing that "as close as these three stick together, so fast should her heart stick to him."

by an assortment of means, including negotiations on behalf of the couple undertaken by family and peers, the ceremonial exchange of rings, drinks, foods, and gifts, the performance of symbolic gestures or entertainments, or the sanctification of espousal by religious intermediaries.

Vows are exchanged in the presence of witnesses and martial commitments are ratified in the presence of family, community, or Spirit—in this we see the essence of betrothal and suitable grounds for reanimating it as a key element in the world culture wedding. As Shakespeare noted in *Twelfth Night*, through the betrothal ceremony, the contract of the bond of love between the couple is sealed.

After the agreement to wed has been sealed and ratified, the festive celebration of the betrothal by gender peers follows. This generally takes the form of the bridal shower and bachelor party, gentle same-sex initiation rituals that prepare and fortify the bride and groom for marriage and its radical change of circumstances. As we'll discover in the next chapter, these traditional acts of prewedding celebration and gift-giving can be transformed into powerful rites of inner preparation, purification, and psychological consolidation that make the bride and groom more responsible, mature, and integral partners.

JAPAN
PALESTINE
CHINA
GREECE
ICELAND
TURKEY
MOROCCO
RUSSIA
BELGIUM
HUNGARY
NETHERLANDS
TIBET
GUATEMALA
ITALY
POLAND

"And All the Ceremony of This Compact Sealed"

Betrothal, as the act of publicly testifying to one's intention to marry, can be accomplished

4

THE

SAGUN

SELF-PURIFICATION AND SANCTIFICATION

Regarded as a psychological relationship, marriage is a highly complex structure made up of a whole series of subjective and objective factors . . . . Whenever we speak of a "psychological relationship" we presuppose one that is *conscious*, for there is no such thing as a psychological relationship between two people who are in a state of unconsciousness . . . . An extreme state of unconsciousness is characterized by the predominance of compulsive instinctual processes, the result of which is either uncontrolled inhibition or a lack of inhibition throughout. . . . A high degree of consciousness, on the other hand, is characterized by a heightened awareness, a preponderance of will, directed, rational behavior, and an almost total absence of instinctual determinants. The reason why consciousness exists, and why there is an urge to widen and deepen it, is very simple: without consciousness, things go less well.

—*C. G. Jung,* "Marriage as a Psychological Relationship"

When Daryl Waters, the assistant music director of the Broadway show *Jelly's Last Jam*, asked Amelia Marshall, a soap opera actress, to marry him, she agreed, but with a condition: "Act right for six months." He did, and eventually they got married. But by his own admission, "It's taken me four years to act right for six months."

One bride, a college professor in her late thirties, staged a women's ritual circle in lieu of the conventional bridal shower. Two dozen women gathered in a geodesic dome in the woods, ex-

changed sacred objects (such as a marriage basket, in which a photograph of the couple was ensconced in a bed of herbs and flowers; a Hindu stone fertility symbol; loaves of bread baked by bride and bridegroom), and shared insights and blessings about relationships. They also played drums because, as one woman commented, "It's a way of remembering that once, a long time ago, to be a bride was to let go of maidenhood."

As preparation for a wedding within the Lubavitcher Hasidic tradition, the bridegroom gave a discourse to his male friends on the spiritual significance of marriage. That was his idea of a bachelor party.

Finally a Manhattan couple was married by a United Church of Christ minister who was also a psychoanalyst, a coincidence the bride found apt. "I spent so much time in my life plumbing the mysteries of the broken heart, it seems poetic justice in some way to be married by a psychoanalyst."

Inner Preparation for the Alchemical Wedding

These four examples highlight an important but neglected element in contemporary marriages: self-purification and inner preparation. Today we usually think of the bridal shower as a mini-Christmas, an extravagance of gifts and goods for establishing a new household, and of the bachelor party as the last chance to be free, wild, and single among one's male peers. But as we take a closer look, we find that prenuptial practices have a deeper, more spiritual importance.

Traditionally the bridal shower and bachelor party were rituals celebrating the imminent loss of maidenhood, virginity, adolescence, and life within the family of one's birth. The idea behind the bridal shower or bachelor party was to mark this important transition from puberty to adulthood, from the family of one's parents to the family of one's making, chaperoned and supported by one's gender peers on the eve of the wedding. Implicit in this ritual was the perception that the woman or man was not otherwise ready or prepared for the marriage without passing through a kind of purificatory shower sponsored by close friends of one's same sex.

Archetypally the wedding is an alchemical process that transfigures a young woman and a young man into the spiritually important roles of wife and husband. The stage of purification, or prewedding inner preparation, provides the flames for the necessary transmutation of personality. Society and our native culture and its rituals are the alchemists; our temperament, gender, sexuality, and identity are the raw materials for transmutation; the gold is a harmonious, mature couple composed of two individuated people, contributing yet another link to the chain of a stable society. How much we exercise this option is our own choice, of course; but as the folkways suggest, it's probably a good idea.

Today, although the sociological motive for a prewedding purification is not the same, the central idea is still sound. Perhaps instead of letting go of maidenhood, we might think in terms of letting go of our old ways of living, our old sense of self as a preparation for marriage. Individual men and women who "work on themselves," who struggle for a deeper self-knowledge and stronger psychological integration before entering a formalized relationship, are bound to experience a marriage that's more mature, nourishing, stable, and supportive of their own further growth.

A premarriage purification ritual today means washing ourselves clean of old attitudes, habits, emotional reactivity, intolerance, selfishness, unreasonable expectations, the taints of past relationships; purging ourselves of our uncommitted bachelor habits and identifications. Traditional cultures accord this purifications stage in the wedding process a high degree of respect, honor, and importance. In the formalized procedures that follow, we find a profound spiritual perception of the nature of man and woman, and the way in which the archetypal structural elements of the marriage ritual reflect and honor them.

With Consciousness, Things Go Well

As Hindu astrologer Ghanshyam Singh Birlaji so presciently remarks, marriage can be the mortar in which we transmute our "minor defects," as the pestle of relationship unmercifully grinds our flaws against its adamant surfaces. Unmercifully? Or is it perhaps a hidden mercy that reveals the naiveté of our expectations of immediate marital bliss? Maybe the happiness of marriage is an experience earned and hard won only after years of nurturing its possibility in a living, intimate, and evolving relationship. That's the sentiment of German poet Rainer Maria Rilke: "For one human being to love another: that is perhaps the most difficult of our tasks; the ultimate, the last test and proof, the work for which all other work is but preparation."

Love is the most difficult task because it requires such a high degree of consciousness, as depth psychologist Carl Jung thought. Wedded love, perhaps ironically, brings us face-to-face with many unacknowledged and even unfriendly aspects of ourselves—that vexing series of subjective and objective factors, as Jung called them. In the context of a pledged relationship, Jung's "high degree of consciousness" doesn't mean some balmy, peaceful, blissed-out state. No, it means the shock of recognition, the creativity of conflict, the unending chore of inner weeding.

As Jungian analyst Daryl Sharp observes in *Getting to Know You,* marriage can be clogged with unconsciousness and burdened with "instinctual determinants," which Jungians call *projections.* Whatever aspects of ourselves we're not conscious of, we're likely to see in someone else, especially our partner, says Sharp. "The question is, are we

then relating to that person at all, or to an unconscious side of ourselves? If we don't see the reality of the other person, we're trapped in a narcissistic bubble. What we don't know about ourselves, we meet in others."

The interval between betrothal and wedding is the perfect time to take an honest look at ourselves, our limitations and shortcomings as well as our strengths. The mirror of marriage will show us these soon enough, so why not consciously begin to purify this energy? Perhaps the most profound troth we can plight when we offer vows to our partner is to do everything we can as an individual man or woman to wake up, to understand our own nature, to try not to project our inner life and unresolved conflicts and desires onto our partner.

Unfortunately Westerners today typically see the interval between betrothal and wedding as not quite enough time to get a million things done—plans drawn up, services contracted, guest lists drafted, clothing designed or purchased, flowers and foods selected, musicians contracted. And if we're not stressed out with overseeing hundreds of details, we're probably luxuriating in the abundance of attention and material well-being, whether it's a bridal shower or bachelor party. For most of us, this interregnum between private intention and public fulfillment is hardly a breathing space; it's an intensely busy time in which nearly all our attention is magnetically drawn outward as we supervise a myriad preparations. But when do we take the time to prepare ourselves?

It's not like this everywhere. All cultures don't tacitly encourage the eclipse of the bride or groom's inner life on the eve of wedding. In certain traditional cultures, the interval between engagement and wedding is a special time for inner work, purification, physical cleansing, and psychological inquiry. It's a solitary time for the bride and groom each to seek an inner experience of sanctification. This is a dowry truly worth bringing to the marriage.

INDIA
MOROCCO
SUDAN
GREECE
RUSSIA
FINLAND
ENGLAND
YUGOSLAVIA
GERMANY
CHINA
TRINIDAD
ROMANIA

INDIA
MOROCCO
SUDAN
GREECE
RUSSIA
FINLAND
ENGLAND
YUGOSLAVIA
GERMANY
CHINA
TRINIDAD
ROMANIA

When you begin to devise your own purification ritual, keep in mind that the most prevalent element in traditional purificatory rituals is the strong belief that there are "demons inside, demons outside." The demons inside are one's subconscious shadow contents, the unresolved trappings of childhood and adolescence; the demons outside are unfriendly spirits and elementals, angry ancestors, and bad-intentioned neighbors. Purification must address both poles of this vulnerability.

Traditional rituals put a strong emphasis on marking the transition in life-state, attitude, and image for both bride and groom. Marriage is a major rite of passage from your former state as a child of your parents (and this is true no matter what your age) to an independent conjugal householder. If we don't understand what the transition from bachelorhood to married means *before* the wedding, we may run into problems later. Becoming a husband or wife is more than joining two households or gaining a new, fun roommate. Men marrying for the first time, especially in their twenties, must be on guard against construing their new wife as another version of their mother; and women must not see another version of their father in their new husband. Didn't Freud tell us that in any sexual act, at least four people are present?

If a relationship is dedicated to waking up and individuating, then this struggle toward recognition of our projections can be a prime aid to growth and understanding. *Dearly beloved, I vow to unmask your projections and I pray you do the same for me.* Such a marriage vow, and its faithful fulfillment, could well keep a relationship dynamic, evolving, and satisfying for decades. The idea behind the purificatory stage of the world culture wedding is to plant this seed of good intention even before the relationship is formalized as a marriage. The couple then presents this living plant to the marriage as a gift.

Purification and the Virgin Sophia

The world culture wedding draws from a rich, sometimes exotic array of purification practices, from anointings with henna and turmeric to ritual baths and fumigations. The consistent theme throughout is the emphasis on cleansing, preparation, consolidation, protection, shielding, and purity, achieved through various means. World folkways stress the externals of purification, the tangible immersions, the need to guard against invisible, hostile dangers, the obligatory solicitations of ancestral spirits, and the supernatural mentors of marriage. This is initiation, the passing with awareness through a critical threshold after a long period of preparation, of arduous inner and outer work. What happens at this stage is a crucial transformation: the *bride* is created out of the woman, the *groom* emerges out of the man. In the world culture wedding, bride and groom are archetypal roles mandated by the "gods," the matrimonial spirits.

According to Hindu belief, marriage is a sacrament, the thirteenth of sixteen life-cycle ceremonies. Says Birlaji, "It is meant to unite two souls so firmly that after marriage, although their bodies seem to remain separate, the souls in them are intended to merge and become one harmonious whole."

But before the sacrament there must be purification. In the Christian esoteric tradition, this stage of inner cleansing was once called "the preparation of the Virgin Sophia." Don't be misled by the word *virgin*, however; the chastity this initiation inculcates has more to do with that part of our being in which live our passions, desires, irritations, angers, bloodlusts, joys, ancestral spirits—the seat of our affective life. In an older time, candidates for initiation did a great deal of inner work, struggling to become aware of their psychological nature, their automatic reaction to events, people, comments, and thoughts. Candidates who had purified the great bulk of this churning emotionality, so that they could choose to respond rather than react automatically, became a "virgin of Sophia." Sophia, among the early Christians and Gnostics, was the wisdom aspect of the Divine Mother and creator of the world of elements in her revelatory mode.

The fruit of this inner work was variously called the alchemical wedding, the inner marriage of soul and psyche; this marriage became the basis, the receptacle, for spiritual energies. A marriage between a man and woman need not differ that much from this initiatory ideal. How else can a couple experience spirituality together unless they create a vessel out of their relationship?

As a strong complement to our inner work, the disciplines of natural health offer a reliable smorgasbord of techniques and remedies for facilitating our overall cleansing. Here are a few: supervised fasting; colonics; change of diet, reduction in the consumption of animal products, or the adoption of a macrobiotic or vegetarian diet; saunas, steam baths, and sweat lodges; emotional catharsis and consolidation through flower essences; smudging with strong herbs; meditation, hatha yoga and *pranayama* (breathing exercises); high negative-ion absorption at waterfalls; homeopathic constitutional "miasmic" housecleaning; supervised retreats at a health spa or meditation center; a relaxing sunny week at the beach; psychological counseling, workshops, retreats, or support groups; active psychological purgation through approaches like reevaluation counseling, rebirthing, and psychosynthesis; journal-keeping to record personal thoughts, emotions, attitudes about marriage.

Anointing the Bride with Turmeric

Our chapter's representative example of inner preparation is the ritual of *sagun*, drawn from India. In the province of Bihar in northern India, the necessity of purification as a preliminary to the Hindu wedding is taken seriously. William G. Archer describes the procedure of sagun in meticulous detail in *Songs for the Bride: Wedding Rites of Rural India.*

About two weeks before the actual joining ceremony, the bride begins her sagun, in which she will ritually enter an isolated, preparatory state. On the day chosen by her priest for commencing, the young woman marks out a square in the household courtyard; this square will assume a sacred dimension as her rituals proceed.

The young woman sits on a stool and unties the bundle, given to her by the priest, containing information about her wedding date. At the same time, female neighbors and relatives establish a supportive atmosphere by singing a variety of songs to her about sagun and Shiva, the cosmic masculine principle and consort to Shakti, the cosmic feminine. The women rim her eyes with collyrium (an eye salve) and rub her limbs with *bukwa*, a paste made of pounded grain and mustard oil. Next she's given an old white sari with turmeric smeared on one of its edges, and a handful of rice and small ornaments; as she receives these, the women and her mother sing blessing songs. Then she visits the family shrine and, bowing before the images of the Hindu *devas* (deities), she offers them her handful of rice. The women rub themselves with oil, feed the bride, then disperse; but from this moment forward, they will gather every evening to envelope the bride with

INDIA
MOROCCO
SUDAN
GREECE
RUSSIA
FINLAND
ENGLAND
YUGOSLAVIA
GERMANY
CHINA
TRINIDAD
ROMANIA

mangal, auspicious songs about Shiva's divine marriage, and to protect her against inimical influences by singing spells. The girl has entered ritual space, made aware of the cosmic archetype of marriage and the necessity for purity.

The next stage is called *maktora,* the ceremony of digging the earth, held at sunrise or dusk five to eight days before the wedding. Here she establishes her ritual space on the family property, connecting with the earth. But first bride and mother must perform some sanctifying preliminaries. The bride acquires a large basket, makes a blessing gesture over it with her stone curry-roller (which she uses for crushing spices), then sets it down in her sacred square in the courtyard. As another preliminary rite, her mother now performs the *manar-puja,* the worship of the drum. She engages the services of a *chamar,* a man from the leather-working caste who has a special drum. She sprinkles vermilion on the drum head, adds rice grains, then positions five betel leaves in a precise manner; when the chamar knocks the drum, the rice and betel leaves fall in her lap; she performs this five times, then it's repeated by some of her women friends, who are also singing the whole time. The mother ties the betel, a copper coin, and rice in a small bundle, then puts them in the basket; already inside the basket is a turmeric-and-flour paste called *aipan,* vermilion powder, and five smaller baskets. As the chamar pounds his drum, five women lift this basket onto the head of the barber's wife, who bears a mattock. (In India the barber occupies an important social role as surgeon, masseur, matchmaker, matrimonial counselor, town raconteur—a unique station somewhat midway between priest and doctor; his spouse is often a midwife.) Singing again, they make a procession to a field on the village outskirts, following the chamar.

At the field the mother and the mattock are sanctified with vermilion. The women use the aipan to make five handprints on her back, as she

uses the mattock to make five small cuts in the ground. The mother makes an aipan handprint on each tiny mound of excavated earth, mixes in vermilion, then puts one mound in each basket. Next, she rinses the mattock using water she carried in a pot, then ties a fistful of earth into a corner of her sari. Back home the women bless the large basket (which contains the five little baskets of sanctified earth) by waving a large curry-roller over it. They set the basket down in the bride's sacred square, then pound uncooked rice five times in a mortar; the rice is winnowed, then put carefully away for use on the wedding day. In a similar manner, the five women invoke their family ancestors as they sprinkle the earth they collected in the field with water then put it into temporary storage. Two days before the wedding, they'll use this earth to make a hearth for cooking the bridal rice.

Approximately five days before the wedding ceremony, the women erect the *marwa,* a bowerlike wedding canopy, in the bride's home, as neighbors and relatives look on. The women cut nine green bamboos, then the family priest affixes a dozen mango leaves and blades of the sacred *munj* grass to the ends of the shoots. The priest holds a stick against the bride's forearm, marks off a measurement, then snaps the stick at the exact corresponding length; using the stick he inscribes a square on the ground, which presumably is a dirt floor. Male family members dig a hole in the center of this square into which they secure a center pole, roofed with thatching grass and bamboos tied with strings of munj grass.

The anointing ceremony comes next, either on this day or the next. First the women assemble a plough, a shaft of green bamboo, and green mango leaves; they bundle them together with grass string and set the unit in the center of the marwa marriage-booth. The barber's wife carries aipan, vermilion powder, the mattock, and the large basket from the earth-digging ceremony, as the women set out for a well, singing songs to the rhythm of the drummer. Once they've arrived the bride's mother touches the base stone of the well with aipan, makes five vermilion marks upon it, then empties several cupsful of water on the ground; the barber's wife scoops up the moistened earth, stows it in the basket, and the women return to the marwa, where a Brahmin priest works the damp soil into a mud platform. Under the marwa again, the women smear a new pitcher with cow dung and assemble various ritual ingredients. Then, as the priest takes up his position, the bride-to-be is at last introduced into this ritually prepared environment.

She sits down on a stool upon which the priest has sprinkled sanctified rice. She places her hands around the cow-dung smeared marriage-pot, then places it on the platform. After the priest fills the pot with water, she drops in a betel nut, a copper coin, and a few grains of rice; she attaches mango leaves to its rim, puts a lid of piled rice over it, and a smaller lid with butter-burning cotton wicks over that. The women take a moment to worship Gauri, one of Shiva's consorts, and her son Ganesh, the elephant god and beneficent remover of all obstacles. Now the barber's wife prepares the turmeric paste and hands it to the priest. He takes five mango leaves and some *dub* grass, dips them in the turmeric, then anoints the young woman's head, shoulders, knees, and feet; he repeats the ritual gesture four times. The married male members of her family and the married male neighbors repeat the priest's gesture on her; as he finishes, each man deposits a coin in the turmeric pot. "By this the girl is increasingly sanctified and, at the same time, slowly, gently, and irresistibly absorbed into the community of the wedded," explains Archer.

When the men have left the courtyard, it's the women's turn to smear the bride's hands, back, and legs with turmeric paste in a collective feminine gesture of anointing—and, as always, of singing. Next they anoint her head with oil, after which they bless the rice held in the young woman's upturned palms. They sprinkle water on the ground around her to deepen this "sanctified state of purity," and carry her into the bridal chamber. For the next three nights, the bride will be similarly anointed by the women, thereby preserving her chastened state of "isolated purity" up until the joining ritual.

This preliminary phase of the bride's sagun is concerned with the creation of a ritually protected, personally unique space—*her* purificatory space—both in the landscape (through the maktora) and in the home (with the marwa) in which her transition from maidenhood to bride will be initiated and completed. The establishment of two ritual purificatory spaces includes familial land and home, and acknowledges a continuity of residency for her even as she prepares to leave both. The women around her invoke the cosmic masculine, Shiva, on her behalf, as an energetic aegis and as the archetypal aspect of her husband as a man; they invoke Gauri and Ganesh, central Hindu deities, to preside over her transition as beneficent, obstacle-removing, and protective spirits. Finally the bride is anointed with vermilion and turmeric as ritual marks of her process of purification. Throughout she is immersed in ritual space and solemnity, which reinforces her awareness that her life is undergoing a profound change; as she moves through these purificatory stages, she appreciates how she is both an individual woman and everywoman, the archetype of womanhood, enlarging her frame of reference into the transpersonal and sacred.

Although these stages in the sagun ritual derive from a patriarchal milieu, in which the virgin daughter is formally chaperoned out of the family nest and into sexual womanhood, the basic structural elements could be usefully copied in our completely different Western context; instead of mother, aunts, and older women, one's gender peers and spiritual sisters could supervise the purification.

INDIA
MOROCCO
SUDAN
GREECE
RUSSIA
FINLAND
ENGLAND
YUGOSLAVIA
GERMANY
CHINA
TRINIDAD
ROMANIA

The Vigil at the Groom's House

The groom also undergoes a purification. He begins by reiterating the bride's ritual of digging the earth and placing it in the sanctified square in the courtyard of his home. During the same hours in which the bride is anointed with turmeric, so is the boy smeared with the ritual paste, as the plough, bamboo stick, and mango leaves are set up in the marwa bower and the pitcher formally set in its position.

Now comes the Farewell Feast of the Five Bachelors. The men of the groom's caste and five young, unmarried male companions join him in a special meal, an act that signifies his imminent departure from their world for the life of a married householder. After the meal the men dig a small trench; as the groom squats over it, the males pour water over him, catching the water in a pitcher as it runs through his hair; the pitcher will later accompany him in his journey to the bride's house. This signifies an act of purification and ablution, his commitment to maintaining and demonstrating his purity in preparation for marriage, and a gesture of respect toward the bride-to-be and the sacredness of marriage itself. With the help of a tailor, the young man's wedding attire—a turmeric-colored dhoti, red socks, shirt, and turban, and a long muslin scarf—is laid out for inspection on the bed; then he puts it all on.

Outside, in the sacred square of his courtyard and accompanied by his mother on a low stool, he squats on a leaf plate. A flower-girl arrives bearing two marriage hats; the mother gets the larger one, the groom the smaller one. The barber's wife arrives to redden their feet and trim their nails—except for the boy's little finger, whose nail the mother cuts herself, then paints red. His uncle drapes him in a cloth and hands his mother five mango leaves, which she puts into her mouth and then gives to the boy. He bites each one, spitting the pieces into her outstretched hands. She wraps the mango stalks with rice inside a whole mango leaf, secures the package with an iron ring, and ties it to his right wrist with cotton thread. The boy rises, sprinkles his leaf plate over the square with rice, bows to the family deities, then enters his litter (a couch with shafts covered with curtains, used for conveyance).

The minute he enters the litter, a band of drums and cornets strikes up a tune. His mother marks his brow with a paste of rice and curds, rims his eyes with kohl, and presents him with the shallow iron kohl container. Then she splits a wick and slab of cow dung into four pieces and tosses them to the four directions. She makes another blessing gesture over him using the curry-roller brought by the barber's wife. The other women present also sing blessings for the groom: "O mother, bless the lovely boy / And your eyes will be soothed / And your heart will be calmed."

That evening brings the vigil at the groom's home. The women companions of the groom's mother convene again in her courtyard, setting up the bridal pitcher in his sacred square, upon which they set a four-wicked lamp; they set the whole arrangement inside the large basket used in the earth-digging ceremony. The *domkach* comes next, marked by the performance of a noisy pantomime. A woman pretends to have been stung by a scorpion; she's attended by another dhoti-clad woman disguised as a country doctor, and four maidservants. The farce turns on the doctor and her assistants attempting to find, by lifting her clothes, where the suddenly mute patient was stung. When they at last discover the (fake) scorpion bite in her genitals, the laughter of the women signifies her miraculous cure.

Himalayan Hindus observe a related purificatory *puja* for the groom. On his wedding morning, the young groom has his hair trimmed before

his ritual cleansing. The area for this ceremony has been plastered with cow dung by the barber, and a Brahmin has inscribed a magical diagram on the ground with flour. He sets a square stool with sacred objects attached over this diagram, and here the groom sits during the ritual. Several men hold a canopy with ritual items on a tray over the groom's head as the Brahmin begins to chant mantras. The groom's female relatives bathe him in a mixture of oil, water, and turmeric, sometimes with horseplay and frivolity. After the bath a male relative carries the groom to a room in his home where the sacred thread ceremony is performed; afterward the groom assumes his wedding clothes of white dhoti, green sash, yellow turban, and veil or garland as the priest performs the Ganesh puja to ensure success in his marriage.

Invocation of the Ancestors as the Wedding Day Dawns

The Bihar wedding preliminaries continue on the morning of the wedding day, when the bride's courtyard is washed and freshly plastered. Ashok tree leaves are tied to specially erected plantain posts at the courtyard's entrance; if possible a fancier marquee is also set up. The barber's wife and the Brahmin priest are on hand this morning, accompanied by the bride's mother and four married women in red saris and *tikka,* the characteristic vermilion brow marks, for the invocation of the household ancestors and deities. The bride's mother sprinkles rice over the curry-stone before them as the women chant:

O Brahma, Vishnu, and Shiva Maheshwar,
Today you must heed my bidding.
O gods who live in the courtyard,
Today you must heed my bidding.

O grandfather who lives in heaven,
Today you must heed my bidding.
O wind and rain and clouds,
You must stay away today.
O black ants and red ants,
You must stay away today.

When all the ancestors have been invoked, the mother grinds rice, puts it in a leaf-cup, folds this near the pitcher, then impresses it with the curry-stone and roller.

Next comes the Feast of the Five Virgins. This is a special meal prepared under the marwa on a hearth made of the earth dug from the field on the previous day. The women circle the bride's head with five platters of *palas* leaves, rice, pulse, curds, and sugar, after which she and four female companions (virgins) take a meal together as the older women sing. After the meal the bride sucks on a single nut; but instead of spitting it out or swallowing it, she maintains it in her mouth until the evening, when she presents it to her husband. After the meal the bride's father and mother, after bathing and dressing in different clothes, sit on stools under the wedding canopy at the feet of their daughter and bind the father's dhoti to the mother's sari; the family priest recites prayers to Gauri and Ganesh.

The bride, her parents, and the priest make one last preparatory oblation: the offering of butter. The priest cuts ten strips of dried cow dung and fixes five on each side of the door opening into the bridal chamber. The father anoints each strip with butter and mango leaves and the mother daubs them with vermilion. Inside the room the priest sets seven more strips of dung against the wall, covering them with a turmeric-dyed cloth; the father and mother repeat their anointings, then set out little trays of moistened flour as an offering to the ancestors. "After this," says Archer, "the bride, her parents, and the priest come outside, the wedding canopy is hung with fancy finery, and the house waits for the bridegroom."

THE CASE FOR COW DUNG AND TURMERIC

*T*he prominent roles accorded dried cow dung and turmeric in the sagun ceremony may seem highly unusual to Westerners. These items, however, have an honored spiritual base in Hinduism.

What Is the Meaning of Dried Cow Dung?

In Hindu spirituality the cow is a foremost totemic image of the Great Goddess, a symbol of the Moon Goddess in her nourishing aspect. For the Hindus it's Nandini, the wish-fulfilling cow who gives milk and elixir and from whose four legs originate the ancient caste system. The celestial cow is also Aditi, the "all-embracing," and the Earth herself, who once assumed the guise of a milk-rich cow. According to one Hindu creation myth, the universe was originally "curdled" from the primordial Sea of Milk from the Goddess-as-Cow; the planet's four primordial rivers flowed like milk from her udders.

For Hindus physical cows—in all their aspects and their five products, whether it's milk, curds, clarified butter, urine, or dung, all of which are used in purification ceremonies—are the sacred, animal representatives of this divine "fountain of milk and curds," a fountain that denotes not only food, but all the earth's water and land masses.

What Is the Meaning of Turmeric?

For Hindus turmeric brings good fortune and wards off inimical spiritual influences. Turmeric, a member of the ginger family, is extensively cultivated in East India as a dyestuff, aromatic stimulant, and flavoring agent. Its distinctive dark yellow-gold color guarantees that it is popularly seen as an auspicious spice, such that any garment marked in turmeric is automatically lucky. Thus in Hindu weddings the bride's garment is turmeric-dyed, her body is turmeric-smeared; and turmeric is sprinkled over the marriage contract and the interior walls of the groom's house.

Turmeric's pedigree may derive from the ancient dramatic text Ramayana, where it is praised as one of the eight ingredients of the Arghya, which is an oblation of respect made to gods and elderly men. It's believed that unfriendly supernatural beings and evil spirits object to the aroma of burning turmeric; in some parts of India, married women dip their hands in turmeric water and anoint their cheeks as a hex against the visitation of Lakshmi, the Hindu Goddess of Sovereignty and consort to Lord Indra. Finally turmeric, being yellow, the color of ripe grain, is associated with the Mother Goddess and her cereal fertility, the ineffable quality of which is offered to both bride and groom during their turmeric anointing.

Seclusion During the Phera

B rahmins in India's Punjab begin their marriage preliminaries often a week before the wedding with the *phera* ritual. In the respective villages of the bride and groom, a priest recites prayers and inscribes the *ganesh* (a swastika-like sign) in red on the forehead of each. In the bride's village, the priest prepares the *chaunk,* a cow-dung-smeared circle of ground over which the sacred fire will burn and around which the circumambulations of the *biah* (formal wedding ceremony) will be made. The hallmark of the Punjabi phera is that during this time both groom and bride remain in seclusion, if not virtually hidden within their respective family homes. During this sensitive time, the Indians believe, the couple is especially vulnerable to occult attack from ghosts (inimical ancestral spirits) or the evil eye (black magicians hired by family enemies to inflict harm).

Hindu women of both families are concerned that the household deities and ancestral spirits be acknowledged and propitiated at this stage to guarantee their benediction and to preempt any mischievous, malevolent actions, or spiritual dangers to the union. In Hindu belief marriage is potentially imperiled because it marks the last of the twelve *samskaras,* a graduated series of purificatory rites to cleanse individuals from the karmic taint accruing from their parents—the proverbial "sins of the fathers." Also, in the Hindu multileveled model of the world and cosmos, spiritual agencies—including the lingering spirits of dead but possibly jealous or irritable deceased family members—are accorded some degree of reality and efficacy. Thus marriage itself is a purificatory event, a positive crisis marking a profound transition out of this tortuous complex, a chance to expiate old injuries and insults. As such the entire marriage process requires precautions and safeguards against "the malice of demons."

We must realize that in traditional societies, where the influence of the priest, barber, medicine man, or shaman is strong, people take the idea of noxious spirits literally. They believe that a host of malingering invisible spirits of ambiguous intent is present in the environment. In the West, where the literal belief in ancestral spirits is not given much attention, the Hindu perception still has a psychological aspect. Here what the Hindus call meddling ancestral spirits and parental taints can refer in our Western context to the unwholesome subconscious presence in the personality of parental attitudes and familial relationship patterns left over from childhood such as resentments, suppressed anger, and unassuaged pain.

For example, a child may grow up knowing his maternal grandmother strongly disapproves of him, no matter what he does; his sense of being held in her disfavor may approach the experience of being damned by original sin. This grandmother enters the child's psyche as an angry ancestor, and her vitriolic presence can corrode the grown man's psychological well-being; it's especially tricky if she is dead by the time the man decides to marry, because then no personal rapprochement is possible. Even so, she must be appeased or else her abiding presence in the man's psychology will undermine his every move. If unacknowledged and unresolved, the emotions stirred up by the grandmother can significantly interfere with the marital relationship. The prewedding purification brings them to light and seeks to discharge their affect so they cannot sabotage our better intentions; ideally the man forgives his grandmother's churlishness and invites her lovingly to his wedding.

In conjunction with their hermitic phera, the couple does not bathe or change their clothes, presumably to maintain an energetic body shield and ritual continuity against these same unfriendly

INDIA

MOROCCO

SUDAN

GREECE

RUSSIA

FINLAND

ENGLAND

YUGOSLAVIA

GERMANY

CHINA

TRINIDAD

ROMANIA

invisible influences. Meanwhile their kinswomen conduct rituals on their behalf, including the daily *maian*. During this, as the bride and groom sit on a wooden plank erected underneath a red cloth canopy, the mother rubs her son's (or daughter's) face and body seven times with a mixture of turmeric and oil. The mother's female companions make jokes and try to prevent her from completing the task, slapping her hands away. She ignores their buffoonery and afterward daubs their faces with the turmeric oil mixture. During maian the palms of both bride and groom (and the bride's soles) are dyed dark red with *mehindi*. Sometimes a turmeric string bracelet is tied to the groom's right wrist as an extra precautionary measure.

Among Rajput or Maratha land-owning families in a Maharashtra Indian village, the marriage preparations are a community affair. The barber shaves the groom, delivers invitations to all the guests, and sets out the leaf-plates. The goldsmith polishes the icons of household deities; a water-carrier greets the bridal party by pouring sanctified water at their feet to counteract unwholesome influences; a rope-maker may halt the procession to ensure good luck; the washerwoman "cleanses" the bride and groom with turmeric on their wedding eve, while her husband inscribes a magic design on the ground then spreads a cloth on the ground so the bridal couple will not actually tread the ground in their transit from litter to bridal canopy.

Removing the Bas from the Virginal Couple

Attention to omens is prominent at Moroccan weddings, explains scholar Edward Wester-marck in his exhaustive study, *Marriage Ceremonies in Morocco*. "A large number of marriage ceremonies spring from the feeling or idea that the bride and bridegroom are in a state of danger, and therefore stand in need of purification and of special protection against magical influences and evil spirits," comments Westermarck. The Moroccans call these inimical spirits *bas*, and they must be driven out of the couple.

The list of purificatory caveats and requirements is awesome because it's so meticulous: bathing the bride and groom; shaving the groom, disheveling the bride's hair; wearing new clothes and slippers; painting the couple in henna, antimony, walnut root or bark, or saffron; purification with flour, bread, wheat; burning incense and candles; firing off guns, making loud music, singing, making the characteristic "quivering" call of the women; employing salt, needles, weapons of steel, and pistols; wearing charms and amulets like silver coins; making a bridal box of oleander branches; hiding the face; dressing up the groom to resemble the bride, while the bride imitates a man's appearance or walks with women dressed identically to herself; prayers, religious songs, and Koran recitations; abstinence from one's home, from eating too much or in public, from speaking aloud, from sitting on the ground, from crossing open bridges. The bride is heavily guarded by her kinswomen on her procession to the groom's household against the possible deprivation of her virginity by magical means by a malevolent bystander. When the bridal procession passes through a village, the bride is sprinkled with milk and henna to avert any evil influences emanating from the new terrain. Not only is the virginal bride in danger, says Westermarck; some of the myriad of Moroccan protective customs may be safeguards for her attendants, kinsfolk, and supporters. "The bride is considered to be not only herself in danger but also a source of danger to others."

This seemingly fanatical Moroccan superstition isn't misogynist aspersion upon the qualities of the Muslim bride, but rather an extreme, precise sensitivity to bridal—in fact, conjugal—virginity and the many ways in which it might be sullied by unsympathetic influences. Underlying the apparent rash of omens and seemingly neurotic superstitions stands a metaphysical perception. Purity of soul and spiritual virginity are highly valued at the core level of these cultures. It's not so much sexual virginity that's in peril as *chastity of the soul* (usually regarded as "feminine" in essence); another expression of the soul is what the occult tradition refers to as the astral body, that subtle sheath around the physical body that carries the life dynamics (often turmoil) of our emotions. It's as if the intensity of protection, safeguards, and purifications arise out of a desire to preserve the bride (and groom) as virgin souls on this unique, transitional day in an unsullied purity unmatched since the Garden of Eden—since before the Fall, to put matters in Judeo-Christian images. If so, then human marriage is a recapitulation of a divine model, the imitation of a heavenly archetype of union between the sexes, when the human was one being, the divine marriage.

Might there be another dimension to this "superstition" surrounding the bride's dangers? Implicit in the Morrocan's purificatory rigor is a profound respect for the original spiritual integrity of the bride. An individual woman entering the bride's stage represents all women, and more: she represents humanity itself in its preincarnational purity. We've lost sight of this sacramental dimension in our Western secularized wedding procedures; we marry by procedure, by rote, but not by true ritual; because ritual is an induction into the realm of the sacred, where the innate purity of the woman and man is implicitly honored and the honoring itself is an experience of the holy.

For example, in one Moroccan village it's customary for the groom's mother to set, upside down in the yard, a mug containing a *didli* (an ornament made of dollar and half-dollar coins threaded on a string of horsehair and worn by women around the forehead). On top of the mug the mother sets an egg; when the groom kicks the mug, this chases away, if not destroys, the evil—that is, any impediments to the successful observance of the wedding. As a related gesture, after the bride has been painted in henna, her attendants tie a kerchief containing an egg around her forehead; the woman who applied the henna then smashes the egg in situ, where it remains—protectively, one hopes—until the next morning. In the village of Hiána, when the groom enters the room where his bride is waiting, he uses a small sword to slash the rope that has been tied from wall to wall in front of the bed; by this gesture he slashes the field of energy set up by the bas around their marital intentions, thereby purifying the room.

Moroccan brides are purified with both water and henna five days before the wedding. Female family members accompany the bride to the bathhouse, bearing candles; once inside they light the candles and utter that remarkably aggressive rapidly trilling, guttural quiver (the *zaghárit,* or "joy cry") to scare off any lurking *jnun* (bad spirits). Three days before the wedding, this ritual is repeated, and seven buckets of lukewarm water are poured over the bride by seven women, presumably to rinse away a disputatious nature in accordance with the proverb, "The water is safety and quarrel there is none."

The procession to the bathhouse, called *Zeffet al-Hammam,* can be a colorful, arresting spectacle, as Edward William Lane noted in his travels through Egypt in the 1830s. Around noon the bride heads "in state" to the baths in a procession headed by musicians with several hautboy and drums. Heading the phalanx are two men

INDIA
MOROCCO
SUDAN
GREECE
RUSSIA
FINLAND
ENGLAND
YUGOSLAVIA
GERMANY
CHINA
TRINIDAD
ROMANIA

INDIA
MOROCCO
SUDAN
GREECE
RUSSIA
FINLAND
ENGLAND
YUGOSLAVIA
GERMANY
CHINA
TRINIDAD
ROMANIA

bearing the utensils and linen needed for the bath on round trays covered with embroidered silk kerchiefs; a *sakka*, who dispenses water to passersby; and another man who bears the *kumkum*, a gilt-silver bottle of rosewater or orange-flower water from which he periodically sprinkles his fellow marchers, and the *mibkharah*, or silver perfuming vessel, in which strong-scented aloes-wood might be burning. Among the bride's companions who walk ahead of her, the married women walk in pairs clad in the black silk *habarah*, while the unmarried women wear white shawls. The bride comes next in the procession, clad in a red cashmere shawl, and walking under a silken canopy, open only in the front, of gay color, such as pink, rose, or yellow, and supported by four men, each bearing a pole; embroidered handkerchiefs trail off the tops of the poles in the light breeze. If it's especially hot, several women will cool her with fans made of black ostrich feathers.

That evening a *m'àllma l-hännàya* (a female henna paste ritualist) paints round henna dots (or stars and crescents) above the bride's wrists and on her fingers, and applies henna to her feet and to the palms and the backs of her hands. Later more of her body is painted: her eyes with antimony, her under-lip with walnut root, her cheeks with ocher speckled with black dots (made from a pigment of wood ashes, pitch, and spices) and white dots. At some point she will also be sprinkled with milk, whose whiteness (signifying light) will avert evil and make her future "white," or lucky. These henna dots remain on her body overnight; in the morning they are stained red outwardly as a mark of ritual completion. But red henna has an inner significance as well, according to some observers. It symbolizes the blood bond between bride and groom, and with members of both families and close friends. The idea is that as marriage establishes a new life and new bloodlines, so do the scarlet henna dots commemorate this genetic and social renewal.

The Wazâra *Anoint Their Honorific Sultan with Henna*

Considerable purificatory gestures and preparatory rites are accorded the Moroccan groom as well. The first is the ritual cleaning of the wedding wheat and corn in the groom's house. White flags mounted on bamboo poles are erected on the roof, announcing the task underway, and they remain until the ceremony is completed. When the grain is cleaned and piled, a bowl containing a raw egg and salt is set on top of one heap, then a dagger is inserted into the grain. The dagger and salt will discourage evil spirits, while the eggwhite ensures that "the wedding shall be without rain and the life of the bridegroom shall be white"—meaning fine weather and a bright life.

Like the bride, the Moroccan groom is also ritually painted in henna on "bridegroom's night," celebrated at his father's house in the company of his unmarried male companions. Musicians play oboes and drums in the yard, giving him "the wish of a good evening." When he appears in the doorway to welcome them, they call back, "Be blessed and lucky." Around daybreak the next morning, the bachelors, carrying four flags and accompanied by the musicians, take the groom for a walk around the village. From this moment until the end of the wedding, the groom is regarded as a sultan and his bachelor friends his *wazâra*, or ministers. They sing to their new sultan: "O great Majesty, O God, O God; the one who is girded with a sword, good luck to him forever, O dear one, O God."

The party of wazâra return with the groom to his courtyard, where they seat themselves in a circle around him. His mother comes out of the house bearing a bowl containing henna paste, an egg, and four candles, and a bottle of water. Setting the bowl and bottle on the ground, she greets her son: "May God be gracious to you." The bride-groom's best man—often called the "sultan's chamberlain" or vizier—takes the bowl, lights the candles, distributes them to the flag-bearing bach-elors, who all kneel before the hooded "sultan." The groom breaks the egg, mixing it with the henna, and asks one "minister" to pour in some water. Slowly stirring the henna paste with the lit-tle finger of his right hand, he sings:

> In the name of God the merciful and compas-
> sionate, O God
> I take refuge with God from the devil, the
> stoned one, O God
> We have made our lord Bulal our leader and O
> God
> We have made our lord 'Utman our leader and
> O God
> We have made our lord 'Esa (Jesus) our leader
> and O God
> We have made our lord 'Alr our leader and O
> God
> His face is like the moon and O God
> Stretch out your hand we shall paint you with
> henna, O my lord
> Stretch out your hand from your sleeve, O my
> lord
> Today your luck has stood up, O my lord.

Then the vizier daubs the right then left palm of the groom with henna, applying some to his own hands as well. Next the vizier instructs the musicians to play as he takes the four burning can-dles and inserts them in the bowl with the henna mixture. He lifts the bowl on his head and dances before the sultan; after him all the wazâra repeat the dance gesture except the last minister allows the bowl to shatter on the ground to banish the *bas,* or "the evil." This final gesture reveals the true intention of the henna ritual, namely, to purify the "sultan" and protect him from injurious subtle or supernatural influences. If he is the sultan then he is a priori holy, and holy people are perpetually

surrounded by dangers; the holiness implies "not only that there is a supernatural energy in the holy individual or object, but also that they are suscep-tible to all kinds of baleful influences," says Westermarck. Henna is the preferred botanical bodyguard because, so Moroccans believe, it's per-meated with *baraka,* a spiritual grace and blessing from God.

Al-Laylit al-Hinna— *Evening of the Henna*

In the contemporary Sudanese pre-wedding cer-emony of *Al-Laylit al-Hinna,* we find preserved (with variations) a concentrated ritual expression of the purificatory use of henna.

After dinner at his father's house, the groom, his close male friends, and male and fe-male relatives make a procession on foot to the home of the bride. The women in the company play the drums and sing, and the unmarried young women might dance as well. Often a man is en-gaged to be chief musician, vocalist, and choir master for the singing women; he covers himself with a robe, anoints himself with perfume, and daubs his eyes with kohl. The groom leads the noisy procession, closely followed by his friends who carry lights, wave sticks, and dance the *'arda.*

After taking refreshments at the bride's home, the groom retreats to a room where he joins his bride seated on a mattress. She's clothed in her wedding costume, and a scarf obscures most of her face and body. Several of the groom's female rela-tives bring henna, perfumes, and a lighted incense burner. They hand the groom a piece of henna, which he transfers to the bride's palms; he squeezes her hands so that the henna stains her skin, which completes the act.

INDIA
MOROCCO
SUDAN
GREECE
RUSSIA
FINLAND
ENGLAND
YUGOSLAVIA
GERMANY
CHINA
TRINIDAD
ROMANIA

BRIDEWEALTH, BRIDE-ALE, AND BRIDAL SHOWERS

*T*he institution of marriage seems to have a strong patriarchal root. Today's fairly innocuous bridal shower, for example, emerged over millennia from what scholars call "marriage by capture." In earliest times men simply took their wives, as it pleased them. Later they were willing to purchase their spouses, by paying what's variously called a bride-price, bride-wealth, witthum, arrha, or beweddung.

The Anglo-Saxon groom awarded his wife a morgengifu, *which was a gift of land; the Jewish groom specified his financial terms for their potential divorce settlement in the* ketubah *marriage contract; the Roman groom had to pay the bride a substantial marriage gift, the* donatio. *The Genoese groom from the artisan class was required to endow his bride with the* antefactum *(money or valuables worth 70 percent of her dowry), and the* tercia *(interest in one-third of his total estate). The sixth-century Germanic groom made a bride-gift directly to his spouse, and the* Morgengabe *(the "morning gift," usually a sum of money), paid the day after the wedding, "in recognition of the bride's surrender of virginity and the groom's acquisition of sexual rights," according to Frances and Joseph Gies in* Marriage and the Family in the Middle Ages.

Much later, in eighteenth-century England, couples who could afford neither dowry nor bride-price had a clever idea: give a party, and have the guests pay. A couple might give notice of their wedding by posting an open invitation in a public place: "Suspend for one day your cares and your labors, and come to this wedding, kind friends and good neighbors." The bride-ale, something like today's sherry-morning and held for a good cause, was usually held in the parish church. The bride and groom provided a party atmosphere—food, games, entertainment, sometimes wrestling, plenty of ale to drink—and then they passed around the collection box. If everything went well, the bride-ale paid for itself and left enough cash for the young, undercapitalized couple—typically servants, trade-folk, and little-holding farmers—to establish their own new household.

Later the bride-ale left the churches and hit the taverns and ale-houses as the penny-bridal. The guests paid for their own drinks and filled a collection box for the couple. In late-eighteenth-century Wales, these events were called bidden-weddings, because the guests—as many as possible—were bidden to attend by a herald, with a crook or wand adorned with ribbons who made his circuit of the local neighborhoods. Those with a few more pennies up front placed an ad in a publication.

Tom the Bidder was legendary in mid-nineteenth-century Wales for his skill at rousing up country-folk to attend bidden-weddings. The Welsh often engaged a local bard to serve as bidder, or Gwahod-dwr. He called in at all the far-flung farms, in swallowtail coat, breeches, top hat, and a long staff decorated with ribbons—the trademark of a Gwahoddwr—making his eloquent rammas *speech at each, listing exhaustively what items would be appreciated as bidden-gifts: a saddle, a heifer, child's cradle, a wagon full of potatoes, a cartload of turnips, a cask of butter, a hundred or two of cheeses, a winchester of barley, "or even a penny-whistle." And of course a little something for himself: "So no more at present. If you please to order your butler, or underservant, to give a quart of drink to the bidder."*

Around the same time as Al-Laylit al-Hinna, the Sudanese groom engages in another prewedding "whiteness" purification exercise involving sorghum and sour milk. Earlier his family planted sorghum seeds in a pot of soil, then covered it with a cloth. When the plant produced a certain amount of foliage, they cut the tops off, then dried and ground them as *bil zarii'a* for Al-Laylit al-Hinna, and as a preparation that would make both bride and groom fruitful. Then the women of the groom's family have a party at which they and the groom eat rice, milk, and a porridge made of sorghum and clarified butter; the groom is also expected to eat a sour milk stew for three nights leading up to this party. These practices turn on the positive magical qualities widely associated with the color white.

Lustration by Water

Prenuptial baths and sanctifying immersions are widespread customs in many cultures, in common recognition of water as the great, unfailing cleanser, the conjugal lustrater.

Bridal couples once took full body baths in water drawn from the Callirrhoë fountain in Athens, with the understanding that the pure waters somehow washed them into a state of virtue. On the eve of her wedding day in ancient Greece, the bride was visited by a special delegation: a young boy playing the pipes, a matron bearing a lighted torch in each hand, and a maiden carrying on her head a long-necked pitcher filled with water from the "Beautiful Spring," a holy fountain arising by the banks of the Ilissos. She fulfilled a long-established Greek prenuptial custom when she bathed herself using this pure spring water. The Greek bride was also expected to propitiate

the water spirits of the spring by tossing in a few coins.

Water played a prominent role in the traditional sixteenth-century Russian three-day wedding ceremony. The second day begins with the ablution of the newlyweds. The bride's best man and matchmaker arrive at her parent's house with the "washing vessels" (a covered copper pot and two basins) and four towels; the groom's best man and matchmaker show up at his house with another set of the same equipment. The groom rises from bed and heads for the soaping room; when his father-in-law learns of his movements, he immediately sends his "washing gifts"—a full set of warm clothes—by the matchmaker in a special casket born on a sleigh.

In Finland on the wedding morning, it was traditional for the bride and her close friends to visit the sauna; afterward her unbraided long hair would be trimmed short as her older female companions and relations sobbed dramatically to display their sorrow at losing a daughter (or niece) from the house, a transition signaled by the haircut and the bride's donning of the *tzepy*, the traditional linen cap for married (and apparently short-haired) women.

For Zulu women it's customary for the bride and her female companions to bathe together on her wedding morning. In the Assam region of India, on her wedding eve, the bride's relatives made a procession, with drummers, musicians, and other women, to the nearest river; there they invoked the goddesses of water for a blessing on the jars of water they would bring home for the bride's lustration. Of course for Hindus the sine qua non for water purification is a prenuptial immersion in India's most sacred river, the Ganges.

In the British Isles, the bridal bath was sometimes limited to the feet. In the Shetland and Orkney islands of northern Scotland, male friends of the groom washed his feet on his wedding eve; if

INDIA
MOROCCO
SUDAN
GREECE
RUSSIA
FINLAND
ENGLAND
YUGOSLAVIA
GERMANY
CHINA
TRINIDAD
ROMANIA

they were wealthy, they used wine instead of water. They tossed a ring into the washing-tub water; the unmarried men dashed avidly for it, understanding that the finder would be the next of them to marry.

Among the G'wi Bushmen of Botswana, the bride fasts in silence and without moving for four days in a wattle circle outside the village. Then the village women collect the bride and groom and shave their heads, and wash their bodies using a sliced juicy bulb as a sponge. Next they tattoo them both simultaneously, intermingling their blood (from the cuts necessary in the tattooing process) as a symbol of their union. When the pattern of cuts has been completed on their bodies, the women rub in a mixture of ashes and medicinal roots to ensure that the cuts will heal as raised blue scars, public emblems of their purificatory experience. Later one of the village elders (a woman) paints identical designs on their bodies using red ocher and fat.

Among the Celebes of Malay, lustration by water was integral to all rites of passage, such as birth, adolescence, marriage, sickness, death, and any critical life period. They called it *tepong tawar,* which means approximately "the neutralizing rice-flour water," a ritual in which neutralizing really means sterilizing the active element of psychic poisons or evil potentialities. The newly wed Malays continued this lustration for three days after their official joining ceremony. In a related purificatory practice, both bride and groom are "fumigated" with incense, then smeared with a "neutralizing paste," to avert ill luck.

A Bath with Tambourines in the Nile

Shortly before her wedding, the young Egyptian woman living in the vicinity of the Nile will perform the jar-filling ritual. She's accompanied by

four female companions in the late afternoon as she fills her jar from the sacred waters. Back home at sunset she washes herself completely with this water, then her mother anoints her with perfume and henna, covering her in a *twada,* a traditional women's wrap. The young bride keeps her face obscured for all but her closest female relatives as a group of her women contemporaries arrive to entertain her with tambourine and song:

> How pretty is the one we are entertaining,
> How we are admiring her.
> The snake in his hole
> has spent a sleepless night.
> He kept one eye on her forehead,
> and the other on her anklets.

Fetching Water from the Three Fountains

In Galicnik in the former Yugoslavia, all weddings took place around the Feast of St. Peter (January 18), beginning at dusk, when the groom (*dzamutra*) and his kinsfolk arrive at the *nevesta's* (bride's) home with a gypsy band led by a man carrying an iron pot of blazing firewood attached to a long pole. They've come to escort the nevesta and her four maiden companions to fetch water from the Three Fountains. The groom takes coffee with her parents, while the bride and her companions sit in another room and sing:

> The rose put forth buds in the *podrum*
> But in the house opened the flowers.
> Here grew up a boy,
> The only son of his mother.
> Lead out the horse carefully,
> That thou break not the rose!
> For the rose has been watered;
> Morning and evening, with water,
> But at midday with tears.

USING THE DREAMBODY PROCESS TO MASTER THE
ART OF CONFLICT RESOLUTION

"*T*he best part of married life is the fights," the writer Thornton Wilder once said. "The rest is so-so." Regardless of how we feel about this statement, conflict is inevitable in any relationship, and if used wisely it can be an instrument for growth. Learning the art of conflict is a necessary element in the purification process of the world culture wedding. What can literally make or break a relationship in this conflicted milieu is how we approach it—do we resist conflict or accept it? Voting on the side of acceptance is Arnold Mindell, Ph.D., Jungian analyst, master of the art of conflict resolution, and author of nine books about his "dreambody process work" model.

Conflict, says Mindell, "is a normal occurrence, a sign of our tendency toward self-balance and development. We need to get into the habit of thinking that conflict may be a chance for personal growth, excitement, a 'meeting with the gods,' a place for discovering the awesomeness of personal life." Conflict is also a catalyst to bring people together. "Conflict is the fastest way to create community, something a group needs in order to understand itself—provided you catch the forbidden edge of the issue that's almost unspeakable."

The edge, explains Mindell, is a half-heard voice of the unconscious. Who's speaking? Mindell calls it the dreambody, which for him encompasses a continuum of effects and processes that expresses itself through dreams, body symptoms, body signals, positions, vocal tones, unintended communications, illness, accidents, relationship problems, synchronicities, and conflicts. Process work means you become aware of the inherent forces behind the apparent issues and conflict, then you act them out, role play them, dramatize them, heighten their affect, and amplify them. When the dreambody message is conveyed loudly enough, you finally get it and the whole field shifts into resolution. "Process work focuses upon the intended and unintended processes, upon what is happening and trying to happen," Mindell explains in The Dreambody in Relationships.

Marriage and relationships are "dreamed up" expressions of the dreambody, too, says Mindell. "You must know both your dreams and your body to survive a relationship. Since we are always dreaming, we are always dreaming others up to be parts of ourselves. At any given moment, both people are simultaneously projecting and dreaming the other up."

Here's a simple example about a couple named Bob and Gayle, whom Mindell helped to "process." As they talk about their relationship, Bob constantly fixes his glasses; Gayle listens to him but faces away. She wants him to pay more attention to her; he says he's very busy. That's the outer case; we see the secondary processes in his fiddling with his glasses and her body position. Mindell asked Bob to exaggerate his double signals and fiddle more with his glasses; soon he put his hands around his eyes, then laughed, saying his fingers were like goggles encircling his eyes. He said he wanted to examine, investigate, and peer at every aspect of Gayle. When she amplified her position, turning even farther away from him, she realized she didn't have time to deal with him and wanted to do her own things.

"How surprised they both were to hear and see the opposite form of behavior coming from their double signals," observes Mindell. In actuality, Bob was fascinated with Gayle and wanted to see more of her; Gayle in actuality wanted less attention from him. "So here the couple's dream was the exact opposite of their normal behavior. Discovering the edges, double signals, dreams, and myths is a step toward discovering the structure of communication and creating a tool kit to give people the richest, most continuous, and fluid relationships imaginable."

INDIA
MOROCCO
SUDAN
GREECE
RUSSIA
FINLAND
ENGLAND
YUGOSLAVIA
GERMANY
CHINA
TRINIDAD
ROMANIA

Now all the guests assemble in the yard, gathering around the bonfire in the iron pot. The bride's relatives distribute chips and small bits of pinewood to each guest for a torch, which is then lit from the bonfire; then they set off following the man with the blazing iron pot. The groom's party walks near the head of the dusk procession, while the bride and her four maidens take up the rear, walking silently and with downcast eyes. One of the maidens is a girl of about eight years, who walks in front of the bride. As they reach each fountain, her task is to fill her pitcher one-third full and to fill her mouth with water, holding it until she reaches the next fountain, when she may spit it out. But she must carry the water from the last fountain all the way back home, spitting it out into the kitchen cauldron; this residual water from the Three Fountains will be heated for the bride's ablution.

Since other wedding processions are out on the steep mountainside this evening on the Feast of St. Peter, one group easily becomes entangled with another. "All of them flame and wander along like a giant centipede," observed Oliver Lodge in his *Peasant Life in Jugoslavia,* "so that the little steep paths and the one road of the village are lighted up with dots and dashes of fire; and the air is filled with the aromatic scent of burning pine-wood." When the pitchers are filled, the group takes a different path home, as they must not retread in their footsteps; later that night the bride washes herself in the water collected from the Three Fountains.

Smudging, Polterabend, *and* Chinese Firecrackers

What native Americans traditionally call *smudging* and occultists call *censing* is usually accomplished by enveloping the individual in a cloud of strongly scented smoke. The intent is to purge the etheric and astral bodies of negative energies, influences, spiritual toxins, and harmful presences. This practice is present in many cultures.

The groom in Sweden and Denmark sewed pomanders of strong-smelling herbs—such as garlic, chives, and rosemary—into his clothes as aromatic antidotes to negative influences. Miss Pardoe, an evidently emboldened British observer of Turkish domestic manners, reported in 1836 that a Turkish mother of the bride performed a kind of smudging as part of her daughter's bridal shower. When the "bridal paraphernalia" had been sufficiently examined, writes Pardoe, the mother strode into the room "carrying in one hand a filigreed silver essence bottle, and in the other a censer of the same material, in which were burning aloes, myrrh, and perfumed woods." She "flung" the strong perfume over everybody present, addressing each individual; to the unmarried she said, "May your bridal follow!" and to the matrons she exclaimed, "May you also see the bridal of your children!"

Another way to purify the ethers around the bridal couple is to make a lot of noise. That's the thinking behind the ancient German custom of *Polterabend,* meaning "noise evening." Well-wishers catalogued the couple's virtues and failings on the day before their marriage; if their virtues predominated, the friends signified their goodwill by making a tremendous racket before the houses of both individuals, presumably to chase away any lurking ill-willed spirits. Often they chucked all the broken, chipped, or defective crockery and glass out the windows, where it would smash definitively, and loudly, on the ground below. Or else they would collect the disposable kitchenware outside and smash it against the sides of the house. House windows were locked, but the front door was left wide open to encourage the demons' hasty departure. The interior walls of the house were sprinkled with water, and all the walls were beaten soundly with flat sticks, to terrorize any residual and surely unhappy ghosts.

The Chinese of old Beijing preferred firecrackers; they were louder, quicker, and took less effort. The Chinese assumed that as a new bride passed various locations in her sedan, she was vulnerable to the approach of evil spirits who could injure her or produce illness. As a protection the custom was to paint the image of a great magician or formidable Taoist priest riding astride a tiger, brandishing a terrifying sword.

In Manchuria two men ran in front of the bride's carriage, flashing a red cloth, presumably to ward off inimical influences; her sedan itself was initially fumigated with strong incense and provisioned with a calendar listing the names of the idols that control the demoniacal hosts. The calendar is also efficacious because the Chinese believed that the cycle of days was originally determined by celestial intelligences, some of whose aegis presumably adheres, if only homeopathically, to their heavenly time reckonings as recorded in calendars. Before anyone entered the sedan, an attendant examined it thoroughly with a mirror, understanding that should an evil spirit catch its image in the looking glass it would be disempowered. When the sedan-chair arrived at the groom's home, attendants secured the doors then released firecrackers around the carriage to scare away the spirits; and before the bride even left the carriage, the groom fired three arrows at its blinds; sometimes they threw coins into the air instead. The Chinese bride was dressed entirely in vivid red; even her head was shielded with a bright red scarf. When she entered the marriage sedan, she took one bite from an apple, but didn't chew or swallow it; she kept it in her mouth until she reached her new home, when she deposited it in a special jar by her bedside as a peacemaking amulet.

In Celtic lands, where the "fairy-faith" was strong, it was commonly known that the Little

People could not abide the clangor of church bells, which was why the church wardens rang them so vociferously on Sundays—to welcome the humans and drive away everyone else. Yorkshire couples crossing a bridge took responsibility for performing their own preemptive exorcisms. The husband would go first to overcome all danger, then the couple would toss small objects into the stream below, so that "it might carry with it every evil wish and ill spell wrought by wicked hearts that day," as Richard Blakeborough puts it in his essay *A Country Wedding a Century Ago.*

World folklore is rife with further examples of these intriguing demon-dispersing techniques. In India the ancient custom was to shoot wedding arrows into the sky, proclaiming: "I pierce the eyes of the spirits who surround the bride." Among the Bhils and Bhilalahs of India, the groom probes the marriage-shed with his sword; or brandishes a long spear four times heavenward then four times over the bride. Roman grooms combed their bride's hair with a spear, the *caelibaris hasta,* presumably to frighten away or neutralize bad spirits of the coiffure. Roman brides wore a wreath of flowers and sacred plants and a flame-colored veil to scare off the "evil eye." Brahmin couples waved censers of lighted camphor before them. Irish men fired guns at intervals over the heads of the bride and bridesmaids on their journey to church; among the Mordvin countryfolk, the best man marched three times around the bridal party with a drawn sword (or scythe), casting imprecations and curses upon any ill-wishers, tangible or otherwise. The Russian best man's task was to walk three times counterclockwise around the bridal entourage, holding a religious icon, as other members of the bridal party cracked whips, fired guns, and made as much noise as possible; then, positioning himself in front of them, he scratched the ground with a knife and cursed all evilly disposed persons and their inspiring spirits. Church circumambulation by the best man was another common purificatory gesture.

INDIA
MOROCCO
SUDAN
GREECE
RUSSIA
FINLAND
ENGLAND
YUGOSLAVIA
GERMANY
CHINA
TRINIDAD
ROMANIA

INDIA
MOROCCO
SUDAN
GREECE
RUSSIA
FINLAND
ENGLAND
YUGOSLAVIA
GERMANY
CHINA
TRINIDAD
ROMANIA

In Thailand, as part of a lay Buddhist wedding altar, a square black table set on the veranda displayed a bronze Buddha, a china pot of burning incense, and a large silver jar of ceremonial water, while the officiant inscribed six white dots in the form of a triangle on the doorstep to discourage evil from entering the house. Another evil-shunning device was the deployment of a flaming red carpet laid down to protect the bridal couple from chthonic evil (just as the bridal canopy shielded them from heavenly malice).

When the Hong Kong bride arrived at her husband's home, she stepped over a small fire of dry grass at the home's threshold to purify her of any "devils" that may have stuck like invisible astral burrs to her personage on the journey from her family's house. German grooms marked all the household goods brought by the bride with consecrated chalk then sprinkled them with holy water. Scottish grooms sprinkled salt on the floor of their bridal home as a protection against the "evil eye."

In Perthshire, Scotland, the bridal couple untied all knots in their clothing (and hair) on their wedding day to symbolically release the evil principle, which would otherwise keep them tightly bound up and constricted. The familiar custom of tying old shoes to the bumper of the bridal car (and its earlier form of throwing old shoes after the departing couple) originates in a belief that leather shoes are an effective charm that dispel unfriendly spirits.

Clothing, either exotic, inappropriate, or cross-gender, is commonly used to foil the apparently undiscerning negative entities in the marital environment. Sartorial interventions such as these are popular among folk cultures: bridal veils, hats, umbrellas, litters, rugs, special shoes, flowers, and rushes. A heavily veiled Chinese bride walked from her private chambers to the bridal sedan wearing her father's shoes. Disguises are a commonly employed ruse: decoy men and women masquerade as the bride and groom or else bride and groom exchange gender costumes. In one wedding tale, a

medieval Christian visitor to the Levant witnessed a Jewish bridal procession led by the bride herself with soldier's helmet and sword with the groom frolicking beside him "in drag" or "cross-dressing" (as we now call it). In old Denmark the bride and groom dressed up in old, unattractive clothes of the opposite sex and avoided being with each other in public until the ceremony.

In India, in a gesture of applied animism, individuals performed decoy, mock marriages with animals, plants, trees, or inanimate objects to distract and confuse the evil spirits who were evidently maintaining constant surveillance. For example, in one instance a woman was publicly "married" to a water pitcher dressed up in a groom's attire. It sounds at first glance like rank paranoia, but if the individual is worried about the interventions of the jealous, malicious, and uncordial spirits of his two former, now deceased wives who do not approve of his current union or any further felicity in his life, then any occultist, Theosophist, Taoist, or psychic will assure you he's being very sensible: unempathetic ancestral spirits lurking in the astral plane can be a definite problem for the psychically unguarded couple.

In fact, the familiar custom of throwing rice after the wedding couple en route for the honeymoon may have originated out of this same defensive attitude, as a way of "giving food to the evil influences to induce them to be propitious and depart," comments Ernest Crawley in *The Mystic Rose*. Even more intriguing, Crawley reports that rather than a symbolic expression of wished-for fertility, throwing rice and other grains as a postnuptial gesture may have been designed "as an inducement to the soul to stay." In Celebes, Malaya, it was thought that the groom's soul was likely to fly away at the marriage ceremony; his friends threw rice at him as an incarnational bribe to keep him in his body. Perhaps that's also why the Greeks poured sweetmeats and flour over the new bridegroom.

ELEMENTALS AND THE VINDICATION OF FOLKLORE

With our attention riveted to the external events and schedules of our unfolding wedding plans, the apparent paranoia of folklore with respect to evil spirits and baleful influences seems remote, if not entirely improbable. Long-standing esoteric traditions had already alerted us to the possibility of invisibly populated tangential worlds, but their views were mostly for the specialists. Then the eruption in the 1980s of occult phenomena, channelings, near-death and out-of-body experiences—and their widespread, often sensationlized media coverage— testified to the possibility of a different accounting of the "neurotic" supernatural fixations of folk customs. We need only to review our recent cultural history to see how significantly our metaphysical parameters have been extended.

- In 1968 Carlos Castaneda published the first in a series of books revealing his astrally tortuous initiation into the "way of knowledge" of a Yaqui Indian sorcerer named Don Juan Matus.
- In 1980 Michael Harner, a Ph.D. anthropologist, published *The Way of the Shaman,* an accessible text that stimulated among mostly educated white young Americans a decade of engagement with the mystical ways of native peoples—astral travel, the human double, ritual, irregularities in time, animal group-souls—and a burgeoning body of literature.
- Lynn Andrews offered her best-selling accounts of a woman's initiation into the occult ways of Canadian Indian wise women in *Medicine Woman*
- From Findhorn (an intentional spiritual community in northern Scotland founded on the visions of mystics Eileen Caddy, Dorothy MacLean, and David Spangler) came reports in the 1960s of communications with the elemental and angelic realms, of meetings with flower devas, gnomes, landscape angels, even the great Pan.

If nothing else, the possibility of the reality of such unsuspected planes of experience has begun to permeate mass culture—that, and the hunger to find them.

In The Magus of Strovolos, *Kyriacos Markides elucidates the practices and insights of Daskalos, a contemporary Cypriot esoteric teacher. According to Daskalos the mind is so powerful that emotionally charged thoughts, whether conscious or unconscious, can take on a life, form, and power of their own. Explains Markides, "Any thought and any feeling that an individual projects is an elemental." Magicians send them purposefully (but not always with benign intent); the rest of us generate them without much awareness; and we may unknowingly collect a congeries of them in our dreamtime." Egotism can create a variety of elementals, Daskalos once told Markides. "We have noticed from experience that when an individual has evil and malicious thoughts against someone, the elementals he creates have the shape of snakes with various dark colors, usually putrid green. They come out either from the heart or the base of the nose. They move towards the person against whom we consciously or subconsciously direct them and they tend to stick to the aura of that person."*

Maybe there *is something to chasing away the evil eye with a bright sword . . .*

Burying the Past and Placating the Ancestors

Marriage, as we've seen, marks a profound psychological cleavage from one's past—whether it's adolescent life with parents, or a successfully negotiated midlife crisis and renewal through a new partnership; but marriage also is about the multigenerational continuity of family lines and the creation of new linkages. In this way settling accounts with one's personal past is equivalent to pacifying the ancestors and family spirits.

Villagers in France's Vaucluse region devised the "burial of the bachelor life" to facilitate the groom's release of his familial and psychological past. This was an elaborate mock funeral, in which his former bachelor life—perhaps vividly represented by an effigy, personal documents, and old clothing—was symbolically buried in a coffin. This is a more severe form of the traditional bachelor party, in which fairly unlicensed drinking, singing, dancing, and frolicking have the quality of a last, desperate fling at irresponsible, adolescent "freedom" on the threshold of adult responsibility.

The Vietnamese devised another way to tame the savage bachelor breast: the *lam re,* meaning, "to be the son-in-law." This is a service period in which the groom performs jobs for the parents of his bride at their home as a demonstration of good character and competence as a farmer and breadwinner. During lam re grooms must cut wood, carry water, and perform other tasks as directed without complaint or inattention, knowing that the critical eyes of the parents-in-law are evaluating his every step.

The Javanese groom chastened himself for marriage by making daily visits to the mosque to stand in cold water up to his chin, reciting his marriage oaths to the priest as his witness. Meanwhile his bride prepared herself by a severe fast, taking only three teaspoons of rice and one cup of hot water every day.

Russian women, upon betrothal, were exempted from most household duties and wore a special mourning dress to signify her sorrow at leaving her maidenhood; friends would hold farewell ceremonies and offer songs of lament at the passing of her innocence. The sadness may be salutary, however. "Weeping bride, laughing wife; laughing bride, weeping wife," advises the old Russian proverb. A small tree that had been decorated to symbolize the bride's free days of virginity and adolescent innocence was dismantled; the bride and groom exchanged small bundles of its twigs, then individually brought them to the bathhouse the next morning for use in their separate ablutions.

Young Russian brides-to-be had another special observance to say farewell to maidenhood. The young woman's maidenhood was symbolized by the *krasnaia krasota,* a wreath of ribbons, flowers, and ornaments twined through a single braid of her long hair. Her female companions unbraid her hair then rebraid it in a single braid for the last time; if her family is wealthy, the girls will interweave strings of pearls and pieces of gold along with the flowers. They sing lamentations, songs prophesying ill-treatment, misfortune; she'd do best if she ran out into open country and purged her grief now before the wedding, they tell her.

> Fall down on the damp earth,
> Upon the burning stones,
> For surely you know, dear sister,
> That our mother, the dampe earth, will not betray you,
> That the burning stones will not repeat it.
> But you will go to strange people,
> You will wipe off the burning tears,
> Do not show your feelings to people.

Young Persian brides were coached through a similar rite of passage on the eve of their wedding. In the evening the maiden was wrapped up in a long scarlet silken veil, set on a splendidly outfitted horse, and accompanied by musicians and all her relations, conducted to her groom's home. During the trip one of her female attendants would hold a large mirror before her, admonishing her to take one last look at herself as a maiden.

Between her betrothal and her wedding day, the Japanese bride will wear white, which for her is the color of mourning; her forthcoming marriage signals her death to her family, girlhood, and youth. White also signifies that she will never leave her husband's house except as a corpse, when she will again be clothed in (funereal) white. On the day of her departure, her parental house is swept out; in older days a purificatory bonfire was lit at the gate, a cleansing rite reminiscent of what's done after the removal of a dead body.

Maybe the ancestral spirits just want some respect; in their view they're still fulfilling their family role as revered elders. In China one of the first items on the agenda after the bride's arrival at the groom's home was for the couple to offer their reverence to the ancestral tablet, making three deep bows to the family roster of generations as strong incense wafts through the room. The ancestor-appeasing practices of the Sumba Islanders in Indonesia arise from their philosophy of a tripartite world: the realm of the living humans, the souls of the dead, and the gods.

"The world that controls the conduct of wedding ceremonies is that of the souls of the dead, the ancestors of a family having particular concern as to how it conducts itself today," as Brian Murphy explains in *The World of Weddings: An Illustrated Celebration*. Immediately after a traditional Filipino wedding, the newlyweds follow a band in procession from the church to the bride's family house. Once there, everyone kneels before an altar to offer prayers for the departed ancestors of both families. In the Breton region of north-

western France, the oldest crone of the village walks straight up to the newly married couple, falls on her knees, and chants a long litany called *De Profundis*, the prayer for the dead.

In Trinidad villagers of Toco who are contemplating a marriage first consult the ancestors and obtain their sanction. They do this through a ritual of reel dances called *sakara*, staged the night before the wedding. For music in the old style they might have a kettledrum, tambourine, and fife; in the 1940s they updated this to a clarinet and jazz bass. While the drum sounds, the younger villagers remain indoors, singing, making offerings of food (white rice, yams, peas, bread, cake, rum, ginger beer) and sacrificial animal blood (from fowl, goat, or pig). A preferred ancestral food offering is *sansam*, made of cornmeal cooked with sugar; they'll also cook white rice with blood from the sacrificed animals and without salt. At midnight a village elder takes the ancestral food, offering it to the ancestors as he speaks frenziedly to them. He sets the corn and rice on banana leaves spread on the ground then adds a libation of rum. He names as many of the ancestors as he can remember and invites those whose names he doesn't know. His head draped in black cloth with a wide red cross in front, he rings a handbell three times then whistles.

As a variation on this form of sakara, the elder performs a ritual that will have a protective value for the groom. He distributes the sakara accompanied by two men and two women, each of whom bears a candle. Using a stick of white chalk, he makes marks on the nearby trees near their base; then he inscribes sacred symbols in chalk around the feet of his four companions and the food; next he marks the foreheads of the two sets of parents with a white cross. He returns to the trees, undresses, makes incantations to the spirits, goes silent for a while, then calls for music. Soon the groom is summoned and the elder rubs his forehead, crown, and feet with leaves gathered from the trees to discourage the activities of hostile spirits.

MAGICAL CORRESPONDENCES FOR PURIFICATION RITUALS

*T*he protocols of Western ritual magic indicate correspondences between the day of the week and the appropriate colors, metals, flowers, spiritual beings, and animal spirits to invoke as protection for one's activities. On a practical level, one could assemble the appropriate items or their symbolic presence for a self-created purificatory and protection ritual during a specially designated day of purification.

A Table of Ritual Elements

	SUNDAY	MONDAY	TUESDAY
Archangel:	Michael	Gabriel	Samuel
Element:	fire	water	fire
Zodiac sign:	Leo	Cancer	Aries, Scorpio
Planet:	Sun	Moon	Mars
Planetary color:	gold/orange	silver/blue	red
Planetary metal :	gold	silver	iron
Incense:	frankincense, saffron	jasmine, patchouli	pine
Flowers:	marigold, heliotrope, night-scented stock, thistles, nettles, sunflower, rosemary	convolvulus, poppy	hawthorn, garlic, cumin
Animal:	wildcat	crab	ram
Bird:	hawk owl	nightjar	falcon

	WEDNESDAY	THURSDAY	FRIDAY
Archangel:	Raphael	Zaphael	Anael
Element:	air	fire	earth
Zodiac sign:	Gemini, Virgo	Sagittarius, Pisces	Taurus, Libra
Planet:	Mercury	Jupiter	Venus
Planetary color:	yellow	purple	green
Planetary metal:	quicksilver	tin	copper
Incense:	sandalwood, cloves	cedar, sage	rosewood, musk
Flowers:	fern, broom, fennel	lilac, borage, magnolia	orchid, rose, violet, mint, marjoram , bergamot
Animal:	dog	bear	cat
Bird:	magpie	eagle	dove

INDIA
MOROCCO
SUDAN
GREECE
RUSSIA
FINLAND
ENGLAND
YUGOSLAVIA
GERMANY
CHINA
TRINIDAD
ROMANIA

SATURDAY	
Archangel:	Cassael
Element:	earth
Zodiac sign:	Capricorn, Aquarius
Planet:	Saturn
Planetary color:	brown/black
Planetary metal:	lead
Incense:	myrrh, henbane, yew
Flowers:	chrysanthemum
Animal:	tortoise
Bird:	raven

Adapted from Michael Howard, *Incense and Candle Burning.*

The elder's companions call out: "Ah, no pass. Ah, good man. Yes, goin' to be a good marriage."

Ramas Bun: *The Solemn Leave-Taking*

The stage at which the Romanian bride and groom take leave of their childhood homes and parental family life is well outlined. This solemn stage of transition and preparation has various names: *iertaciunea* (forgiveness), in which the departing son or daughter requests forgiveness from the family for having erred in any way during youth; *belciug* (bounty, wealth), in which the son or daughter receives the parent's blessing; or *ramas bun* (leave-taking), in which the departing young adult is exhorted to fare well.

The format for ramas bun is well articulated for the bride and groom, the immediate family, bridesmaid, flag-bearer, godparents, cook, violin player, and future wedding guests who act as collective witness. Technically the bride and groom participate in ramas bun separately at their individual family homes. A close friend of the family or a local religious official delivers a sermon on holy matrimony, the "gifts" of marriage, both happiness and difficulty, bliss and sorrow. First the deacon toasts the groom. Then the son takes the glass, faces his father, and asks him for forgiveness, while wishing the family to prosper in his absence. It is often a tearful moment. The father responds with a blessing: "God give you luck, a good mind, and understanding throughout your life. Heed the words you have just heard. God give you life." The groom next toasts his mother, and may request her absolution as well; she toasts him in return; then everybody toasts him, and all glasses are clinked to the accompaniment of the violinist. The same steps are repeated with the bride.

O HYMEN! THE NUPTIAL GODDESSES AND GODS

*A*ll our attention so far has been with ambivalent ancestral spirits and bad-mannered elementals—
are there any good spirits out there, gods and goddesses of the wedding, perhaps?

The Greek goddess of weddings and patroness of the wedding night and honeymoon was Hymen
(or Hymenaeus), whose color was yellow. Alternatively, as some scholars prefer, Hymen was the marriage
song personified, mythopoeically created from the practice of reading an epithalamium, or nuptial poem
of praise, at the wedding service, when a chorus of maidens sang the praises of the bride and groom and
entreated Hymen to look favorably upon the match.

Hymen's gender is in dispute; the classicists contend Hymen was the son of Apollo and one of the
Muses; the feminists claim her as their own. Classical poets portrayed Hymen in a saffron robe, bearing a
clear taper. In one sculpted frieze, Hymen is depicted as a winged male being bearing a flaming nuptial
torch, as Pronuba (Roman Juno; Greek Hera) joins the right hands of the bride and groom. "Bees are still
called hymenoptera, veil-winged, after the hymen or veil that covered the inner sanctum of the Goddess's
temples, the veil having its physical counterpart in women's bodies," explains Barbara Walker. "Deflo-
ration was a ritual penetration of the veil under the 'hymeneal' rules of the Goddess, herself entitled
Hymen."

Hera, the Queen of Heaven and bride of Zeus, was revered as the goddess of marriage, especially
on the island of Samos, which was entirely consecrated to her worship. "Bring wine and the Muse's
charmful lyre, that we may sing of the far-famed bride of Zeus, the mistress of our island," sang the
Samian poet. Artemis was the goddess of all maidens; when Greek girls reached an age of ten years, they
were consecrated to her in the Brauronia ritual (Apollo got the boys). As the young woman's wedding ap-
proached, her father made sacrifices and obeisances to the tutelar gods of marriage, who might include
Zeus, Hera, Artemis, the Nymphs, or the Fates. The sacrifice, called progameia, was in effect a dedication
of his daughter, represented by some shorn locks of hair, to the deities invoked. On the wedding day itself
the couple made an offering to Aphrodite.

In Viking Scandinavia a representation of the god Thor's hammer was used to consecrate the
bridal pair; the blessings of the goddess Var, who hears the wedding vows, were requested. Var was sometimes solemnly invoked at weddings as the sign of Thor's hammer was made over the couple, according to
accounts preserved in the Eddas. "Then said Thrym / the chief of Thursar: / Carry in the hammer / to
consecrate the bride / Lay Mjöllnir / in the maiden's lap / Wed us together / with the hand of Var." In
Denmark sacrifices were offered to the goddess Freya (the spiritual aegis of Friday) in expectation of conjugal fertility.

In Hindu India, before the bride enters the world of mortal men through marriage, she belongs to
the three Vedic gods: Soma, the moon; Gandharva, a fertility spirit and offspring of Brahma; and Agni,
the fire-god. To facilitate the marriage, the groom must pray to these spiritual beings to cede the bride to
him; during the marriage ceremony, the couple acknowledges Agni through their circumambulations of
the ritual fire. All the Hindu spiritual beings are invited to participate in the wedding. Similarly the
Greeks and Romans had their personifications of the marriage-fire spirits, Hestia/Vesta, and household
deities, the Lares, and Penates, all of whom required suitable propitiation on the wedding day.

Dulha Deo is a richly drawn spiritual personage preserved in the original Dravidian cultures of India, although it couldn't honestly be said his life was marked by good fortune. Once he was a human groom on his way to collect his bride, when a stroke of lightning transformed him and his horse into stone. Since that illuminating day, Dulha Deo was regarded as a marriage divinity worthy of animal sacrifices, floral presents, songs, and kitchen ceremonies with oil and turmeric. An alternative accounting of Dulha Deo has him borne as a child upon his uncle's shoulders en route to meet his promised bride. They both felt an uncontrollable urge to meet each other faster that day, and as they leapt desirously toward each other, they were turned to stone—even the uncle. At least among the Gonds of India, that's why ever since it's always been the bride who went to collect the groom.

The Benediction on the Mandoa

The Mundas of India observe two prewedding purificatory ceremonies. The first, called *Sasang-Goso*, takes place a few days before the marriage, when helpers raise a mud-pulpit called *mandoa* in the courtyards of the bride and groom. They plant a thin *sal'* sapling at each of the four corners of the pulpit, and three more saplings—a sal', a thin bamboo, and a *bheloa*—in the center. All seven trees are smeared with a rice-flour paste then individually encircled with a cotton thread. Beginning three days before the wedding, each evening the bride and groom spend time sitting on their respective mandoa, where a female relative anoints them with a mixture of mustard oil and turmeric paste.

On the night before the wedding, a benedictory ceremony called *chuman* is performed at the homes of both bride and groom. The groom dons turmeric-dyed clothes and sits in his mandoa; his female relatives cup rice and young grass blades in their folded hands. Then, one by one, they anoint the feet, thighs, shoulders, and cheeks of the groom. As she touches the groom's cheeks, each woman kisses her own hand, completing the ceremony. The identical blessing ceremony is performed with the bride at her home that night.

Russian Bridesmaids and the Sham Ceremony

In earlier days in Russia's Apsheron Peninsula, on the morning two days before her wedding, the bride would be escorted by women relatives to the bath. The *uzalan* (a beautician) plucked out fine

INDIA
MOROCCO
SUDAN
GREECE
RUSSIA
FINLAND
ENGLAND
YUGOSLAVIA
GERMANY
CHINA
TRINIDAD
ROMANIA

facial hairs and aligned the woman's eyebrows, but otherwise the bride remained secreted behind the curtain and was seen by nobody else. At home in the evening the bride, wearing a *duvag,* or bridal veil, was presented to a party of merrymakers assembled in a large room of the house. Musicians played the accordion, double drum, and tambourine, as speakers eulogized and glorified the bride's qualities. The women exclaimed something like this: "We have brought you a bride, placed the wedding shawl on you, and wish you happiness and wealth. Beautiful is the moonlit night / On this night rejoicing is all around, apply henna to the bride, the groom is restless this night."

Meanwhile the bride sat in a privileged position on a mattress in the middle of the room with two trays with sweets and lit candles before her. Two bridesmaids stood beside her, each holding a lighted candle, or *sham*—the central feature of the Sham ceremony—never quenching them but allowing them to naturally burn out as the evening wore on. Apsheron villagers believed that fire had magical protective potency of value to their family and clan; further they believed that as the bride was illuminated with candles on both sides, so was she protected and safeguarded from inimical spirits.

The Mikvah *and Family Purity*

The Orthodox Hebrew wedding protocols place a high value on prenuptial sanctification. First the groom participates in a special prewedding Sabbath called the *Aufruf,* in which he is called to recite the blessing over the Torah. His congregation acknowledges his forthcoming marriage with extra *mazel tovs* and by throwing nuts and raisins at him in the synagogue, an observance called the *bevarfen,* no doubt with fertility antecedents. Ac-

cording to the Talmud, guests at weddings made a practice of passing wine by the couple then throwing wheat, grain, and nuts at both bride and groom, exclaiming *pe'ru u-re'vu,* "be fruitful and multiply."

The bride begins her practice of "family purity"—*taharat ha-mishpachah*—four days before the wedding with a *mikvah.* Family purity is a Jewish sexual hygienic custom whereby a week after her monthly menstruation the woman immerses herself in a ritually prescribed water bath called the mikvah, during which she recites a special blessing praising God for sanctifying her people with the Commandments and for providing instruction regarding the rite of immersion (*tevillah*). After this she was "purified" and available for renewed sexual activities with her husband. The mikvah-tevillah requirement imparts a monthly cycle of abstinence and renewal to the marital relations between the Orthodox Jewish couple; this encourages the couple to perceive their relationship as periodically sanctified and blessed, cleansing their conjugal psyche—family purity, in short. The bride's duty, then, is to perform mikvah for her wedding, following the same procedures and with the same devotion as for her monthly tevillah.

In some traditions within Judaism, the groom also takes mikvah. "It is good support for the soul," explains one authority quoted in Maurice Lamm's *The Jewish Way in Love and Marriage.* "He should silently confess his wrong-doings during the immersion, for it will help him shed the external trappings he heaps upon himself. If, for some reason, he cannot get to the mikvah, he should intensify his study of Torah. That will purify him."

Both bride and groom are encouraged to fast from daybreak until after the ceremony in the *chuppah,* or marriage canopy, later in the day. The wedding day is considered a time of unilateral forgiveness, when bride and groom are absolved of their "sins," flaws, and shortcomings. Like Yom Kippur with its fasting, wearing of white, and recitation of confessional prayers, it's a day for taking spiritual inventory and making repentance (a true change of mind). Symbolically mikvah is about self-purgation, cleansing, an admission of one's faults, mistakes, inadequacies, commissions, omissions, and errors ("sins"), and a heartfelt request for forgiveness. Here it's a matter of spiritual orientation: we seek self-forgiveness, or we request forgiveness from others, or we forgive others, or we ask the family spirits and saints to forgive us. Forgiveness in this sense is a key element in the prewedding purification, possibly the inner heart of the variety of cleansing, protective, and sanctification rituals we have considered in this chapter. According to the admonition of the "saintly Shelah," also cited by Lamm: "The groom and bride need to sanctify themselves very, very much as they prepare to enter the chuppah, because of what the Sages said: 'God forgives them their sins.'"

The world culture wedding transforms the bridal shower and bachelor party, traditionally genteel rituals for separating from one's familial household to establish a new independent one, into occasions for serious inner work in the company of gender peers and in solitude. During sagun we appreciate that even as we are individuals with unique biographies, as bride and groom we move within a mythically charged atmosphere, embodying roles in a divine ritual mandated long ago by the ancestors, the gods, and the original patrons of marriage.

As bride and groom, we move as archetypes with the sacred marriage once called the *hieros gamos,* the subject of our next chapter. As archetypal players in the divine wedding, we appreciate that our marriage potentially includes all of nature, the planet itself; and we see that just as astrology counseled us in the wisdom of finding the right time, so too can it help determine the right place.

INDIA
MOROCCO
SUDAN
GREECE
RUSSIA
FINLAND
ENGLAND
YUGOSLAVIA
GERMANY
CHINA
TRINIDAD
ROMANIA

"A High Degree of Consciousness"

We need "a high degree of consciousness" to make our marriage a true psychological relationship, said Carl Jung. While the effort to impart more awareness to our relationship is a lifelong struggle, we can usefully plant seeds for the habit in the earliest stages of our commitment. This is the basic idea of sagun, the stage of self-reflection, purification, and inner preparation before the wedding.

Matrimonial folklore offers us various rituals and devices to accomplish this inner cleansing—turmeric and henna pastes, vermilion dyes, lustration in water, incense, noise, firecrackers, placation of ancestors with food and prayers—while the disciplines of natural health provide numerous techniques for mind-body integration.

5

THE

HIEROS GAMOS

MARRYING WITH THE EARTH IN MIND

> Standing stones, which are firmly anchored down into the earth and therefore act as a focus for the Earth Mother's energies, were frequently visited and rituals performed with the expectation of ensuring fertility or curing barrenness. Earlier in the marital sequence, couples visited certain holed stones to seal their betrothal . . . In some places actual marriages were performed at holed stones . . . The link of wedding celebrations with ancient sites in folklore and custom echoes the ritual dances that were once presumably held at such sites . . .
> —*Janet and Colin Bord,* Earth Rites: Fertility
> Practices in Pre-Industrial Britain

Equally as important as naming the day for one's wedding is finding the appropriate place for the ceremony. Should a wedding always be held in a church? On the other hand, is there a reason, besides the obvious one of ecclesiastical allegiance, why so many weddings have been held in churches? We'll consider both questions in this chapter.

Increasingly, since the 1960s and the unconventional, self-expressive "New Wedding," innovative couples have moved their nuptials out of the church and into entirely novel venues—sandy beaches, city parks, country clubs, mountaintops. Even a partial list of places where couples have married reads like a gazetteer of the unfettered imagination: on a sailboat, underwater, in a hot-air balloon, under a waterfall, in a formal botanical garden, atop flagpoles, by the ocean, on a rocky cliff, on trapeze bars, while skydiving, in a snow-storm atop a 9,000-foot ski mountain, with dolphins, in a train's dining car, on a roller-skating rink, on horseback, in an airplane circling Las Vegas, while waterskiing . . .

Virtually any place imaginable and physically accessible has been (or undoubtedly will be) chosen as a wedding site in lieu of the conventional church or synagogue. Some couples are content with the fast-serve walk-through nuptials offered by marriage chapels: in 1992 the Marriage Chapel at City Hall in Manhattan married 13,126 couples in civil ceremonies lasting less than five minutes. In Las Vegas, Nevada, A Little White Chapel issued 79,235 marriage licenses in 1992, performing drive-up ceremonies for $25 so that couples in a hurry needn't leave their car to become husband and wife.

At the more imaginative end of things, a Bronx, New York, couple recently staged their ceremony on the pitcher's mound of the playing field of the Bronx Yankees, a baseball team for men over thirty-five. All participants wore baseball uniforms, the men made an archway of baseball bats with flowers strapped to the shanks, the wedding ring was borne on third base, and the minister was dressed in an umpire's uniform.

Another New York City couple exchanged their vows at the Central Park Zoo, against ambient sounds of seals, sea lions, and tropical birds. A couple from upstate New York traveled by mahogany motorboat (as did their 180 guests sporting orange life vests) to a one-acre island in the Upper Saranac Lake in the Adirondacks; there they enjoyed an unarguably bucolic wedding ceremony in a spare, knotty-pine chapel flanked by evergreen trees. Legend has it that an even more indomitable couple and their bridal party traveled by dog sled across the frozen lake one winter's morning for a wedding ceremony in this same cabin.

A Manhattan couple, fond of mountain climbing and high-peak skiing, invited sixty-five guests to their weekend wedding at a ski resort in the mountains near Salt Lake City. Guests joined the adventurous couple in morning ski outings, afternoon hot tubs, and the sense of a communal camp-out. "I can't think of a better place than the mountains to contemplate and experience those truly important things in life—family, friends, love, and skiing," said the groom.

Considerations of convenience, expense, and availability generally dictate the locales we choose for our weddings. If we are traditionally religious, the church or synagogue is our first choice; if we are iconoclastic, lapsed, or of mixed denominations, exotic, unique, and flamboyantly unconventional locations have a strong attraction. But might there be a hidden principle overlooked or unexplained by today's wedding conventions that might put the issue of "finding the place" in a new light?

I believe that there is. This principle is called *geomancy,* the science of landscape energies and configurations and their influences on human beings. Like astrology, geomancy—the science of finding the right place—should have a prominent place in putting together the world culture wedding. Geomancy puts the wedding ceremony firmly in the spiritual dimension by including the earth as a factor in the ritual. Marrying with the Earth in mind is a central element in the world culture wedding.

Geomancy, a traditional intuitive science once practiced in both European and Asian cultures (notably China, where it's called *feng shui*), explains why churches—the old European cathedrals, many of the old parish churches, and some of America's oldest churches as well—are often the best places for a wedding. Geomancy also teaches us how many landscape sites are equally as good, regardless of whether they have structures on them or not. It isn't simply the sanctity of the structure or its architectural felicities, but its specific location and topographical orientation that make all the difference. In Europe, megalithic structures such as stone circles preceded the installation of a church at the same site by many centuries. Pagodas and royal burial grounds in old China, and stupas and temples in India and Tibet, were strategically situated according to geomantic principles to maximize the beneficial influence of the earth energies.

ASTRO-CARTOGRAPHY—HOW TO FIND THE BEST PLACE ON EARTH FOR YOUR WEDDING

*A*useful first step in finding the right place to wed is to employ the services of a new field of astrology called astro-cartography. Back in the 1970s, Jim Lewis had a brilliant idea. Why not take the insights and mechanics of astrology, plot them out for the Earth itself, match them up with the specific birth data of individuals, and put it all on computer? The result was his now popular astro-cartography mapping, charting, and interpretive services, concentrated in what's called a relocation chart, now handled under the auspices of Astro-Numeric Services.

Normally birth charts analyze the significance of time (cosmic and solar system time as expressed by the movements and angular positions of the stars and planets) with respect to the time of birth of an individual. Astro-cartography adds the element of space to these interpretations, working off the assumption that one's internal birth chart remains sensitive and reactive to one's changes of environment, residency, and location: "How we relate to the Earth as a whole whether or not we are conscious of it," as Michael Harding and Charles Harvey, professional astrologers who work with this innovation, explain in Working with Astrology. "Our chart is in a continual spatial relationship with the Earth which mirrors its synchrony with the planets."

Here's how astro-cartography works. You provide exact data about your birth time and location; Lewis's computer uses this data to generate a planetary map depicting your individual extra-planetary cosmic influences. As a complementary interpretive tool, Lewis's system also generates a locality reading, a personalized astrological analysis of your immediate region of habitation with respect to your life map.

The personalized natal chart is inscribed in crisscrossing lines across the geography of the globe. The lines, says Lewis, "identify places at which planets occupied powerful positions at the moment of your birth. The map is valid for your entire life and identifies places where you will find maximum potentials for manifesting parts of yourself, symbolized by the planets." For example, if you live within a couple of hundred miles of where your natal Mars line is inscribed, this helps "you get in touch with your Mars potentials, such as assertion, masculinity, and enthusiasm—more than in other places." Further, there are times (in astrological parlance, transits and progressions) in a person's life when individual lines temporarily activate the influence and disposition of one's natal planets. Information gleaned from a survey of one's astro-cartographical domain can become immediately practical as a tool for self-understanding; and, not surprisingly, some people use the Locality Reading to assess the potential suitability of marriage locations.

If you were to order a locality reading for feedback on a proposed site's marriage prospects or the likelihood of finding a suitable mate, the key information in your study would be the placement and movements of Venus. This means integrating the data from the astro-cartographical charts of a couple, comparing the placement of their planetary Venus lines, and striking a geographical compromise. As of 1992, Astro-Numeric Services reports they have assisted over eight hundred clients in using their "Venus Zone" Locality readings to locate conjugal mates.

Love and marriage mates, if they are ever to be found, are most likely located under your geographical Venus lines. "Venus areas of the world are among the most desirable for many people. Here is where mercy, friendship, benevolence, conviviality, marriage, romance, though not so much sex, enter the life and people met here may become lifelong friends." Specifically, the line in which Venus lies on the descendant (horizon) is the most favorable for matters of marriage and partnership. "This is probably the best place to get married, especially for women," says Lewis. "Harmony and cooperation are projected outward, and thus return, though you let others do most of the work in relationship." Under the Venus influence, "we see the 'quality' of social relationships or marriage as important."

ENGLAND
HONG KONG
JAPAN
MOROCCO
EGYPT
IRELAND
AUSTRALIA

What qualifies both the old churches and the sacred but nonecclesiastical sites as geomantically suitable for weddings is the empirical fact that they provide a heightened energetic ambiance that uplifts consciousness. We feel better, healthier, more vibrant, energized, wakeful, even reverential at such sites. This kind of positive energetic milieu can only enhance whatever social rituals we enact under their aegis. And as native peoples and geomancers alike will attest, when positive, life-affirming human rituals are performed at such geomantic nodes—sacred sites, power points, numinous apertures—it has the effect of inviting the Earth itself to participate in the nuptials.

A Planetary Nexus of Wedding Sites

Avebury, a massive stone circle complex in south-central England, is probably Europe's largest, most majestic megalithic site. Nearly twenty-nine acres in size, its odd-shaped but imposing stones tower up to twelve feet tall. Unlike Stonehenge (its better-known neighbor, also in Wiltshire and some thirty miles south) it's not fenced in; it's not guarded; it doesn't exact an entrance fee; and there's even—surprisingly, for anyone other than the British—a small village with a topnotch natural foods restaurant *inside* the circle. Sheep graze unrestrictedly amidst the stones, people picnic on the rim of the henge, and the air exudes antiquity. This is where I'd most like to marry—because as any geomancer will tell you, Avebury, like most other megalithic sites around the earth, has an energy that's almost palpable, and that energy or "vibration" can become part of your wedding.

Ever since the publication of British megalithic scholar John Michell's landmark studies in

the 1970s—*City of Revelation* and *The View Over the Atlantis*—interest in geomancy has been growing. "A great scientific instrument lies sprawled over the entire surface of the globe," declared Michell. That instrument is a vast complex of sacred sites—megalithic circles, unusual hills, stone chambers, medicine wheels, caves, earth mounds, mountains, old churches—all apparently linked by straight running lines of subtle energy called *leys*. Contemporary writers, like Doris Lessing in *Shikasta* and Carlos Castaneda in *The Eagle's Gift*, speak in fictional or philosophical terms of ley line phenomena, while well-known spiritual figures like Peter Caddy, cofounder of the Findhorn community in Scotland, and his original colleague, the visionary David Spangler, speak about "centers of light" occupied by deliberate human communities and linked with other light centers by telepathic and oral means. Others speak about "lines of light," "cosmic power points," an "etheric web of energy," "a mysterious stream of terrestrial magnetism," and an intricate planetary "acupuncture" system of lines and points. These all fit within the province of geomancy.

According to this burgeoning group of basically independent and inspired landscape probers and dowsers, the planet has, in addition to its tangible geological terrain, another contoured surface, an "etheric geography" that we can map, chart, and interact with creatively. By analogy it's useful to conceive of an etheric geography or earth grid matrix as a planetary version of the system of acupuncture meridians and acupoints, as described by classical Chinese medicine. According to this view, the human body is crisscrossed by numerous lines of energy and still more numerous treatment nodes; the entirety of this system exists somewhere between the physical and the "etheric" layers of the human body. In the case of acupuncture, the proposition that the human body is a webwork of energy lines and nodes has been empirically substantiated through thousands of years of clinical practice. Geomancers propose that the earth has a similar system, but on a larger scale; the meridians are what dowsers call ley lines, while planetary acupoints are what we commonly call sacred sites or power places.

Quite often it's at these "geopoints" or ley line intersections that we find the stone circles, older churches, temples, pagodas, and stupas. The Harmonic Convergence of August 1987, for example, was the first mass recognition of this planetary web of etheric geography; at that time estimates suggest that several million men and women voluntarily sought out geopoints for meditative and ritual purposes during a three-day period. In earlier days such geopoints were regularly resorted to by native peoples, shamans, oracles, occultists, and saints for initiation, vision quests, and training in the Mysteries. And folklore suggests that such places were often visited by ordinary men and women seeking boons, healing, blessings, fertility, or a special place for life transition rituals.

The planetary nexus of sacred sites represents the etheric body of Gaia, our planetary Spirit. The Gaia Hypothesis, as proposed by British atmospheric chemist James Lovelock in the late 1970s, proposes that the Earth is a unified, purposefully self-regulating organic being; feminists, ecologists, and mythographers since the introduction of Lovelock's theory have extended his geophysiological model into the domain of mystic perception and sentient attribution, claiming, in effect: Gaia lives! So when we evoke the idea of a planetary acupuncture system, we are describing the multiple energy points in a spiritual being the size of our world. The Gaia Hypothesis may take us into esoteric terrain, but the proposed model has practical applications for the world culture wedding. "It would seem as if the hidden current which flows through the land can be tapped at certain points, much as an electric socket on the skirting board of our sitting room enables us to 'plug

in' to the current and put it to use," explain Janet and Colin Bord in *The Secret Country: More Mysterious Britain,* one of their valuable series of Earth mysteries handbooks. The hidden current—Earth *ch'i*—is available at these sites and may form the energy ambiance of our rituals, heightening our sense of spirituality. Participating in these possibilities of the landscape is what marrying among the stones is all about.

The abundance of sacred, numinous places around the Earth are elements of a living ecology, "special nodes of concentrated vitality," suggests James Swan, a scholar of the mysteries of the landscape and "the spirit of place," in his *Sacred Places: How the Living Earth Seeks Our Friendship.* Swan reminds us that it was the naturalist Pliny the Elder who coined the term *geomancy* to describe "the art of reading the subtle qualities of a place to discern what actions might best be conducted." Linking cultures, Swan further points out that the venerated Chinese oracular text *I Ching*—which came out of a culture intimate with the science of Earth mysteries—offers a paradigmatic view of the esoteric dynamics of landscape, habitation, and human awareness: "Heaven and Earth determines the places," states the *I Ching.* "The holy sages fulfill the possibilities of the places. Through the thoughts of men and the thoughts of spirits, the people are enabled to participate in these possibilities." Let's consider a few representative examples from Celtic, Chinese, Japanese, and Moroccan cultures.

ENGLAND
HONG KONG
JAPAN
MOROCCO
EGYPT
IRELAND
AUSTRALIA

Marrying Among the Stones of Gaia

In an earlier time, British couples were joined on the front steps or porch of the parish church, as Geoffrey Chaucer's Wife of Bath noted in his fourteenth-century *Canterbury Tales:* "Husbondes at chirche dore have I had five." Still earlier, when the megalithic milieu flourished in Celtic lands, the betrothal and wedding ceremonies were clearly linked to the Earth. British couples might stand upon a particular stone—usually a commemorative slab for a local saint buried underneath—on the church floor during their ceremony for an extra benediction. Scottish couples wedded at special ceremonial sites in the landscape, where they passed their hands through an opening in a menhir (standing stone), known variously as the "plighting-stone," "betrothal stone," or "bridal stone." At Lairg in Sutherland, a "Plightin' Stane" was built into the church wall and used regularly for making marital pledges and sealing betrothals. On the holy isle of Lindisfarne off the north coast of Great Britain, brides once stepped upon the Petting Stone immediately after the wedding service to ensure a fortunate, fruitful marriage.

Newly married couples in the village of Doagh in Ireland's County Antrim ratified their union by clasping hands through the human-sized Holed Stone. The same function was reserved for the Stone of Odin near Kirkney in the Orkney Islands, such that an unwed couple who clasped hands through its bored hole and pledged their vows were regarded as married. Further south, on the Isle of Man, the stone rings in the churchyard of Kirk Braddan were formerly used during the wedding ceremony, when couples clasped hands through their central cavities. At Lanark, in County Strathclyde, Scotland, wedding parties visited the Marriage Well on the day after their service and toasted the couple with the holy water. On the Scottish island of Colonsayup, until the early nineteenth century, marriages were held at Sithean Mor, a mound regarded as a large fairy enclave.

The Wedding Walk at Amah Rock

Extending eastward off the Bowen Road in Hong Kong is a footpath known locally as the Marriage Road that winds its way through scenic terrain for a couple of miles until it reaches Amah Rock. Since the time of their remotest ancestors, engaged couples of Wanchai district take this walk to pray for a fruitful marriage. They pause at the confluence of two torrents descending in spumes and spouts from Magazine Gap; reading an inscribed marble tablet, they understand this is the Living Water, whose perpetual musical sound is a balm and a companion. Their path takes them through a deep ravine, up a steep track, and through a welter of butterflies, as they begin to discern the spur of a massive granite outcropping—Amah Rock. Finally they clamber up a flight of undressed granite steps to the shrine and altar atop Amah, where they find thick ritual incense sticks inserted into the ground and a half-dozen small paper banners—the *Chao Hun Fan,* or "Spirit flags." Behind the altar, snug against the higher vertical stone face of Amah, is an oblong granite block, more like a bench, and clearly worn smooth from thousands of visitors who have sat here to rest and pledge their marriage vows.

"The Amah stands a gaunt sentry over the stone sanctuary," observed V. R. Burkhardt, who reported on his visit to Amah in the early 1950s in his *Chinese Creeds and Customs.* It seemed evident to Burkhardt that Amah was not a coincidental geological freak of nature, but a deliberately sculpted geomantic shrine, an attitude tacitly endorsed by the unending stream of supplicant Chinese couples. The Chinese here are convinced, says Burkhardt, that "there's a divinity that shapes their ends, and

that his propitiation will ensure that children bless the union"—and, we might append, for them Amah holds the key.

The couple kneels before the altar, inserts their incense sticks in the ground, clasps their hands, and engages in silent prayer. Then, pouring out a libation on the ground, they set fire to a written request—a square red talisman with three-inch sides within an envelope decorated in designs of the Goddess, with words beginning "Nine Heavenly dark ladies . . . "—for spiritual protection. Their document also includes the couple's personal names and prayers: "May the Spirit of the Goddess protect the stone shrine. . . ." The document may also include the characters for the seventh—Tzu Sun Niang Niang, she who grants posterity—of the Nine Niang Niangs, specialized protecting deities according to Chinese belief. When the document is burned up and becomes ashes, it becomes absorbed by the site, thereby becoming readable by the invisible spirits. "The Amah Rock's virtues are not only confined to engaged couples," Burkhardt comments, "but it is also a place of pilgrimage for married women who wish to retain the affections of their husbands which show signs of waning."

Wondrous Inada-Princess who had been designated to be a sacrifice to the dragon; after Susa-no-wo slew the dragon, Wondrous Inada Princess agreed to marry him. Susa-no-wo explored Izumo Province to find a particularly lovely spot for the wedding; at last he found a place that afforded him such pleasure that he exclaimed, "My heart is refreshed." Thereafter the site was known as Suga; and after he became the lord of Izumo Province, the Great Shrine of Kitzuki was erected at Suga in his honor. According to Japanese legend, all the Japanese deities assemble at Kitzuki at 4:00 A.M. on the first day of the tenth lunar month (called the "month with gods, *Kami-ari-suki*") to arrange all the marriages that will occur in Izumo during the next year. According to Shinto belief, the whole of the Japanese countryside is the land of the gods, filled with sanctuaries like Kitzuki and traditions of gods, spirits, fairies, or ancestors. Sanctuaries like Kitzuki are clearly geopoints, landscape sites that have positive terrestrial energies that have been geomantically enhanced by the precise placement of temples for the benefit of human visitors.

A Wedding at the Place Where "My Heart Is Refreshed"

The Great Shrine of Kitzuki in Izumo Province, Japan, is the place where the gods gather every year to make all marriage arrangements. It all began when Susa-no-wo the Storm-god was expelled from the Plain of High Heaven. As he wandered along the River Hi, he rescued a girl named

Stones of the Bride

Not far from a tiny village in Andrja, Morocco, there is a series of standing stones generally believed to be the petrified remnants of a once living bridal procession. The legend has it that one day, while a bride was being conveyed to the bridegroom's village in an *ammariya* (a closed "bridal box" born on a donkey's back), she was seized with diarrhea. After one of her attendants committed an impropriety with the *rgaif* (thin, unyeasted cakes made with butter and oil), suddenly the entire procession was turned to stone as punishment for the transgression.

The bridal procession may have ended badly for these women, but they became permanent, petrified mentors for succeeding generations of young women anxious to marry who visited the site as if it were a shrine (called afterwards a *haus*). They visit the megalithic ammariya on three successive Thursday afternoons, because Thursday is the day on which Moroccan brides are frequently conveyed to their new home with the groom. Then they visit the site for three Fridays before sunrise; while at the haus, they deposit several dolls, representing brides and grooms, adorned with strands of their hair; then they step over the dolls three times with their legs spread apart, presumably to evoke fertility. When the prominent marriage scholar Edward Westermarck visited Morocco in the 1920s, he found many instances of miraculous stones with salutary effects, such that he could comment: "Even ordinary stones are sometimes treated as though they were sentient beings."

As a coda, the Merry Maidens, a standing stone circle in Cornwall, England, represents, according to local legend, the petrified bodies of several dozen once merry young women who danced without restraint on the Sabbath and were punished by petrification. The equivalent story is claimed for the three stone circles at Stanton Drew in Avon; here, too, members of a wedding party were petrified after dancing to music on the Sabbath played by the Devil. Other stone sites in France, Gambia, and Pakistan also carry claims to represent petrified wedding parties. Legendary "just-so" accounts like these are always strongly tainted by institutionalized morality, whether it's Christianity or Islam; but if you're a dowser, geomancer, or occultist, you might sense the real message in the folk memory by reversing the story: feminine spirits, deities, divinities, or spirits of

place periodically visit the standing stones and imbue them with life-affirming energies available to all human visitors—including betrothed couples—who might dare to rub up against them seeking a marital boon.

Inviting the Earth to Participate

The world culture wedding aims to include the landscape and the spirit of place in the planning and ceremonies. But where can we find such a sacred spot?

Fortunately, this search is getting easier every day. A steadily increasing volume of guidebooks to geomantic locations fills the bookstores, revealing an unsuspected and vast spiritual estate all around us. And as glamorous and potentially transcendent as the prospect of wedding among the stones of Avebury or at the base of Egypt's great pyramid of Giza might be, we can still stage a geomantically significant ceremony virtually anywhere—even in our cities. These, too, have their specially charged (if overly concreted) nodes within the planetary web of energy, as the geomancers tell us. The services of a competent dowser, psychic, local folklorist, feng shui master, or Native American can help identify the geomantic anatomy and possibilities of any neighborhood, pasture, or hill.

According to the geomancers, the webwork of the landscape energies and connections is as complexly intricate and multilayered as the interpenetrating nervous, muscular, circulatory, and lymphatic systems of our own bodies. This means that we can reasonably expect to find a place with some geomantic significance virtually anywhere, and certainly close to home. In New England, for example, sometimes the oldest churches in the oldest inhabited towns were sited according to geomantic principles, and would therefore make suitable venues for a wedding with the earth's participation. In many instances state and federal parks, National Forests, and other specially preserved wilderness areas contain geomantically enhanced features or geopoints. Many human-made structures—such as New York's Church of St. John the Divine and San Francisco's Grace Cathedral—have an ingrown *habit* of spiritual iconoclasm and unconventional observance that permeates the air and can support a geomantic wedding. We can identify some of the important urban geopoints by considering where people went in their cities to observe the Harmonic Convergence.

How can we invite the earth to participate in our wedding when we position ourselves at a geopoint? Again, we must resort to a worldview once common among traditional cultures. This older philosophy acknowledged the constant interaction and the web of interdependent activities between macrocosm and microcosm. In this case the macrocosm is the Earth and the microcosm is the individual human; the place of interconnection between Gaia and humanity is our own active, focused spirituality.

We learn from the geomancers, mystics, and esotericists that there is a kind of subtle energy feedback loop between humans and planet through the webwork of sacred points on the surface of Earth; a mind-body interface in which humanity is the mind, Gaia is the body, and consciousness is the life force transiting between both. Prayers, benedictions, joy, meditations, invocations, and positive rituals offered at geopoints (which are like planetary treatment nodes) are amplified and then channeled into the life body of the planet. Gaia listens through her geopoints to the wishes of men and women.

It sounds fanciful, but geomancers insist that we can especially contribute to the psychological well-being of Gaia by casting our best wishes (expressed as rituals, prayers, meditations) into the receptive ethers at the sacred sites around the planet. For example, in their healing practices, acupuncturists sometimes burn special herbs over a bodily acupoint in a procedure called moxibustion; our spiritual practices conducted at geopoints become a form of geomantic moxibustion. These healing vibrations "feed" Gaia with spiritual nutrition; Gaia can then feed humans back through these same geopoints with energies supportive of expanded consciousness and heightened perception. The system is mutually supportive.

The Russian metaphysician G. I. Gurdjieff once called this feedback system "reciprocal maintenance." According to Gurdjieff, animals, humans, nature spirits, the planetary spirit, and celestial beings mutually support one another in an interdependent system. As Gurdjieffian scholar J. G. Bennett explains, "Full renewal requires full mutuality. It is by Universal giving and receiving of energies that Cosmic Harmony is maintained. The commandment becomes: 'Fill your place in the Cosmic Harmony or perish.'" A wedding ritual, with its high degree of joy, celebration, and affirmation, can be such an obligatory contribution to cosmic and planetary harmony.

Following Gurdjieff's analysis, then, when we offer our wedding celebrations as reciprocal service back to the planet, we are fulfilling our obligations as part of this reciprocally maintained network. It's a simple gesture of spiritual ecology. Working through the geopoints, Gaia feeds our nuptials with heightened spirituality, and we feed Gaia with our purest aspirations. That's how geomantic understanding can introduce an extra dimension to our wedding rituals. The idea might seem a little outlandish today; but when we examine some of the basic concepts in mythology, its deeper relevance comes slowly into view. Foremost

ENGLAND
HONG KONG
JAPAN
MOROCCO
EGYPT
IRELAND
AUSTRALIA

ENGLAND
HONG KONG
JAPAN
MOROCCO
EGYPT
IRELAND
AUSTRALIA

among these mythological antecedents is the *hieros gamos*, the sacred marriage, which mythologists contend is the divine model for all human marital unions.

Sacred Marriage of Heaven and Earth, King and Goddess

The sacred marriage, which the Greeks called hieros gamos—the marriage of heaven and earth, of the King and the Goddess, of the King and his Queen, of the King and the Land, of the Gods and Goddesses—is a concept loaded with significance. "Marriage with the earthly representative of the Goddess, in the form of the queen, was essential to the position of kingship," explains mythographer Barbara Walker. In fact, a marriage at this level was at the basis of the original meaning of "holy matrimony." As Georg Feuerstein explains in *Sacred Sexuality: Living the Vision of the Erotic Spirit*, "The holy intercourse between God and Goddess was reenacted on the human level by the temple priestess and the divinely appointed king or the high priest."

The institution of the hieros gamos was the divine model for human wedding rituals, recounts myth historian Mircea Eliade. Human marriages replicate the original "hierogamy," and through a

RESOURCES FOR IDENTIFYING SACRED PLACES IN NORTH AMERICA

The following are reliable guides to geomantically significant sites in North America that might become the "right place" for your world culture wedding.

- *Lost Cities of North and Central America,* by David Hatcher Childress. Stelle, IL: Adventures Unlimited Press, 1992.
- *Sacred Sites: A Traveller's Guide to North America's Most Powerful, Mystical Landmarks,* by Natasha Peterson. Chicago: Contemporary Books, 1988.
- *Earth Memory: Sacred Sites: Doorways into Earth's Mysteries,* by Paul Devereux. St. Paul: Llewellyn Publications, 1992.
- *Sacred Sites: A Guidebook to Sacred Centers and Mysterious Places in the United States,* edited by Frank Joseph. St. Paul: Llewellyn Publications, 1992.
- *Sacred Places: How the Living Earth Seeks Our Friendship,* by James A. Swan. Santa Fe: Bear & Company, 1990.
- *The Search for Lost America: The Mysteries of the Stone Ruins,* by Salvatore Michael Trento. Chicago: Contemporary Books, 1978.
- *The Earth Changes Survival Handbook,* by Page Bryant. Santa Fe: Sun Books, 1983.
- *Terravision: A Traveller's Guide to the Living Planet Earth,* by Page Bryant. New York: Ballantine New Age, 1991.
- *Manitou: The Sacred Landscape of New England's Native Civilization,* by James W. Mavor, Jr., and Byron E. Dix. Rochester: Inner Traditions International, 1989.

WEDDING FEASTS OF THE LITTLE PEOPLE

*L*egends of the fabulous, improbable "Little Folk"—fairies, gnomes, sylphs, brownies, pixies, lep-rechauns, fees, corrigans, and many others—are as indigenous to the British Isles and Old Eu-rope as are the enigmatic megaliths and numinous sacred sites. According to Welsh and Saxon folklore, even the Little People have their wedding customs. So as a coda for our wedding with the earth in mind, here are two folk accounts of Celtic Fairyland nuptials among the "Good People of Peace."

Saxony: The Little People's Wedding

The little people of the Eilenburg in Saxony planned to celebrate a wedding, which is why one night they slipped through the keyholes and window-slits of the castle to enter the great hall, tumbling onto the floor like brightly clad peas. The sudden noise of their arrival woke the old count, who rubbed his eyes in disbelief at the sight of so many tiny visitors. One of them acted as herald and addressed the half-awake count, courteously inviting him to join their wedding festivity, with the stipulation that he alone of the human folk in the castle would be present.

"Since you have disturbed my sleep, I will join your company," said the count, agreeing to their terms. He became aware of other members of their party: torchbearers, musicians, and an interesting lit-tle woman with whom he sought to dance.

Then, inexplicably, the spritely dancing halted, the merry music ceased, the room hushed, and the entire party dashed for the door-slits. The bridal pair, and the heralds and dancers attending them, craned their necks upward to a hole in the ceiling through which the old countess was avidly—and with-out permission—watching them.

The same courteous personage again bowed before the count, thanking him for his hospitality, and casting a dire prediction: "Since our wedding and our festivity has been thus disturbed by another eye gazing on it, your race shall henceforward never count more than seven Eilenburgs." Then the little people vanished from the room, leaving the count to ruminate on this genially delivered curse on his fu-ture generations. "The curse has lasted till the present time, and one of six living knights of Eilenburg has always died before the seventh was born," concludes folklorist Thomas Keightley, in his 1880 World Guide to Gnomes, Fairies, Elves, and Other Little People.

Wales: The Phantom Wedding Procession

An old woman once lived in Edern, Wales, on a small farm called Glan y Gors. One day, on her return walk from the fair at Criccieth, she paused near a bog when she heard the sounds of considerable talking (clebran) and chattering (bregliach). Soon she beheld a crowd of men and women walking to-ward her. She darted out of the way and crouched behind a fence as they passed noisily by.

When they were out of view, she resumed her journey homeward. In almost no time she heard, then saw, them again—the same rowdy, marching crowd. As before she hid herself, this time with rising fear and annoyance, saying to herself: "Here I shall be all night!" She didn't recognize any of them, nor did her neighbors afterward, when she recounted the event. Nor could she understand what all their cle-bran and bregliach meant; it wasn't Welsh or English nor any tongue she knew or had ever heard of.

According to folklorist John Rhys, who first published this account in 1901 in his Celtic Folklore, she had witnessed a Little People's phantom wedding procession. "What the old woman of Glan y Gors thought she saw looks by no means unlike a Welsh wedding marching on foot, especially when, as I have seen done, one party tried—seemingly in good earnest—to escape the other and to take the bride away from it."

kind of sympathetic magic reestablish the union of heaven and earth. In the early spiritual texts of India called the Upanishads, the husband says "I am Heaven," and of his wife, "Thou art Earth"; in the later Atharva-Veda, each ceremonial gesture in the wedding copies a divine prototype and primordial event that occurred outside of time. For example, the groom says that just as Agni the exalted Fire God grasped the right hand of Earth, so does the husband grasp his bride's hand.

The ancient marriage rites, says Eliade in *Cosmos and History,* are based on a cosmogonic structure. "It is not merely a question of imitating an exemplary model, the hierogamy between heaven and earth; the principal consideration is the result of that hierogamy, i.e., the cosmic Cre-

ation. Every human union has its model and its justification in the hierogamy, the cosmic union of the elements." Since the marriage rite is based on the archetype of world creation, its repetition in human societies constitutes a ceremony whose purpose is the "restoration of integral wholeness." In this way the world is regenerated with each reenactment of the hierogamy through a wedding ceremonial; marriage regenerates time itself and its expression as the yearly round, assuring wealth, fecundity, and happiness for the human couple, their society, and all of creation.

The king's loss of queen often meant a dissolution of the hieros gamos at all levels and the bonds that wove society and environment together. In Western mythic traditions, says Walker,

A VISION OF CAMELOT

*I*n The Phenomena of Avalon, *a recent Celtic work of high vision and near fantasy, Gino Gennaro recounts a psychic impression of the original days of King Arthur's Camelot situated at a primary megalithic site in England, which subsequent researchers have identified as Avebury stone circle in Wiltshire. According to Gennaro, Camelot was a kind of megalithic solar clock, timed to record the movements and influences of the celestial bodies; the Arthurian family's task was to prime, correct, recalibrate, and receive the heavenly radiations through a daily ritualized wedding at midday between "Goddess Earth and other heavenly planetary deities."*

Everybody participated in the observance of this daily cosmic marriage, says Gennaro, from royal princes to humble bakers—it was also the choice time for new weddings. "Exactly at noon in every castle and village, the groom and the bride led the way to the chosen glade, preceded by the musicians, followed by four bridesmaids representing the four seasons."

Meanwhile at Camelot, as the sun's rays reached their daily zenith, the arch-priest "proceeded to celebrate the global marriage between earth and heavens with the ceremonial act of placing the wedding ring, symbolizing infinity, upon the fingers of the young bridal pair who had the fortune to represent the finite terrestrial world." As the arch-priest concluded his oblations, "triumphant nuptial music spread out over the land, and all the brides and the grooms of the Earth led the wedding dance."

So through this high ritual observed within a powerful megalithic enclosure, the world was kept in balance. We see vividly in this example, even if we disbelieve its contents, the way the hieros gamos operates on behalf of the Earth in the context of the planetary grid system of geopoints.

King Arthur's loss of his royal queen and wife, Guinivere (through an adulterous liaison with Arthur's best friend, Lancelot) precipitated the ruination of the land of Logres, transforming it into the dire Wasteland. As Parsifal correctly observed in John Boorman's film *Excalibur!* in his concluding remarks to a dying Arthur: "You and the Land are One."

In Ireland the land was regarded as Sovereignty, who often presented herself as a loathsome hag who transformed herself into a comely maiden with the embrace of the king. "The relation between Irish kings and their realm is often portrayed as a marriage, and the inauguration feast of a king is called a wedding-feast," explain Alwyn Rees and Brinley Rees in *Celtic Heritage.* The country, initially, is a hag with deranged mind; but when she is united with the rightful king, "her countenance is 'as the crimson lichen of Leinster's crags . . . her locks . . . like Bregon's buttercups,' her mantle a matchless green." Irish legend maintained that no one could ever be king in Ireland without drinking the ale of Cuala, the water from Sovereignty's well, or *derg flaith*, which means "red ale" and "red sovereignty." As the Reeses comment: "Sovereignty is a bride, the server of a powerful drink, and the drink itself."

The divine marriage between the world-making ancestral couple is a motif found worldwide in creation myths in Central America, Egypt, India, Greece, China, Mesopotamia, and Australia. Here, too, among the Australian Aborigines, there is an account of the "great cosmic copulation" between the primal couple—the All-Mother *Waramururungundju* and All-Father *Baiame.* According to cultural historian Robert Lawlor, in his *Voices of the First Day,* the existence of the divine marriage here "suggests the Aboriginal belief that they can experience the vast creative process through ecstatic dance and sexuality. They, and all the world, share in the currents of life emanating from this cosmic union."

Greek myth recounts the celestial marriage of Hera, Queen of Heaven, with Zeus, King of the Gods of Olympus. All the gods brought gifts to the wedding, the most significant of which was Mother Earth's gift of a tree bearing golden apples, which would later be guarded by the Hesperides in Hera's private orchard on Mount Atlas and sought by Hercules as his eleventh labor. The wedding night of Zeus and Hera on Samos lasted three hundred years; the celestial penumbra of positive influence produced by this sustained hieros gamos, Robert Graves suggests, might have later formed the basis of the Samian sacred year of ten thirty-day months. At any rate their union is construed as a personalized metaphor of the marriage of Heaven and Earth.

It's not only the cosmically royal marriages that have import for human life. We mustn't overlook the Fairyland marriage of Oberon and Titania masterfully evoked in Shakespeare's *A Midsummer Night's Dream.* As the human couples—King Theseus of Athens and Hippolyta, Hermia and Lysander, Demetrius and Helena, and the farcical Pyramus and Thisbe—pursue their wooings and wedding commitments, the nuptials of Oberon and Titania are enlivened with the dancing and singing of their fairy attendants: "Hand in hand, with fairy grace / Will we sing, and bless this place."

Ultimately the hieros gamos exists as a model for human benefit and aspiration. The marriage rite, explains Mircea Eliade, "serves as the exemplary model not only in the case of marriages but also in the case of any other ceremony whose end is the restoration of integral wholeness." So marrying with the Earth in mind might mean taking on a very big lover. Annie Dillard evokes this fairly majestic notion of a bridegroom as big as the world in her *Holy the Firm.*

Every day is a god, each day is a god, and holiness holds forth in time. . . . I wake in a god. I wake in arms holding my quilt, holding me as

ENGLAND
HONG KONG
JAPAN
MOROCCO
EGYPT
IRELAND
AUSTRALIA

ENGLAND
HONG KONG
JAPAN
MOROCCO
EGYPT
IRELAND
AUSTRALIA

best they can inside my quilt. Someone is kissing me—already, I wake, I cry, "Oh," I rise from the pillow. Why should I open my eyes? I open my eyes. The god lifts from the water. His head fills the bay. He is Puget Sound, the Pacific; his breast rises from pastures; his fingers are firs; islands slide wet down his shoulders. Islands slip blue from his shoulders and glide over the water, the empty, lighted water like a stage. Today's god rises, his long eyes flecked in clouds. He flings his arms, spreading colors; he arches, cupping sky in his belly; he vaults, vaulting and spread, holding all and spread on me like skin.

Ravishment on the Nuptial Barge

Perhaps it's not conventional for men to fantasize about their dream wedding, but I did, and still do. Within the fanciful elements of this imagination lie the seeds for a possible deepening of the marriage ceremony into a spiritual ritual that knits the worlds together in a joyous hierogamy. What worlds? The celestial and terrestrial, Heaven and Earth—all the old dichotomies of matter and spirit.

I used to have a terrific fantasy about my wedding. I was a teenager, subject to extensive imaginings. It first came to me when I was lying on a small plastic float out on a lake, staring into the empty blue sky above. Summer droned and baked all around me as I dragged my fingers in the cool water . . . It would be a three-day affair on a grand English country estate—lake, deer park, formal gardens, gazebo, fountains and waterways, stately rows of beech trees. We'd have hundreds of acres in lawns and rose walks and open woods through which to ply our wedding celebration—plenty of room for peacocks, doves, and swans, too.

During the first two days, we'd ease our way into the party atmosphere, with long, relaxing walks or rides on horseback, midday concerts at the gazebo—preferably Baroque and exclusively Bach, if I had my way—leisurely mid-afternoon lunches on the infinite lawns, theater, mime, poetry, and recitations around five o'clock, and dinner by candlelight by lakeside at twilight as the dew moistened the verdant summer grass. Miraculously it wouldn't rain or grow overcast or sultry; the weather would be balmy throughout and there would be no insects, but an amplitude of songbirds. We'd have a hundred guests, all of whom I liked immensely, because in my fantasy I'd be popular enough to have that many close friends and cordial enough to want to invite them. My bride and I would be generous, cultured hosts willing to fête our friends unreservedly—of course, we had lots of money—so for a few days, we all would live in an unblemished nuptial paradise.

Just before dusk six trumpeters would summon all the guests to the last gazebo before the lake, the lilac one at the brow of the hill and at the top of the walkway that leads elegantly down to the dock. It would be the summer solstice in June, so twilight wouldn't begin until around ten o'clock at night. We'd all be dressed up to the hilt for this. The hundred of us would gather in ranks of four abreast and begin our slow, measured promenade down to the lake as the six trumpeters play a marvelously complex, mellifluous fanfare that fills the early evening air with rich, crystalline curtains of music. Six guests would bear our banners and pennions: insignias of scarlet dragons and golden griffins and a special design my wife fashioned of the blue-white earth inside a brilliant green emerald under a fiercely yellow sun. These were our bridal flags. It was a large lake, and remarkably we had a flat-decked boat large enough to accommodate our entire party. In the center of our nuptial barge was a wooden pergola festooned

ENGLAND
HONG KONG
JAPAN
MOROCCO
EGYPT
IRELAND
AUSTRALIA

with yellow roses and shiny green leaves while two dozen other varieties of flowers—iris, foxglove, delphinium, baptisia, nasturtium, salvia, peony—bloomed gloriously, almost wantonly, in ceramic pots. The water was glassine and silvery, reflecting the fading blue glory of a magnificent day of sunshine, greenery, and sociability. The water's stillness inspired our own appreciative silence as groomsmen poled our barge out across the broad dish of lake.

I stood with my bride under the rose pergola, holding her hand fast. We were silent, all us of, attentive, reverently calm, a hundred of us breathing spontaneously in unison, our unified breath like a wave of air rolling over the barge in synchrony with the waves lapping underneath it. The sweet perfumes of sandalwood incense, herbal pomanders, and smoldering sage and rosemary scented the moist evening air. We were awaiting a sign.

When the oboists suddenly burst into a melody, we knew it had been given: we sighted the first star of the evening, Venus. We handed all our guests a yellow rose from the pergola's prodigious hoard and a three-foot lilac candle from an open cedar chest. My bride and I each made our welcoming talks, extolling the joys of friendship and the epiphanies of love. We became aware of the moment, awakening to its fullness. There we stood: under the rose-dimpled pergola, encircled by a human wreath of well-wishers, on a nuptial barge sporting more flowers in bloom than the gardens of Eden, drifting placidly on a still lake under the cerulean canopy of a night sky only now scintillating with virginal pinpoints of light, the celestial fireflies of a billion stars. We made no further moves; what would happen next wasn't ours to initiate.

Then it came. It was like an irresistible swoon of warmth, a rosy diaphanous cocoon of affection, an embrace of inestimable scope, a sussur-rus of wings and whispers and love from above, and we sighed into its unrelenting regard as if a galaxy of stars had descended upon our wedding barge like a sparkling crown of heaven rendering us aflush in ineffable bliss. I could make out wings, transparent, billowing sails of wings spangled in stars and eyes blazing adamantly as suns and tender smiles huger than the lake and voices like jubilant chorales and hands aflame with the benedictions of doves—and somehow none of this up-welling immanent glory in any way ruffled the awed stillness among whose folds we languorously floated.

Time dissolved, the barge melted away, as we wafted within this matrimonial aegis of angels until we couldn't stand the happiness anymore, and the tall scarlet candles beside the pergola and the tall lilac candles in our guests' hands seemed to suddenly light themselves. As if waking suddenly from a magnificent enchantment, the musicians started up, fountaining ribbons of nocturnal melody upon soft radiant faces over-brimming with joy. And so we were married.

Ritual Wedding Dances Among Gaia's Stones

Most of us, of course, do not live near stone circles, and might find it almost impossible to make arrangements to hold our nuptial dances at a place like Avebury, Stonehenge, or the Merry Maidens. But whether there are stones (or structures) present is not the point; wedding ceremonies and even dancing form symbolic stone circles at Gaia's geopoints.

As geomancy attests, it's fairly easy to locate geopoints or sacred sites at nearly any place on the

ENGLAND
HONG KONG
JAPAN
MOROCCO
EGYPT
IRELAND
AUSTRALIA

planet—in urban and rural settings, with facilities (such as churches, cathedrals, and temples) or undeveloped (parks, hills, mountains). Such geopoints are advantageous sites for the world culture wedding; correctly sited according to these criteria, your wedding—with its mood of exaltation, delight, and spiritual focus—is also a vibrational gift to the planet.

Each wedding is an imitation of the hieros gamos, the sacred marriage based on an exemplary divine model. As such, it provides the rationale for marrying with the Earth in mind. The hierogamy recapitulates the story of the creation of heaven and Earth and the cosmic union of all the elements, and thereby accomplishes the "restoration of integral wholeness." When we hold our wedding service at a geopoint, we assure that the high vibrations of our human marriage will be registered by the planet in honor of its divine marriage with the cosmos.

In the next stage of our wedding ceremony, we erect the holy altar and wedding canopy from which the rites of marriage will be conducted and to which we lead all the members of the wedding in the ceremonial bridal procession. This we address in our next chapter, but with an interpretive twist: in the world culture wedding, the bridal procession *is* the holy altar.

THE

CHUPPAH

BRIDAL PROCESSION TO THE HOLY TABLE

The indissoluble tie which hallow'd Altars sanctify.
—*Dr. Syntax Combe*, Consolation, *1820*

In the *sagun* ritual, the bride and groom are created out of the fires of purification and sanctified through the ceremonies of protective cleansing. The woman emerges as bride, the man arises as groom—transfigured, pure souls each. In the *hieros gamos* stage, the couple acknowledges their participation in a primordial cosmogonic ritual drawn from a divine source and in imitation of many levels of union and sacred marriage. Now, as "chaste virgins," endorsed and escorted by the community, they process to the conjugal altar, that "high place and holy table," for the handfasting and nuptial blessing, and the second transfiguration into wife and husband.

Normally we think of an altar (from the Latin *altare*, meaning "a high place") as a raised platform, a ritually decorated and adorned holy place, on which to make offerings or observances to the deity. The altar—variously called holy table, hymeneal altar, God's board, Communion table—

is the sanctified place from which ceremonies are conducted and blessings imparted, the meeting place for transactions between human community and numinous audience, the high place for the "sacrifice" of male and female individuality for matrimonial union, the shrine of human reunion with divinity. We usually think of processing *to* an altar; but in this chapter I'd like to invert this image and suggest that in the world culture wedding, the bridal processional *is* the altar.

The Bridal Processional as Community Altar

The processional is a unique moment of unconditional community acceptance of the woman

GREECE
TURKEY
RUSSIA
SERBIA
POLAND
BULGARIA
ROMANIA
JAVA
VIETNAM
LAOS
THAILAND
KOREA
TIBET
CHINA

and man as worthy, deserving, precious, and honorable. The couple may never again experience such unconditional love from their community and family; but for the duration of the wedding, they move through holy, sanctified space and are unblemished and beyond criticism. Through the procession the community *honors* the couple and their intentions; this honoring establishes a spiritual atmosphere in which the joining ritual can be performed.

The processional is much more than family members and close friends squeezing down a church aisle in a two-minute stroll as the organ pumps out the wedding march from Wagner's *Lohengrin.* Groomsmen, bridesmaids, best man, flower maidens, bride-pages, matron-of-honor, parents, siblings, relatives, neighbors, flowers, candles, cakes, veil, torches, music, flags, the sponsors and officiants—these are all ceremonial bridal implements on the high table of the processional, the sanctified space in which the marriage will be made.

Every altar needs a covering, an aegis that sanctifies its ritually numinous space. In the Judaic tradition, this is the *chuppah,* the bridal canopy, a cloth tapestry (*tallit*) spread over four poles to form an open bower, sometimes festooned with floral bouquets. Traditionally the Jewish marriage ceremony is performed under the chuppah, set in the open air, usually in the courtyard of the synagogue; in earlier days musicians would accompany the bride on her procession from her parent's home to the synagogue. The Talmud records that originally the construction of the chuppah was the groom's father's responsibility; he would make the staves from a cedar or pine tree planted at his son's birth expressly for his future marriage.

The Talmud tells us of the chuppah's divine origin. God made ten *huppot* (life containers, known to Qabalists as *Sephira;* ten Sephiroth constitute the *Otz Chaim,* Tree of Life) for Adam and Eve and will build such huppot for the pious in the world to come. According to Hebrew legend, the wedding of humanity's first couple was celebrated with inimitable pomp. Angels surrounded the wedding canopy as God pronounced the nuptial service; after this blessing the angels danced and played musical instruments for the pristine couple who resided in ten bridal chambers of gold, pearls, and various precious stones specially prepared for them by God. The ten bridal chambers made of different jewels is another reference to the ten huppot, or vessels of light (Sephiroth) that comprise the Tree of Life. This alone corroborates the concept we explored in chapter 5, in which we viewed the hieros gamos as the exemplary model for the sacred marriage based on a cosmic archetype. In the Hebrew interpretation, Adam and Eve represent the primordial and thereby timeless human couple standing under the wedding canopy. The canopy, or chuppah, with its four poles (the four elements: earth, air, water, fire), or ten huppot (the Sephiroth or life vessels), represents the whole of Creation.

The structure and rites of our mundane weddings recapitulate a primal spiritual marriage consecrated in heaven between the archetypal forebears of humanity. The wedding canopy we construct for our earthly wedding is an imitation of the canopy of angels and jeweled bridal chambers at the divine wedding of Adam and Eve, as recalled in Hebrew myth. In this metaphorical sense, the elements of the traditional Elizabethan wedding procession, for example—musicians, flower bearer, bride, pages, bridesmaids, family, relatives, friends, flower girl, ring bearer—represent a moving altar, a nimbus of delight enveloping the bride and groom with good cheer.

Traditionally the chuppah symbolizes the groom's home and his matrimonial, sheltering munificence, to which the bride is ritually conducted; more specifically the chuppah signifies the bridal bed, in which they will soon consummate their marital union. In some accounts the chuppah is taken to mean the wedding itself. The chuppah also signifies the establishment of a new home, a fragile common roof for both partners; in a broader liturgical sense, the chuppah symbolizes the covenantal marriage of God and the Hebrews. Sometimes the chuppah itself is used symbolically; in medieval France the Jewish groom covered the bride's head with his personal ritual tallit to symbolize his sheltering her.

Within the Hebrew context, the chuppah also stands for the groom's home because in the many traditional cultures, the joining ritual is performed, not in a church or temple, but at home in a specially sanctified space—the bridal canopy or "marriage bower"—and in the multigenerational presence of both families. The bridal canopy, concisely symbolized by the Hebrew chuppah (and as we'll see below, exemplified in numerous other folkways), is the ritual altar, the high place and holy table within the groom's home, upon which the bridal procession represents the living, moving, affirming components.

"Bride of Mine, Now Cease to Grieve"

Let's open this section with a description of an Albanian processional that exemplifies this expanded idea of processional as altar. The processional for the Albanian bride makes its way through a stream of songs and salutations. The bride is dressed in her wedding finery and jewels at dawn, then she stands in the home's reception room, motionless, silent, veiled, and with downcast eyes, her hands crossed over her chest, until the procession begins. Around ten o'clock a dowry cart arrives from the groom's party to collect her goods and baggage. *"Per heir!"* "Good luck!" everyone shouts as the cart sets off; several women accompany the cart, sprinkling its contents with holy water.

Then the procession begins: all the males of the groom's party and his father escort the bride who sits upon a gaily caparisoned horse. She has been led down the stairs of the house, covered in a long cloak and veil, supported on both sides as if infirm. Attendants hold silken curtains around her, so that she is seen by nobody outside the house until she has mounted her horse. Then the women sing to her:

> Our fair bride is on the way,
> Like a pink, so fresh and gay.
> In the courtyard is the bride,
> She's a rose that's open'd wide.
> On the stair the bride see now,
> White as jasmine is her brow.
> Now she comes within the room,
> Her neck is like the lily's bloom.
> "Bride of mine, now cease to grieve,
> Let not sobs thy bosom heave."
> "Bridegroom mine, can I be gay?
> I've my father left today.
> From my home for ever torn,
> It is meet that I should mourn."

As she passes through the familiar streets of her maidenhood, she inclines her head three times in a small bow of respect and farewell. The same precautions for dismounting are observed when the bride arrives at the groom's home. Women of the groom's house receive her and gently escort her to the nuptial chamber, where she is seated on soft cushions. The women attending her now raise her veil using a ceremonial silver dagger, and it's their duty to offer this song of womanly praise to her:

> How beautiful she is, the bride!
> May God preserve her!
> Her eyes for coffee cups might serve,
> May God preserve her!
> Her cheeks the rose's inmost fold,
> May God preserve her!

Like cypress is she tall and slight,
May God preserve her!

May God preserve her—and him—indeed. Amidst the paraphernalia of the processional that we'll meet in this chapter—nosegays and posies, music of violins, gongs, tambourines, hautboys, the trilling *zagharits,* volleys of joy, rifle shots and camel sedans, mock combats and tolls, rosemary rushes, laments and dirges, red-lacquered gift boxes, dried figs, tiaras of orange-blossoms, signs against evil spirits, white horses, the bedding train, hymeneal torches and epithalamia—the world culture wedding processional conveys the bride and groom safely to the altar, to the sanctified enclosure of the bridal canopy. The conveyance itself is the formation of the altar, the holy table from which the spiritual aspects of the wedding will be conducted once the couple has been brought safely into its ritual space.

I say "safely" because the care, precision, and thoroughness with which the community executes the procession suggests that in this moment of transition and transfiguration, the couple is precious and vulnerable. Safety is paramount, but it's a spiritual safety, an integrity at the soul level that's at play. In the sagun stage, the couple enters individual sanctified space for a purifying private moult; now in the chuppah stage, the transfigured bride and groom emerge into a collective sanctified public space for a communal adoration. Sagun is private, inner, transformative; chuppah is communal, outer, celebratory. Throughout, the couple has been vulnerable, requiring protection. Is someone about to attack them? No, but they're precious all the same in the sense that somehow underlying the details of the wedding in all its guises a spiritual drama unfolds, a concentrated pageant about the creation, birth, and fulfillment of the twofold human.

The couple is precious and honorable—this the bridal procession tells us, and this we acknowledge with the procession. The couple itself is the holiest object on the altar, not for their individual sakes, but on behalf of humankind, for whom they stand as representatives. The bridal procession is the moving tableau of ritual implements on the high table—the space of the altar expressed as time—with which sacred space and the invocation of the holy are ordered; the community that forms the procession creates the chuppah out of itself. The single man and woman before us in this moment represent the totality of all men, all women. Through them we may behold the living archetype of the sundered primal couple; here, in this individual man and woman standing expectantly under the chuppah, they wait on behalf of us all for spiritual reunion. Reunion, not as a surrender of individuality, but as its extension, its fulfillment, an enrichment of its dialectical twofoldness. For as Rilke reminds us, "Only in the dual realm do voices become eternal and mild."

Nuptial Torches and Epithalamiums

The Greek processional is a richly dramatic affair. Here we'll consider a composite, representative impression of the Hellenic bridal journey drawn from classical and contemporary sources.

It all begins Wednesday night, when the homes of both bride and groom "start the leaven." With family relatives present, the mothers begin baking breads and wedding cakes from freshly milled flour and "untouched water," presumably from a sanctified spring. A young boy holds a sieve over the long wooden kneading trough, which is set in the middle of the room; in some instances he holds a sword and sits at one end of the trough, while at the other sits a young girl who pretends to help mix the dough but actually hides a wedding ring and small coins in it.

At first everyone is silent. Then as the sifting progresses, they exclaim *"Kalorizika!"* ("Good luck!"), tossing coins into the sieve, and members of the party outside the house fire off three rifle shots to announce the progress to the village. Relatives take pinches of wet dough and daub the faces of bride and groom. Close to midnight, after a late dinner, the groom's party visits the bride's home for dancing, singing, drinking, and more rifle-firing, all of which may well continue until daybreak.

On Thursday the women kneaders assemble again to divide the leavening dough into portions in hopes of finding the ring and coins secreted in the mixture the previous day; when it's found the groom redeems the ring from its lucky finder with a small present. All portions of dough are now returned to the central mixing trough as the women set about in earnest to make the *propkasto,* the largest of the wedding cakes. In the afternoon the groom and his party set the propkasto over a bowl of water, and with the bride's female friends, dance three times around it while singing "the song of the wedding cake." Then the propkasto is shattered into many small pieces, mixed with figs and other fruits, and showered upon the heads of the couple; as the children scramble for the delicious morsels, the party throws a great quilt over the bride and groom, as an additional symbolic gesture of abundance and fertility.

Friday sees the display of the dowry, another key preparation for the processional. Women from all over the village arrive in the bride's home, bringing basil, rice, and cotton for good luck. Next comes the "filling of the sacks" with the spoils of the dowry, but first the bride's mother stows a copper saucepan into one of the large empty homespun sacks; then the bride packs up her household equipment and clothes into several sacks, as her women relatives toss in coins. When the sacks are filled and the household goods (mattresses, cushions, and covers) are piled up, the women sprinkle it all with rice and attach sweetly aromatic herbs in between the layers of clothes; they might stuff the mattresses with herbs and coins, too. This is the signal for dancing in the courtyard. Meanwhile the groom dispatches several male companions equipped with jugs of wine to canvass the village with invitations to his wedding day dinner; evidently they sweeten the invitation by offering cups of retsina; the bride's father, too, distributes party invitations. Back in the kitchen, the women begin preparing the special wedding dishes including loaves of bread inscribed with symbolic patterns.

On Sunday, the preferred wedding day, friends, relatives, and peer escorts gather in the homes of bride and groom; often they dance in the courtyard as the bride dresses. A small delegation of the groom's male friends, ritually called the *Vràtimi,* sets out to collect the *koumbaros,* the nuptial sponsor, who is the groom's godfather (or one of his sons, if he's deceased). The koumbaros is expected to provide two large white candles tied in a bouquet of orange blossoms for use in the joining ceremony, and sufficient silk for the bride's wedding gown. Once arrived at the koumbaros's home, they hoist a white flag, adorned with the images of apples and sweet herbs, then take the koumbaros back to the groom's home.

The "sewing of the wedding standard," usually undertaken Saturday night, is itself an important preparatory ritual in the Greek wedding. In some instances the wedding flag flies from the roof of the groom's home until the marriage has been consummated. The wedding flag is more than a news report on nuptial events; it's understood to symbolize marriage itself, the "joining of noble youth with virgin maid," as one observer said. "Whose is the wedding standard, noble and red?" sing the participants. "It is the standard of the bridegroom." The standard-bearer is an adolescent virgin, usually the groom's nephew, aged sixteen to twenty, whose parents are both alive. It's his job Saturday night to sew the flag (which in modern times tends to be the Greek national flag) to the seven-foot pole, at the top of which he affixes a Christian cross; onto the three points of the cross

GREECE
TURKEY
RUSSIA
SERBIA
POLAND
BULGARIA
ROMANIA
JAVA
VIETNAM
LAOS
THAILAND
KOREA
TIBET
CHINA

the boy impales apples or pomegranates as fertility symbols; finally, at the top of the pole but below the cross, he ties a handkerchief and two strands of wool (one red for virility, one white for purity). As the boy prepares the flag, the groom's party of men sing wedding songs, but when he finishes, it's time to dance. The standard-bearer leads the young men in a dance—there are musicians present—holding the freshly made flag with his right hand above the group. After dancing he sets the flag into the thatch of the groom's roof over the right-hand side of the doorway for the night. In the morning he'll collect it, mount his horse, and lead the pennioned procession to the bride's home.

The female companions of the bride (among the Vlach of Turkey) also prepare a nuptial flag called *flamboro* for display above her house beginning a week before the wedding. They visit the forest and select a long branch that terminates in five twigs; onto one they fasten an apple (Venus' emblem, symbolizing love and maternity), onto the other, four tufts of red wool (symbolizing household thrift and industry). They carry the flamboro in triumph back to the village, after which they establish it on the roof of the bride's home.

Now the procession can begin, usually in the late afternoon. As the procession leaves the house of the groom's parents, the groom's mother pours out a libation of water and puts down a girdle (or sash) before him at the gate, and he steps over both. First in line is a young boy carrying the white nuptial flag, then the priest and the groom's extended family. Alternatively the procession might be headed by a girl bearing a large jug of scented water. Accompanied by music, shouts, and gunfire, and with the groom mounted on horseback, they process to the bride's home where the flag-bearer establishes the wedding flag on the roof. He may also go by "car," the ancient Greek sedan (or minichariot) pulled by horse, mule, or oxen. The groom dismounts, strides up the steps of the house, and is greeted by the bride's mother

who offers him wine, a ring-shaped biscuit, and a boutonniere of marjoram, basil, and other herbs wrapped in a white handkerchief. He kisses her hand, she kisses both his cheeks; he drinks the wine, pins the boutonniere to his lapel, and asks for her blessing. She might lightly sprinkle him with water from a dipper made of flowers. She may also touch the nape of his neck with a censer of incense and give him a gift called *embatikion,* which is "the gift of in-going"; then, she lays a folded blanket across the threshold, with a stick resting on one corner. The groom steps forward with his right foot, snaps the stick, then enters the house followed by all his relatives, each of whom presents the bride with a modest sum of money. She bows to the four directions, in effect making the sign of the cross with her body movements.

As the wedding ceremony will be performed at the groom's house, the next phase of the procession gets underway: the conveyance of the bride. If the groom came by "car," the bride will sit in the middle between the groom and his *paranymphos,* or best man. The Vràtimi load the bride's dowry and household gear into the "car" or upon muleback, while others discharge guns to frighten off inimical spirits and generally heighten the excitement. The bride's mother tosses a piece of raw cotton onto each dowry sack, presumably as a symbolic blessing that the marriage will enjoy the fruits of the soil; when the processional arrives at the groom's house, his mother repeats the gesture. If they're proceeding to a temple, they will be presented with an ivy branch to symbolize the indissoluble matrimonial bond.

During their dusk journey, the couple may be showered with cottonseed, rice, small coins, sweets, the crimson petals of spring anemones, or rose and myrtle leaves, their way illuminated by pine-flares. The car itself follows the torch-bearers, whose nuptial flames were ritually lit by the bride's mother. It might be the bride's mother herself who, like Hymen, carries the foremost nuptial torch kindled at her family hearth. The bride wears a tulle veil down to her shoulders and a satin gown trimmed in orange blossoms, both bride and groom may be wearing orange-blossom (or myrtle) chaplets, and onlookers call out blessings and nuptial poems, called epithalamiums (meaning "before," *epi,* "the bridal chamber," *thalamus;* also sung after the wedding before the bridal bed) against the sweet trills of the flautists and the heavenly ripples of the harpists. For example:

Today the sky is fair,
And bright today the morning;
Today they hold their wedding,
The eagle and the dove.

Or:

I leave a "farewell" for my village, a "farewell"
for my kin;
And I leave for my mother three phials of bitter
savor;
From one she will drink at morning, from the
second one at noon,
And from the bitterest one of all, she will taste
on holidays.

Or they might chant the *Hymenaeus,* from the conclusion of Aristophanes' comedy *The Birds:*

Jupiter, that god sublime,
When the Fates in former time
Matched him with the Queen of Heaven
At a solemn banquet given,
Such a feast was held above,
And the charming god of Love,
Being present in command,
As a bridegroom took his stand
With the golden reins in hand.
Hymen, Hymen Ho!

When they reach the groom's home, it was once customary to burn the axle of the car (or smash the saddle) to symbolize the irreversibility of their journey to a new life. As they stand in the glimmering twilight at the threshold of the groom's house, its door frame garlanded in flowers, sweetmeats are showered upon them. The groom's mother, who may be holding a lighted pine-torch in each hand, has her assistants present the bride with a small pot of honey. She dips her finger into it and uses the honey to inscribe a cross on the door; she might get a quince or honey-cake, made with walnuts and sesame seeds, as a goodwill gesture for a sweet and fruitful life. The bride's maidens serenade her at the door sill: "Bless thee, bless thee, lovely bride! Bless thee, happy lover! We'll renew our minstrelsies when the day is dawning, and the bright-throated singer cries first his note of warning. Hymen, Hymen, wish us well, in our wedding festival!"

The Meeting of the Wedding Trains

The Russian Usviat wedding ritual traditionally takes up three days, from Friday through Monday, as it moves through its schedule of events, from *zapoiny* (engagement) to *zastol'e* (feast). Like the Greeks the Usviats start their wedding festival with baking the *karavai* loaf, in this case on Saturday night, at the homes of both bride and groom.

The baking of the karavai, a round white loaf decorated with pinecones and images of birds and animals, is the responsibility of the bride's godmother, who supervises the work of the *karavainitsy* ("wedding loaf women"), her female helpers. The women sing while they bake: "The pine stood thirty years. The karavai bakers are drunk. But today the karavai is not baked by nightfall." For the bride possession of the karavai acts as the key of admission to cross the threshold of the groom's house. Each wedding participant gets a slice of the bread "for the sake of a well-fed life."

Alternatively the bride's cohorts may bake sweet *klubtsy,* a pastry in the form of intertwined rings, while the groom's party brings *baranki,* ring-shaped rolls.

The karavai, also known as the gift cake, is the principal component of the *nadel* ritual, the next phase of the Usviaty wedding celebration, when gifts are presented to the bridal couple. The karavai baking is followed by a formal party of nadel, or gift-giving, for the bride, groom, and their friends. Surrogate parents—the marriage godparents—have a prominent role in all the activities and occupy a place of honor at the party table. With the *druzhka* (best man) and *bol'shaia boiarka* (bridesmaid), the godparents have the most active roles in the wedding. The marriage godfather conducts the groom and bride to and from the nadel table, and the marriage godmother bakes, slices, and distributes the karavai, and supervises the ritual tying of the bride's kerchief.

A prominent feature of such parties is an emblem of the bride's beauty. This might be a decorated pinecone, meant to symbolize the bride's pulchritude; afterward the pinecone becomes the groom's property. As a variation the bride's beauty might be represented by a white towel with lace inserts, made by herself; she wears this draped over her head like a veil during the party. At end of the party, the bride's best friend presents the lace towel to the groom, saying, "Our 'beauty' was merry and playful. Now she will be yours. Love her as we loved her. Live with her in the same harmony as we lived with her." The groom receives the towel and deposits it inside his shirt, resolving to honor their request.

The bride gets a *tsvety,* a garland of white and red wax flowers with a ribbon to wear as a chaplet, while the groom, the druzhka, and bol'shaia boiarka get a miniature, hand-sized garland. The marriage godfather conducts the groom, his best man, and the bridesmaid around the nadel table three times in the direction of the sun. Relatives

and children approach and briskly toss coins onto the karavai, swinging their arms exaggeratedly; the more *nadeliashki* ("money given"), the happier the marriage. The bride makes laments—"Endow my little head with a lucky little share, and a good little fate"—whose motifs are echoed in the responses of all the other women present; all of this is set against the sounds of live music. As the women make their laments, they toss more coins, kissing the bride or groom. When the nadel is finished, the bride's mother ties up the tablecloth with all the nadeliashki into a knot, and everyone departs.

The next day the "merging of the wedding processions" takes place: the wedding party meets the couple on the road to the church, or the groom's contingent encounters the bride's "train." The groom's processional has a precisely delineated cast and hierarchy of characters: in the front are the *korovainiki* (loaf-bearers) and *svechniki* (candle-bearers), then the priest with a cross; next come the druzhka on horseback; then the groom. Other dignitaries of the groom's wedding may also be present in the processional or awaiting them later: the *tysiatskii* (master of ceremonies), the *svakha* (matchmaker), *spal'nik* (gentleman-of-the-bedchamber), and other service personnel such as the *movniki* ("masters of the bath"), musicians, tambourine players, and buglers. The bride's party would potentially include the matchmaker, bridesmaid, and *postel'nichii* (bearer of the bedclothes), not to mention the "true lords, sitting lords, and members of the procession."

It was customary as recently as the 1960s for the groom's procession, mounted on horses, to stage a mock attack on the bride's train and attempt to kidnap the bride or block the bridal train with wagons. But the essence of the combat/kidnap ritual is preserved even with the use of modern motorcars. The groom and druzhka travel separately, in a sedan decorated with ribbons and flowers, while the rest of the procession (both bride's and groom's) travel in buses or open trucks decorated with birch tree branches. The two sets of wedding trains advance rapidly toward each other, playing "chicken": they speed past each other, turn around, and meet. Meanwhile there is competition between the choirs of both parties over which is singing more gracefully and loudly. In the days before automobiles, the bride's cart was defended by her male relations, galloping about on horseback; immediately before the cart was the "merryman," who sported a long skewer in each hand with cooked meat or bread at the tips. Next to him walked a companion with a dripping wineskin or beer-barrel. Passersby received a small portion of bread, meat, and wine as they encountered the procession.

As the two processions meet, they sing, "Berry rolled to meet berry." Coarse jokes are bandied between parties; then each side puts forth a counterfeit groom and bride, until they are chased off with laughter. The road at both ends of this tumultuous meeting of two trains is barred in as many as twelve places; anybody who wants to pass through is charged a ransom, usually a couple of bottles of vodka. The roadblock might be a "living fence" of people linking hands, a cordon of flowers dug into the ground, a felled tree, several tables and stools, birch poles linked with ribbons, a long white ribbon held by children, or even two mounted herdsmen. Inhabitants of nearby villages find the *poezdy,* the antic meeting of the wedding processions, entertaining. They put on holiday dress, stand on their fences, and give their blessings. In the old days, when the bride's party traveled by *droshky,* it was decorated with flowers and *kolokolets,* melodious chimes whose tinkling would frighten away the unclean spirits. There were also musicians present, playing bagpipes, mandolin, and drums, and sometimes children running on ahead making a terrible racket beating iron spoons against each other like cymbals.

Somewhat secretively, while the two parties wrangle, the real groom is meanwhile trying to kidnap his bride to avoid the required "ransom"

payment. The druzhka and bol'shaia boiarka are heatedly trying to negotiate the best deal: "We have a rich bride with an education," declares the bol'shaia boiarka. "We will not yield her for less than cognac and truffles." The druzhka replies, "Here is a liter of vodka, the tail of a herring, and a pound of candy!"—except he tries to palm off a bottle of mineral water in place of the vodka. Usually the deal is cut with an authentic bottle of vodka and chocolate candies, after which the bride and her bol'shaia boiarka hop aboard the groom's train. As a variation of this mock reenactment of the wilder, less cordial days of "marriage by bride capture," the bride's father might lock his gates to the groom's procession, refusing him entry until a ransom was paid. Or the bride's party would barricade the road against the passage of the groom; his best man had to call upon all his eloquence and stock of wine and sweets to bribe his way through.

The last phase of the Usviaty proceedings prior to the joining ritual is the meeting on the porch between the couple and their parents. Often fabric has been laid on the ground as a nuptial carpet for the bride for perhaps ten feet, leading up to the porch or door. When she steps out of the carriage, she puts her feet on a sack of rice; or she might be presented with a pot of pilaf (rice with meat and spices). Carrying a napkin-covered tray, the father offers the couple bread, a salt cellar, and two filled glasses. The mother holds a religious icon in one hand, the hem of her skirt in the other. The couple drinks part of the beverage, then tosses the rest over their shoulders, smashing the glasses on the porch for good luck. They might also each be given a slice of bread "so they will be well-fed all their lives." As they enter the house, the mother sprinkles them with grain, candy, and money that she has been clutching in the upheld hem of her skirt—"so they will be healthy, happy, and have many children." Or they might enter the house by passing under living arches made by the upraised hands of the parents, who are clutching bread and

GREECE

TURKEY

RUSSIA

SERBIA

POLAND

BULGARIA

ROMANIA

JAVA

VIETNAM

LAOS

THAILAND

KOREA

TIBET

CHINA

NUPTIAL COLORS THEY WORE—AND WHY

Married in white, you have chosen right
Married in green, ashamed to be seen,
Married in gray, you will go far away,
Married in red, you will wish yourself dead,
Married in pearl, you will live in a whirl,
Married in brown, you will live out of town
Married in blue, love ever true,
Married in yellow, you're ashamed of your fellow,
Married in black, you will wish yourself back,
Married in pink, of you he'll aye think.

Unattributed folk-saying, in Ethil Urlin, *A Short History of Marriage*

Lest we mistakenly think the bride always wore white:

- Yellow was the nuptial color for Roman brides, and a substantial flame-yellow veil their chief sartorial insignia.
- Yellow was favored by eighteenth-century American brides, especially in the form of heavy brocade.
- Yellow was the sacramental color of Hymen, Greek patroness of marriages.
- "A person wearing yellow slippers which are always clean and bright is thereby protected from the evil eye," says Moroccan marriage expert Edward Westermarck, "and people will respect him, he will never suffer want, and his face will not turn yellow."
- In the Russian *Domostroi* wedding ritual, the bride wears a yellow summer dress, white virgin's crown, and red sarafan (the mark of a married woman) on the first day, and a white summer dress the next.
- Turkish brides often wore a softly billowing silken inner outfit of blue and yellow embroidered with pure silver, and a long red velvet "nightshirt" style of overdress.
- Red, for the Chinese, is the color of joy, fire, the sun, phoenix, summer, the South, happiness—the luckiest of all colors. Everything from invitation cards to the bride's dress, veil, and processional sedan is red.
- Bengali brides always wore red saris, although brides in western India chose green or yellow saris.
- The Japanese bride, too, frequently wore a red kimono during the sake joining ritual.
- The Egyptian bride wears a red dress underneath an extensive red (or white) veil, or a red cashmere shawl that hangs down tentlike from her crown, so that she resembled a red cone.
- The Scots shunned green as the "fairy color" because it was the Little People's chosen hue—and the Scots didn't want to encourage them to attend their weddings.

- Zoroastrian brides of Persia a century ago were veiled from head to foot in a green silk robe.
- Korean brides wore a dress with a bright green waist over an intensely red skirt.
- Moroccans favored green because, as the color of lush vegetation, it embodied a lot of good luck.
- The mid-nineteenth-century English bride's attendants might alternatively dress in pale blue, pink, lilac, or pale green.
- The Siamese bride preferred a sarong of sky blue, the color of sincerity, and a pink shawl, the color of love and loyalty.
- Gold, the color of divine power, the splendor of enlightenment, immortality, radiance, the highest value, and the essence of the sun, is the preferred bridal color among Indonesian royalty. One princess bride, wearing a scarlet skirt wrapped in purple and gold sashes, was bound from hips to chest in strips of gold lamé; her forehead was studded with gold leaf, while gold flowers, with a ruby heart in the middle, made a sparkling circlet on her head; and gold leaves and tiny gold flowers trailed from her head down to her shoulders. Her bridesmaids, said one observer, "looked like a row of golden chrysanthemums."

salt. A winter coat has been laid on the floor inside the house and near the pantry for the couple to tread upon "so they will be rich."

Another aspect of the old-style Russian processional is the "bedding train." This involved the transportation of the bride's dowry and bedclothes, often in five enclosed wagons, from her family's home to her new household. The first wagon contained an icon and samovar and a "dish-boy," a young lad who held a tray with an enormous sugar loaf decorated with ribbons and a packet of tea wrapped in silk. In the second wagon sat the bride, holding her porcelain and a silver salt-shaker; the third wagon carried the bride's featherbed, satin blankets, large pillows, sheets, and bolsters; and the fourth wagon bore a plush rug and furniture. Riding in the fifth wagon was the bride's aunt and perhaps her mother with the "dowry list," the inventory of goods in transit. The matchmaker could also be found in the fifth wagon, holding a live turkey festooned with ribbons and a cap.

The Svatovi *and Their Jester*

A few days before a Serbian wedding, the groom's father must turn into a *buklijas,* a flask-bearer. He fills a flask with his best brandy, decorates it with flowers, hoists a *torba* (a gaily woven sack) over his shoulder, and sets out to personally invite all the wedding guests. He calls on the future godfather of all children issuing from the marriage, then the *starojko* (the chief witness), then the *ever* (best man), then the home of the bride, and finally the households of his own kin, and finally friends and neighbors. He proffers each person he visits a drink of brandy, and together they toast the health of the couple. The now

GREECE
TURKEY
RUSSIA
SERBIA
POLAND
BULGARIA
ROMANIA
JAVA
VIETNAM
LAOS
THAILAND
KOREA
TIBET
CHINA

invited guest tops up the buklijas's flask with more brandy and pins a handkerchief, pair of socks, shirt, or towel onto his torba, which is a kind of traveling sartorial bulletin board.

Then, on the wedding day morning, the members of the *svatovi* (the wedding guests who will collect the *mlada,* or bride) gather in the courtyard of the groom's father. A fleet of buggies and fiacres—it can be as many as twenty—are decorated with garlands of pink, white, and gold chrysanthemums and green leaves; the bridles of the horses are trimmed with flowers, colored streamers, and trailing white scarves. Sitting in the first carriage ride the *mladozenja* (groom), his parents, and his godfather. An accordionist plays, the young men whoop, and the party's rear is brought up with bachelors on horseback. The procession's leader and standard-bearer, the *vojvoda,* carries the Serbian flag, considered indispensable in weddings.

But as the svatovi approaches the bride's house, the vojvoda calls a halt. He must surmount an obstacle laid before them by the bride's household. They've lashed a swaying willow pole ten feet long to a treetop; at its top they've fastened a small gourd and a white handkerchief. The vojvoda must retrieve these trophies on behalf of his svatovi before they can expect admission at the bride's home. The vojvoda gets some degree of help, if only comic relief, from the antics and buffoonery of the *vojvodski momak,* the official wedding jester. This happy fellow—who is dressed up as the bride with a long flaxen braid pinned to his cap, a necklace of red peppers, garlic, and corn kernels around his neck, and a squawking chicken under his arm—acts silly, inspires merrymaking, sings lewd songs, and generally acts up in the face of all solemnity. All of this is intended to distract and confuse any evil spirits present and keep the evil eye off the bride—even nasty sprites enjoy a show.

Between the formidable presence of twenty floral fiacres and the hen-assisted antics of the jester, the male relatives of the bride finally show

their faces. Inside the courtyard the female relatives survey the incoming groom's party and brazenly review them, particularly the groom, in song:

Come forward, come forward, beribboned wedding party,
So we can see, so we can see, who is the bridegroom—ii ih!
Is he better looking, is he better looking,
Than our maiden—ii ih!
What have we given, what have we given?
Gold for lead—ii ii ih!

As her female relatives toast the groom for his pitiable aspect, the bride remains cloistered inside the house. Soon her mother-in-law and her female relatives visit her and present their gifts, traditionally a necklace of gold coins, but in recent years, a stout pair of shoes and stockings. Then women of both families dress the bride in her wedding costume, a high-necked, long-sleeved white dress with gauze veil. They leave her to rejoin the drinking, carousing party outside plying the long food tables.

Somebody fires a rifle shot, which signals the bride's brother to ceremoniously escort his sister to the head of the table, where she greets all her new in-laws by kissing their hands. She and her groom stand at the head of the banquet table until everyone has eaten their fill, while her sisters, female cousins, and girlfriends pin corsages onto the jackets and blouses of all the guests. Then the *dever*—the bride's official guardian until the wedding ceremony—wearing a long white sash across his chest, accompanies her in the lead carriage as the svatovi caravan resumes its progress, this time, with the guests shouting and waving brandy flasks above their heads, destined for the church in the groom's village for the vencanje, or joining ritual.

Polish weddings in the eighteenth century also had a clown. On the day of the wedding, all the guests were woken up by a band of traveling musicians who went house to house with their musical reveille. They varied their program according to the desired mood of the guests, playing sentimental songs to evoke tears of reminiscence, or wild dance tunes to encourage revelers to dance off their excesses of vodka. The musicians collected all the guests, and in the wisecracking company of the *badchan,* the ceremonial clown or jester (in Germany he was called *marshallik,* "the little marshal"), would escort them in the procession to the church. The badchan was a professional comic who cracked jokes and poked fun at all the wedding dignitaries—the bride and groom, their families, and all the bigshots of the community. If the badchan had anything to say about it, solemnity was not allowed.

"With their garlands of flowers and vine leaves, their songs and strains of wild music, their gleeful shouts and gay laughter," wrote Victorian wedding scholar Lucy Garnett in *The Women of Turkey and Their Folklore* (1891) of Bulgarian customs, "this wedding procession presents the appearance of an ancient chorus of Bacchanals wending its way by mountain-path and ravine to some old shrine of the vinous god." The procession is led by a male guest, who displays the groom's flag surmounted by an apple. As they near the village, the *nunco* (best man) and other nuptial functionaries greet them with baskets of fruit and cakes, flasks of wine, compliments of the nunco, who is personally transporting the bridal crowns and a goat with gilded horns. Once arrived at the gate of the groom's house, the flag-bearer enters first, impaling his standard in the courtyard, followed by the bride, who dismounts her horse. Wedding guests sing: "O Maldever, O Stardever, why linger thee outside? Dismount, dismount, and enter now thy husband's house, O Bride!" She does, but first she bows three times to the guests, then, taking one corner of a handkerchief proferred her by her father-in-law, she's led into the house.

The White Flag of Purity and a Carpet of Sweetmeats

The wedding procession of the Romany Gypsies of Spain, which is part of their overall wedding festival that lasts three days, is led by a man sporting a long pole with a white handkerchief fluttering at its tip. For the Gypsies this symbolizes the bride's purity. Behind him walk the betrothed couple, then their closest friends, then a "rabble rout of Gypsies, screaming and shouting, and discharging guns and pistols," as one observer noted.

When the party reaches the church, the standard-bearer inserts the pole into the ground, but then the crowd proceeds past it for another venue, a day of drinking, dancing, feasting, and carousing. As much as a ton of sweetmeats is prepared (often in the form of sugar-coated egg yolks), then strewn as an edible carpet on the floor of a large room to a depth of three inches. In the evening a signal is made and the bride and groom enter this specially carpeted room to dance the *romalis;* they're joined by the remainder of the party, who also dance excitedly to the strumming of guitars and the snapping of castanets. Soon the sweetmeat carpet is pulverized, the floor turned to mud, and the clothes of the dancers soiled to the knees from the splattering of egg yolks, sugar, and fruits. During the three days of celebrations, the doors are kept open to all casual visitors, whether Gypsies or not.

The Wedding of the Dead

For Transylvanians (a people within Romania), marriage is a form of symbolic death—which

GREECE
TURKEY
RUSSIA
SERBIA
POLAND
BULGARIA
ROMANIA
JAVA
VIETNAM
LAOS
THAILAND
KOREA
TIBET
CHINA

GREECE
TURKEY
RUSSIA
SERBIA
POLAND
BULGARIA
ROMANIA
JAVA
VIETNAM
LAOS
THAILAND
KOREA
TIBET
CHINA

means the best way to approach the processional is to consider it a funeral and ply it with dirges. After all, the bachelor lives of both groom and bride will momentarily be radically transformed. So the groom's male friends sing a dirge *pa drum* (on the road), using images evoking the uncertainty of the dead departing this world in a casket, and expressing sentiments intended to provoke in the groom a brief purging of grief for the loss of his bachelorhood, his family, and youth.

> On the road that I am taking
> There is neither a well nor a stream
> To temper my longing.
> There is neither a well nor a spring
> To temper my sorrow.
> The road to Cluj is long
> But that of yearning is longer.
> The road to Cluj ends;
> That of yearning, never.

White Horses, Floral Palanquins, and Mock Combat

In Norway the bridal procession to church, on horseback in summer, on sledge in winter, and by boat in the lake country, was accompanied by fiddlers and drummers. When U.S. President John Tyler married in June 1844, his procession down New York City's Fifth Avenue after leaving the Church of the Ascension was visually arresting: he sat next to his much younger wife, who wore white chiffon, white gauze veil, and a circlet of white flowers, in an open barouche, drawn by four white horses.

The nineteenth-century English novelist William Makepeace Thackeray published a reliable description of a wedding procession in his novel *Vanity Fair,* highlighting its essential: a glass coach.

This was a horse-pulled canopied carriage with ample glass windows on all sides and streaming white ribbons; for a time it was an instantly recognizable signature of a wedding in progress.

"In some of the rural parts of this country," wrote the English folklorist W. T. Marchant in *Betrothals and Bridals* (1879), "it is usual to fix a floral rope across the street on the day of a wedding; all who pass through on that day have to pay a toll."

The Armenian groom, wearing a flesh-colored gauze veil or silver net over his face, neck, shoulders, and chest, rode to the church on horseback. Behind him rode the bride, entirely veiled in white, and holding one end of a girdle, of which he held the other. An attendant walked alongside her horse, tending the reins. Alternatively the couple walked to church holding opposite ends of the wedding girdle, the bride escorted by two matrons and the groom by a saber-clad friend, as their family and relatives accompanied them with burning tapers and musicians.

In seventeenth-century France, the groom led the procession, escorted by two near kinsmen and followed by married men, then bachelors, in pairs. Next came the bride, wearing a coronet of white flowers or pearls on her brow and escorted by two close kinswomen; behind her came female friends in pairs, each wearing smaller coronets in imitation of the bride's. At the tail of the procession walked a man bearing plates of bread and wine as offerings for the church service.

If you happened to have been in Persia in October 1867, when the king was married to his cousin, you would have seen a procession with state-of-the-art pomp, circumstance, and ostentation. The bride's cavalcade was preceded by one hundred horses, mules, and camels, laden with servants, carpets, tents, and the bridal impedimenta. Next came a regiment of horses with rich housings, then drawn by six horses the bride's carriage, whose wooden shutters concealed the princess. Behind this came mules pulling palanquins with drawn curtains to maintain the privacy of the bride's female retinue. At the end of the procession, you would have seen numerous military officers and governmental dignitaries on "beautifully caparisoned horses," escorted by musicians playing violins, trumpets, and tambourines. Most remarkably the princess's lavish processional from her home to the king's lasted thirty-three days.

The royal procession of England's Princess Elizabeth, daughter of King James I, when she married Frederick, the Elector of Bohemia, in 1613, had comparable grandeur, according to an observer (quoted by Peter Lacey in *The Wedding*) who registered his awed impressions: "Her vestments were white, the emblem of innocence; her hair disheveled, hanging down her back at length, an ornament of virginity; a crown of pure gold upon her head the cognizance of majesty, her train supported by twelve young ladies in white garments, so adorned with jewels, that her passage looked like a milky way."

The traditional Javanese processional has dramatic elements of mock combat. Men walk with spears that are struck by other men; sham soldiers festooned in peacock plumage and horses' tails and armed with shields, darts, and swords, dance and engage in mock combat. Completing the procession are the groom and his male cohorts, women carrying ornaments and household goods as bridal presents, drummers, and all the invited guests. When the procession arrives at the bride's home, she conducts her husband-to-be inside to a seat of honor; as a simple token of his intention to share his future good fortune with her, he presents his wife with a portion of rice, which they eat together from the same bowl. In some instances she washes his feet when he first enters the house, or wipes his feet after he has trodden upon the raw egg left on the threshold.

The old-fashioned Burgundy wedding in north central France, which lasted three days, began with a procession of drummers and fifers, ribbons and sweetmeats, and a host of *dames d'honneur*, the bride's women attendants. The bride and groom spent a great deal of time distributing sweetmeats to guests who in turn showered them, in a fertility ritual called "the sowing of the married pair," with golden kernels of corn from upper windows along the street, calling: "Scarcity and want shall shun you, Ceres's blessing now is on you."

In Scotland the bride is escorted, arms linked, in procession with the bridesmaid on one side, the groomsman on the other. Her two companions each flourish white scarves and handkerchiefs in their hands, waving them about her like fans. At the rear of the bridal procession come two young girls similarly holding white scarves "in festoon," while at the procession's fore, pipers play 'Fye, let's a' to the Bridal."

The Welsh practiced a playful game of bridal party lockout as part of their traditional processional. On the wedding eve, all the guests assemble at the bride's home; the sound of music alerts them to the imminent arrival of the groom. During this brief distracting moment, the bride and her family are sealed up in a room and all doors to their house locked. Outside everybody clamors strenuously for admittance, but no progress is made until a bridesmaid pries open a window enabling the groom to climb through, after which he flings open all the doors and the guests stream through and improve their dispositions through taking large quantities of spiced wine and cake. In the morning the formal journey to the church begins as two separate processions, originating at each family home; at a certain point the bride's and groom's processions merge, as a harper plays "Come haste to the Wedding."

In her processions from parent's home to church to groom's residence, the British bride of the Tudor period was accustomed to a constant "noyse of musicians" and the "great noise of harpes, lutes, kyttes (violin), basens (cymbals), and drooms, whewyth' matrimonial celebrants troubled the whole church," as the Bishop of Exter, Miles Coverdale complained in the mid-sixteenth century.

GREECE
TURKEY
RUSSIA
SERBIA
POLAND
BULGARIA
ROMANIA
JAVA
VIETNAM
LAOS
THAILAND
KOREA
TIBET
CHINA

Cavaliers and the Bonaventura

In a typical shepherd's wedding in nineteenth-century Corsica, the bride, dressed in white, her head wreathed in orange blossoms, sets off on a white mare escorted by armed cavaliers of her groom's party. They periodically punctuate her procession with rifle shots in the air, making "a volley of joy." Several of the cavaliers, who had ridden on ahead, return with fresh bouquets, which they present to the bride with a kiss and a compliment in verse. When the processional crosses a stream, the bride soaks a *canistroni* (a wedding pastry) in the water and launches an olive branch or flower down the stream, to symbolize the abundance, peace, and happiness that will flow through her marriage. She may kneel by the stream and anoint herself with the pure water, letting it sprinkle out of her upheld palms over her head and face; murmuring an old prayer, she may request that these lustral waters purify her.

The procession moves on with the cavaliers singing *lamenti,* until the bride is met at the threshold of her new home by her mother-in-law, who presents her with a spindle and key then sprinkles her with rice and corn as a gesture of abundance. This is the *bonaventura,* the fortunate welcome, which the cavaliers commemorate by another volley of joy with their rifles.

The Ride of the Bridegroom and the Bride's Camel

The Moroccan groom, dressed in his new clothes with a big turban and silk cord and his face covered by the *hâyek* (veil), leaves the mosque on his wedding day and mounts a saddled mule. Both groom and bride will be in procession today. His chief vizier, *wazâra,* scribes, and other male assistants are with him today, all dressed in white, and several of them wave handkerchiefs at him, just as they would to honor the passing of the real sultan, because on this, his wedding day, the Moroccan groom is an honorific sultan. The "ride of the bridegroom" proceeds slowly; the huntsmen in the train fire off volleys of gunpowder, musicians make music, and the scribes and wazâra sing: "O Muhammed O he who is shaded by the veil, on you be the peace of God; and O beauty of the turban, on you be the peace of God."

During the bridegroom's ride, if they pass a *ràuda,* or religious cairn, they pause and pelt the cairn with stones to drive away or kill *Yiblis,* bad spirits who may try to join their processional. After the ritual pelting, the groom faces East, raises his hands in the *fâtha* gesture, and whispers in a barely audible voice (because he's not supposed to talk aloud before the wedding: "I am under the protection of God and the Prophet Muhammed." The rest of his entourage repeat the gesture, then they continue on to his home, accompanied at some distance by women who make the distinctive zagharit "joy-trill."

When they arrive at his courtyard, they find a carpet is laid out for them (a present from the bride); the vizier lifts the groom from his mule and sets him down on a cushion upon the carpet where he remains, surrounded by the unmarried scribes holding the groom's ceremonial flags. There is continual music, gunpowder play, and food until sunset, although the groom himself abstains from eating. The groom's mother brings four large candles, which are lit by the vizier and set before the groom where he sits on the carpet. Then the "Sultan" and his wazâra perform their sunset prayers.

The bride must be fetched, too, and for this Moroccan tribes have many local variations in procedure. Among this diversity one thing is con-

sistent: the groom most often isn't part of the bride's procession. Here's a pastiche drawn from the customs of several different tribes:

A delegation from the groom's village sets out to fetch the bride, in the morning if she lives far away, or at sunset, if she's local. The procession, which includes the full range of the groom's female relations, brings with them a mare led by the groom's mother with two women on either side of the saddle, their hands on the stirrups; on the saddle is the groom's young brother or cousin, who carries a flag for the bride. The women bear small gifts for the bride of dried fruit and boxes containing mirrors, antimony, walnut root and bark, and sweets to prevent hoarseness. If the procession reaches the bride's home by sunset, they are fed and entertained; at midnight the bride is painted with henna, and at dawn she is clothed in her bridal clothes and veiled. A brother or paternal cousin lays part of his tunic out on the ground before her as a rug to prevent her from touching the sullied ground; she takes three steps upon it, dropping several coins as a gift, then is lifted onto the mare. As the procession moves along, there is music, drumming, the ubiquitous zagharit, and small gunpowder explosions.

It's not always a mare the bride rides, however; far more dramatic is her sealed conveyance inside the *arägn* on camelback. The arägn is a sedan frame made of four wooden posts covered in cloths; sometimes it's commodious enough to accommodate four other young women. In front of the man conducting the camel walks the *luzîra*, a woman who carries a flowerpot on her head containing a sweet-scented plant. The women sing: "A house of good people whereto the road will take her; if there are good people, there are all kinds of good things."

Victoria de Bunsen, an English woman visiting Turkey in the 1930s, provides us with a vivid impression of this conveyance. The bride was "covered from head to foot with an enormous veil of violet gauze, and her face beneath was adorned with pieces of gold paper pasted on with white of egg," she wrote in *The Soul of a Turk*. "From the open window we could see the flaming torches of the bridegroom's procession . . . It was a wild and romantic scene, the women on the balcony craning their heads and waving their arms in welcome, against the starlit skies, the dumb bride with her downcast eyes under the flickering oil lamp inside, the noisy shouting procession in the street." Edward William Lane, an Englishman who visited Egypt in the 1830s and witnessed a traditional wedding, was strongly impressed with the *mesh'als*, which were pole-mounted multiple flame torches. "The mesh'al is a staff with a cylindrical frame of iron at the top filled with flaming wood, or having two, three, four, or five of these receptacles for fire . . . [which] brilliantly illuminate the streets through which the procession passes, and produce a remarkably picturesque effect."

Honoring the Spirit of the Soil

In Vietnamese villages the bridal procession effectively begins on the night before the wedding with festivities at the groom's house. Friends, relatives, and neighbors gather for a meal in a gay party atmosphere of candlelight and music, and present the groom's father with presents. The celebrations may easily continue until daybreak, when they drink tea until it's time to assemble the procession. The family erects an altar before the house dedicated to the Spirit of the Soil; another altar, honoring the family ancestors, has already received offerings of fruit, rice, alcohol, and tea. When everything is ready, the groom dons his traditional blue robe and the party sets out for the bride, each taking his prescribed position in the procession.

A close male friend of the groom leads and acts as chief assistant—de facto, the best man—

GREECE
TURKEY
RUSSIA
SERBIA
POLAND
BULGARIA
ROMANIA
JAVA
VIETNAM
LAOS
THAILAND
KOREA
TIBET
CHINA

TIARAS OF ORANGE BLOSSOMS AND
NUPTIAL FLOWERS

*I*f one is an American contemplating flowers for a wedding, in the land where "bigger is better and more is desirable, too," the temptation can easily become not which, but how many. That was evidently the sentiment motivating multimillionare Sid Richardson in his florally legendary 1960s' Texas wedding, which used 2,300 camellias, 1,700 Easter lilies, 500 gardenias, 1,000 bride's roses, 1,000 snapdragons, 1,500 peach-blossom stems, 500 bunches of violets, 200 azaleas, 170 white lilacs, 12 pink magnolia trees, 5 flowering peach trees, and 12 flowering crab-apple trees.

Traditional folkways, however, were somewhat more subtle:

- The Roman bride carried three wheat ears in her hand and wore "a chaplet of flowers or hearbes upon her head," noted William Vaughan in his *Golden Glove* (1608). Nuptial garlands were often made of myrtle sprigs, sacred to Venus and thus an emblem of love, or olive, especially if these plants were native.
- Chaplets of roses, nuptial crowns of wheat-sheaves or corn-ears, or other floral wreaths, were highly favored by European and English brides; often the leaves and blossoms of these chaplets were fitted on a hoop of thin metal worn around the head.
- Myrtle, highly respected because of its enduring freshness, was seen as the flower of constancy in duty and affection.
- Nineteenth-century English bridesmaids carried bunches of yellow chrysanthemums.
- The strewing—or "strawing"—of flowers and herbs before the wedding procession as a floral carpet was widely practiced in Elizabethan England so that bridal couples could walk to church on flowers. Minor poets of the day attest to the ubiquity of the custom: "Enter a maid strewing flowers, and a serving man perfuming the door," wrote one commentator in 1609; "The wheaton ear was scatter'd near the porch / The green bloom blossom'd strew'd the way to church," said another in 1796. This practice continued well into the nineteenth century: "The author was present at a wedding in Ightham, in Kent, in 1862," wrote Edward Wood, "when the old women and children of the village scattered wild flowers before the bride as she left the church after the ceremony."
- Rosemary was a popular choice, because it is "for remembrance" and tenacity of memory. In seventeenth-century English weddings, often rosemary was first dipped in scented water; sometimes a branch of rosemary might be "gilded very fair, and hung about with silver ribands of all colors." Rosemary sprigs might also find their aromatic way into the bridal bed on its inaugural night. In the sixteenth century, it was customary for the bridesmaid to present the groom with a bunch of rosemary bound in ribbons first thing on his wedding morning.
- "Gilt rases of ginger"—that is, dried gilded roots or sprigs of ginger attached to the bride's sash—in complement to rosemary and ribbons were part of the floral accouterments of the seventeenth-century plain country English bride.

- In the ancient Roman wedding procession, the torch carried by the young boy was whitethorn (*Spina alba*), regarded as a powerful protective against hostile magic.
- Wreaths of orange blossoms, bonnets trimmed with orange blossoms, and a jeweled tiara laced with orange blossoms became enormously popular in England, Europe, and America beginning in the 1830s. This was probably due in part to the inarguable fact that few fruit trees are as prolific (hence, fertile) as the orange.
- Combinations were appealing, especially among the wealthy who could afford the floral finesse. A bouquet of orange flowers might be displayed on one side of the bride's lapel, with a full-blown white rose pinned on the other. Britain's Princess Augusta, for her marriage in 1843, "wore on her head a wreath composed of orange flowers and myrtle and a tiara of sapphires and diamonds and was covered with a very large and most beautiful veil of point lace," commented the *Illustrated London News*. Almost a century later, when the present Queen Mother of England married in 1923, she wore a narrow headband of myrtle leaves and two white roses and orange-blossom sprigs above each ear.
- Robert Herrick, in his eighteenth-century poem "Hesperides," lists the wedding flowers of his time: ladysmock, pansy, rose, prick-madam, gentle-heart, and maiden's-blush. Primroses, violets, and sprigs of gorse also found their way into nosegays.

carrying gifts of gold earrings, rice alcohol, a red silk wedding robe, and large, circular hat for the bride to wear on the return procession and during the joining ritual. Next comes the groom; he's carrying a big round red-gold lacquered box containing *mam trau cau*, the traditional wedding gifts of betel leaves and areca nuts, which symbolize unity and fidelity. The red lacquer wedding boxes might also contain gifts of brocade, silk, taffeta, and jewelry. Groom and best man are accompanied on both sides by assistants bearing long-handled mandarin parasols; behind them trail more male kinsfolk carrying black umbrellas; behind them come younger married women and maidens dressed gaily in pastel colors and gold necklaces. At the rear of the procession walk the elderly women dressed in black. The groom's mother will not join, so that her absence and noninvolvement in the procession and its negotiations will be understood to mean the future lack of friction between her and the daughter-in-law.

Meanwhile kinsfolk and friends are gathered at the bride's home in expectation of the arrival of the groom's procession. When the groom appears, the bride's parents greet him, and his best man formally informs them that they are here to collect the bride; he sweetens his announcement by presenting them with small glasses of rice wine, the areca nuts, and betel leaves. The bride's family might push the matter a bit and ritually refuse the groom entry, although the payment of an entrance fee in a red envelope, plus an eloquent speech delivered by a trained orator, helps his cause. They accept and place the gifts on the ancestor's altar, covering them with a red-bordered cloth, as the groom's party enters the house. Sometimes the groom's mother visits the bride's house and presents her with pink chalk to symbolize the rosy future she'll have (white chalk, in contrast, signifies death and misfortune). The bride's father bows before the shrine of his ancestors, asking their permission to present his new son-in-law. The groom makes a gesture of respect to the bride's family by

GREECE
TURKEY
RUSSIA
SERBIA
POLAND
BULGARIA
ROMANIA
JAVA
VIETNAM
LAOS
THAILAND
KOREA
TIBET
CHINA

bowing before their ancestral altar, then before his bride's male, then female kinsfolk. After this he presents the wedding clothing to this bride, who is waiting in a room within.

In the second phase of the bridal procession, which begins at an exact time prescribed by the astrologer, they return to the groom's house through the rice paddy fields. Before they leave the bride's house, the entire family, except the father, makes lamentations about the loss of such a fine daughter. On their arrival, before entering the house, the bride and groom clasp burning incense in their hands and bow before the altar to honor the Spirit of the Soil. Inside the house, as they await the beginning of the wedding ceremony, they find the male elders appropriately seated before the shrine of the ancestors, while the women sit on the periphery in the shade, near the trays of betel leaves, areca nuts, and lime pots. The house is attractively and ambitiously decorated, according to the means of the family's budget; palm fronds are tied to pillars and beams, chairs, chinaware, and chopsticks are laid out, the brass altar accouterments are polished, fresh candles are made ready, silk and satin hangings drape the altars.

Wedding processions in Laos run along similar lines. As in neighboring Vietnam, the auspicious timing for all aspects of the wedding is meticulously plotted by the village astrologer. The procession comprises the groom's parents and relatives, village elders, family friends, and is conducted to the bride's home by young women and girls, but not widows or divorcées. Members of the procession carry offerings for the gods and presents for the bride's family, such as betel, tobacco, cakes, meat, fish, and bedding; gongs, drums, and singing keep their procession festive. It wouldn't be accurate to say the bride's family welcomes the procession with open arms—or at all. They're in hiding and have bolted the door. A clever, disputatious elder, chosen by the bride's family, accosts them verbally with the finesse of a prosecuting attorney

hot on the trail of obvious deceit. "Why have you come?" he demands. If the groom's party wants to prevail, they must put forth someone equally dexterous with wit and words, praying their side will emerge victorious in this battle of the "lawyers." Generally the bride's party will settle out of court for a huge sum; after more negotiation they reduce their demands and accept a bottle of beer. Finally, before he enters the house, a brother or cousin of the bride washes his feet as he stands on banana leaves over a flat stone to ensure he enters his father-in-law's house pure of heart and body.

Muang Song's Elephant Ride to Fetch the Nymph of the Jungle

Kumut Chandruang, in *My Boyhood in Siam*, describes a wedding procession he observed in Thailand in the 1930s.

Nang Onn's beauty was formidable, which was why Muang Song's bride was widely known as the "nymph of the jungle." Muang Song and his male friends gathered at the edge of the village, several fields away from Nang Onn's home. Not long after sunrise, he was dressed in his finest red *panung* and a green silk jacket—and he was sitting on a decorated elephant borrowed from the local monastery, while his friends were on horseback. Some carried gongs, while others held long drums over their shoulders. They started percussing with these as the elephant-horse cavalcade moved briskly and ponderously (depending on what you were riding) across the fields. The villagers, some of whom, along with their dogs and children, joined the rear of the procession bearing their wedding presents (often braying or bleating domestic animals), cheered them on with calls of "Ho-hi! Ho-hi! Ho-hi!"

Everything was moving smoothly until the procession was halted at the gates of the bride's home by two angels—well, almost, explains Chandruang. The obstructing angels were the two diminutive but no doubt cherubic brothers of the bride who made it clear (coached by their mother, standing behind them) what the conditions were for any further processional passage. "Do you bring the wedding gold with you?" they asked, beginning what would prove to be a very long, precise catechism. Then they asked Muang Song if he brought gifts; yes, he replied: ducks, chickens, three goats, two pigs, a calf, banana trees, sugar canes. "Before you pass this golden gate to your precious wife, to live together on a pile of silver and gold, do you have anything to offer us angels?" Muang Song's tendered bribe of two golden rings got the gates opened for him and his best man and got the acquisitive angels off his back.

But now the mother barred the gates, demanding further booty. "Declare your gifts as I call your names," she commanded. This roll call netted her a pig, a jar of rum, one hundred duck eggs, a goat, and a good luck charm from a magician. But this was a wizard with an eye for business. When he entered the house, he told the bride's father it would be haunted by evil spirits unless he exorcised them in a special ritual that would set him back one hundred duck eggs, five chickens, and one large pig's head. Then the two fathers exchanged greetings: "Today my heart is blooming with joy," said Muang Na, the groom's father. "Through our son and daughter, we shall be linked together with a golden chain." Kamman, the bride's father graciously replied: "Your grandson will also be my grandson." Which inspired Muang Na to add: "May the protector of all life bless them!" After this the yellow-robed priests arrived, had their feet washed by the little "angels," refreshed themselves with tea and areca nuts, and got on with the wedding.

Sending Silk in the Bride's Gift Box

The traditional Korean prewedding procession and gift-exchange ceremony is based on the ancient Six Etiquettes, established by the Chinese neo-Confucianist Chu Hsi. Confucian etiquette requires the groom to wait outside the bride's home on his wedding day until he's invited inside by a family member. What happens between the time he leaves his home and the time he gets inside his parents-in-law's gate is subject to local variation, as the following descriptions make clear. One of the matrimonial rites is *napp'ye,* "sending silk."

On the day before his wedding, the Korean groom, dressed in his wedding hat, belt, and coat, visits his bride's village riding a white horse. As he departs his village, children throw ashes after him, as a beneficial charm against the "gods of the plague." He's accompanied by his nearest male relative (but not his father) or a *tabokhan saram,* a "lucky person," who is perhaps a family servant or hired porter, but at any rate somebody who is harmoniously married and whose firstborn was a son. The tabokhan saram bears a gift box (wedding chest), which is the traditional *pongch'i ham,* a container of modest bridewealth. Additional servants may be present, carrying large paper umbrellas. The whole matter—day and hour—has been carefully scheduled through consultation with an astrologer to be the most auspicious. He may also have as companions various attendants who walk with large paper umbrellas.

The tabokhan saram or relative walks alongside the mounted groom carrying a black lacquer box wrapped in pink cloth and containing bridal gifts. Sometimes his face is painted black, making him appear clownish, so that the formal confrontation between the families is enlivened. The gifts vary: a blue silken shirt bound with a red

GREECE
TURKEY
RUSSIA
SERBIA
POLAND
BULGARIA
ROMANIA
JAVA
VIETNAM
LAOS
THAILAND
KOREA
TIBET
CHINA

ribbon, a red skirt tied in blue, the marriage con-tract folded in a long envelope; further, there might be gold or silver rings or cosmetics.

When they arrive at the bride's house, which is festively lighted with paper lanterns, torches, and candles,, they're greeted by a desig-nated "lucky person" of the household. She accepts the gift box, places it on the *pongch'i ttok* (ritual rice-cake), serves the gift box–bearer liquor, and bears the box into the bride's chamber: "Here's a lot of good fortune coming in." Selecting gifts from the sealed box is a kind of divination of future childbirth. Without looking, a family member draws out the first of the two silk-wrapped gifts: blue wrapped in red means the firstborn will be male, red wrapped in blue foretells a girl. The bride's gift box is delivered, but it won't be until the next day that the master of the house delivers the bride.

Early the next morning, the groom per-forms the next ritual in his wedding travail—send-ing duck. Wearing his special red and green hat at the back of his head, he repeats the mounted jour-ney to the bride's house. On this procession the groom travels with a full retinue: before him, two servants with paper umbrellas; behind him, his best man, followed by two lantern-carriers, a wooden-duck carrier, and six female servants dressed in green and blue. (Instead of a wooden duck, a live goose might be involved. The duck is a zoomorphic stand-in for the goose, which is Korea's and China's classical marriage symbol, rep-resenting conjugal fidelity, monogamy, felicity, bearer of good tidings, and beauty.)

The bride's family has laid out rice-straw mats in the front yard in expectation of his arrival, but they keep him waiting outside for some time for good measure. The groom deposits the wooden duck on a table on the porch, then as fast as possi-ble, anyone from the bride's household snatches the duck away; the equation seems to be, the faster the removal, the greater the fidelity. Duckless, the groom bows four times before the empty table.

An Arrow-Flag, a Flick of Beer, and the Wheel of Life

When the Tibetan bride is ready to depart her family home in Lhasa, two things happen. A senior servant in the groom's family puts a turquoise crystal in the top of her headdress and plants an "arrow flag" on her back near the neck, as he extols the positive virtues of both. The *da-tar*, or arrow flag, is an arrow four feet long adorned with green, white, red, blue, and yellow silk stream-ers, emblematic of five blessings. A small mirror dangled off the da-tar as well, as a talisman against evil spirits.

Now the groom's party is ready to trans-port her. Preferably she rides on a mare with a foal because this is a lucky sign; as she departs, her family calls out: *"Yang ma shor!"* ("Be not lost luck!"). If the priest is making the procession with her, he'll commence their movement with a ges-ture to scare off any lurking "demons": he bran-dishes a painted prayer scroll, attached to a long will branch, that reputedly carries spiritual po-tency from a high lama.

On the journey she's offered beer two times from a small pot. She refuses but flicks a couple drops with the thumb and index finger of her left hand as an offering for the (thirsty) gods. This lit-tle gesture makes sense to her because, raised in a Buddhist culture, she's carrying a picture scroll of the Wheel of Life. This represents a fundamental teaching of Buddhism, namely, that existence is a vast wheel with six tangential worlds like spokes, twelve interdependent stages of existence, and three essential qualities and causative principles at the hub of the Wheel of Life: a rooster (lust), a pig (greed), and snake (anger).

When the party arrives at the groom's house, the bride dismounts on a stack of several dozen sacks of wheat and rice. Servants are present, but the groom's parents don't greet her; they're sitting in hierarchical fashion on their cushions inside. The bride enters the house with her retinue, but nobody rises to greet her; she takes her seat next to the groom and accepts tea, beer, barley-meal, and rice. The elderly servant once again extols the good qualities of the da-tar. The groom's parents now present their gifts to the couple, which include ceremonial scarves, and their blessings; then the relatives and friends reiterate the gesture, wishing the couple prosperity and abundant joy. Later the couple must visit his oracular shrine together and make offerings in the chapel of his guardian deity, the *Gon-kang,* because in leaving her family, she has sacrificed the protection by the household gods and must come under the protection of her husband's deities.

Sir Charles Bell, in his visits to the Tibetan plateau in the 1920s, which he reported in *The People of Tibet,* observed an intriguing variation on this format among upper-class families in Sikkim. Not only does the astrologer determine the best day and hour for the bridal procession, but he specifies the years in which the bridesmaids must have been born, the colors for the bride's cushion and pony, what food she must take first to her new home, as well as the birth year for the person who first serves her food at her husband's house. "And if a suitable person of the age, so divined, be not forthcoming, he also prescribes the necessary steps to be taken to counteract the evil that might arise from such discrepancies," comments Bell.

The females in the bride's party hold as foremost the desire to make the expedition auspicious, but their means strike the Westerner as a little odd. They wish the bride to bear as many bold, heroic, and quarrelsome sons as possible, so they bar the groom's path with a fence of thorns and fight off all people who approach with thorny sticks. The groom can ameliorate their vehement attack if he pays them a small cash fee; the bride's parents pay him back one-fifth of this as "effacer of the thorn-wounds." Later it's all forgotten, and the

groom's party is treated to a fine dinner sans thorns, sticks, and anti-attack fees.

The Red Sedan Bridal Chair

On his wedding day morning, the Chinese groom dispatches a wonderful decorated bridal chair, an empty red sedan, replete with embroidered designs, red cloth hangings, and shuttered glass windows on four sides, carried by four hefty men. The groom travels to the bride's house in a less ostentatious blue sedan, and his father's sister, or cousin, or father's brother's wife, rides in another one; these are carried by the groom's cousins. The three sedans process to the bride's home as a brass band and the constant explosion of firecrackers keeps the atmosphere lively.

When the red sedan arrives, the bride, wearing a robe of red or deep pink and a scarlet satin veil, is conveyed into the sedan, often along a specially laid red carpet, by one of her older brothers or an uncle, as her mother weeps and her father watches in silence. The sedan's curtains are drawn shut so nobody may see the bride during the procession; two of her brothers, or cousins, accompany the chair, carrying the key to the sedan door. But before the sedan departs, her parents may take a bed-quilt by the four corners, holding it at waist level off the ground; then one of the bride's assistants tosses four rice-cakes into the air, one at a time, so that they'll land on the quilt; when they do, it's bundled up with the crackers inside. This is considered a good luck omen.

Customarily the bride's considerable dowry is conveyed simultaneously, and this is available for public viewing—and gawking: two leather chests, three tables with drawers, two red-lacquered stools, six pairs of shoes, fifteen suits of cotton cloth, an abundance of cosmetics, writing implements, and smaller household goods. When the sedan arrives at the groom's house, the groom is presented with the key; opening the sedan door, he beholds his wife for the first time.

Paving Her Way with a Carpet of Soft Rushes

The procession was the high point of Elizabethan weddings in England. First the bridesmaids had to knot yards of rope with fresh flowers to hang through the house; then they had to lay down a carpet of roses and soft rushes between the bride's house and the church door; and they had to prepare numerous favor bouquets for all the guests to wear. The groom's attendants were equally industrious on the wedding morning. They decorated him with rosettes and ribbon streamers in the colors selected by the bride; they also trimmed his beard and hair. As compensation the bridesmaids got silk scarves, the groomsmen, gloves.

Around ten o'clock in the morning, the staff at the bride's house began to hear flutes, horns, drums, and cymbals outside, summoning them to the procession. Accompanying the musicians were the groomsmen who had come to provide escort for the bridal party—which the general public regarded as an entertaining spectacle, worth watching—to the church.

The order of members of the processional was important. The musicians topped the line, followed by a flower-bearer with a silver bride's cup wrapped in ribbons and containing a gilded rosemary branch. Next came the bride, flanked by two pages; then her bridesmaids, bearing either bride-cakes or gilded wheat sheaves, both considered to be fertility symbols. The bride-cake would be sliced into small pieces and tossed into the air above the

bride and groom, like confetti; then a few pieces would be slipped through the wedding ring. Following the bridesmaids at the rear of the procession were the parents, relatives, and friends of the couple. The musicians and a young girl carrying a basket of flowers and a little boy carrying the wedding ring on a cushion led the final bridal procession into the church and up to the altar.

The Procession to the Hallowed Altar

The bride, groom, family, and extended community have now assembled at the holy altar, the chuppah, whatever its cultural expression. The physical altar itself may contain various spiritual impedimenta of the particular faith involved, but in a more profound sense the community bridal procession to the church or wedding facility has itself formed the sanctified altar from which the marriage will be performed. In joyful imitation of the divine model of hieros gamos, the community has formed a corona of support, love, and affirmation around the couple on their way to the altar tacitly acknowledging that this couple, no matter how ordinary or undistinguished, is a bona fide expression of the archetypal male-female couple whose primordial marriage was consecrated in heaven.

The processional complete, we move next into rituals of joining: the nuptial blessing that consecrates the bond between woman and man at the wedding altar.

7

THE

CUNUNIE

RITUALS OF JOINING BY CROWNING, HANDFASTING, AND BLESSING

In Hebrew, both the word for a man, Eesh, and that for a woman, Esha, are composed of three letters, two of which are identical: Esh—meaning fire. The additional letters represent God's name. Thus, the Talmud explains, when a man and woman live together harmoniously they add the presence of the Almighty to their marriage; however, if their marriage is unhappy the only common factor is the presence of a consuming fire.

—Hayyim Schneid, Marriage

During the wedding ceremony of Margo, thirty-two, a ballerina, and Mitchell, thirty-five, a venture capitalist, their rabbi read passages from their love letters to each other from the year of their engagement, thereby imparting an intimate tone. "It was not until our first date was twenty-four hours old that my mind locked onto the seriousness of what was happening," confessed the groom.

Another couple, Julie, thirty-five, a television writer, and Ralph, fifty-one, a radio announcer, staged a ceremony, conducted jointly by Roman Catholic and Episcopal priests, that was a blend of scripture and comedy. When the couple recited short tributes to each other, Julie quipped: "I love you so much that I'll even listen to you once in a while."

When Angela, twenty-two, and Wayne, thirty, planned their ceremony neither was a member of a congregation and they wanted a ritual free of sanctimonious attitudes. They were lucky to find "the good vibes pastor," Reverend Bill Kalaidjian, pastor of the Bedford Park Congregational Church in the Bronx. What Angela and Wayne most appreciated about his ceremony was the soulful way he recited their marriage vows.

"The tone and rhythm in his voice—it was like he understood love," said Angela. "That will stay with me for a lifetime."

Implicit in these three examples of contemporary wedding ceremonies is the desire to deepen the moment of joining at the altar. As we noted in chapter 1, iconoclastic Western couples increasingly find the standard protocols of the Judeo-Christian marriage ritual unsatisfying, irrelevant, staid, and generally inadequate. Some couples shrug their shoulders and focus on making the reception meaningful, personally tailored to their temperaments and life-style; other couples take the joining ritual in hand, redesigning it, incorporating new elements drawn from diverse cultures, or from their private lives. Underlying this search for freshness and originality in the joining ritual is a tacit admission that we've lost sight of what it is that *marries* us—the spiritual agency that enters the ritual space of the *chuppah* and, through the officiant's hands—whether it be priest, rabbi, minister, roshi, or imam—accomplishes the joining.

Something must enter the chuppah and its holy altar and marry us; otherwise it's a secular formality. Sensing this absence, couples try to fill the empty space with a myriad of clever embellishments that will give their ceremony individual uniqueness. What we really want, I propose, is a reconnection with the transcendentally spiritual, a breath of the Spirit upon our joined hands as we stand before the altar.

Transfiguration by Blessing— The Thing That Happens

As Hayyim Schneid reminds us in the chapter's opening epigram, in Hebrew only one letter separates man (*Eesh*) and woman (*Esha*). As different sexes we share the fundamental aspect of our human nature, which is cosmic fire, or *Esh*. According to Hebrew tradition, God added its own name, *YH*, to the names of the divine couple; to Adam went Y (*Yod*), to Eve, H (*He*). By this gesture God meant that as long as the man, *Eesh*, and the woman, *Esha*, walked in spiritual observance of God's commandments, the divine name (*YHVH*, the Tetragrammaton) would shield them from harm. But if they went astray, the Yod and He would be removed, leaving only Esh, the consuming fire. This leads us to a vexing question implicit in the world culture wedding.

What happens during a joining ritual that *marries* us?

Sometimes we get so busy and distracted with designing the details of a wedding—especially in the new world culture wedding, where so many interesting choices are available—that we lose sight of the essence of the joining ritual. What is it—the engagement, the stephanotis bouquet, Mendelssohn's wedding march, the liturgy, the oath-taking, the ring, the handclasp, the kiss, the congratulations, the wedding feast, the honeymoon—that catalyzes this mysterious transfiguration we undergo from man and woman to husband and wife? It must be right in front of us, somewhere in the ritual; it must take only a slight adjustment of vision to see it.

My wife and I were married by a justice of the peace. He's a neighbor, a man about my age who has a couple of riding horses, a huge pile of unstacked cordwood, and a big white house with lots of lilac bushes on a knoll. One day he came over for tea and signed a document, *marrying* us. When it can be this simple, what is this marrying?

Marriage, said the great medieval theologian St. Augustine, is a permanent union, a sacrament, with three discernible "goods": *fides*, fidelity or faith; *proles*, offspring; and *sacramentum*, a sacred bonding, and solemn obligation of two people and two lineages of family descent. The Roman

Catholic church has long recognized matrimony as one of seven sacraments commissioned directly by the Christ, construed as a spiritual being. "Marriage is not merely a *viniculum* ("link, joining"), but also a *sacramentum*, a solemn obligation," notes liturgical historian Kenneth Stevenson, contemplating Augustine's insights in his *Nuptial Blessing: A Study of Christian Marriage Rites.* He also cites a view by Fulgentius of Ruspe (467–533), who regarded marriage as the work of God, contending that "the Lord joins a married couple in a 'link' by *faith,* favors them with the gift of a *blessing,* and multiplies them with the increase of *children;* it is from God that come *fidelity* between partners, *love* for each other, and *fruitfulness.*" As Frances and Joseph Gies comment in *Marriage and the Family in the Middle Ages,* "With marriage accorded the status of sacrament, a nuptial blessing by the priest seemed no more than logical."

The *nuptial blessing.* That's the missing contemporary element, the undeniable transfiguring experience of spiritual presence, the thing that happens at the moment of the joining: the blessing by rite or pronouncement that hallows, consecrates, and makes holy.

I take heart in learning that this was the line of thinking Paulinus of Nola (353–431) pursued as he contemplated the Italian wedding of Julian, son of the bishop of Benvenuto, to the daughter of the bishop of Capua. As Kenneth Stevenson reconstructs it today from the scanty text, the ritual begins in the church:

> The bishop blesses with his hand, bestowing the grace of Christ, with angelic help, giving justice and peace; and, in a recognized manner, he places a veil over the shoulders of *both* the man and woman, and blesses them, and so Christ gives them reverent hearts through the chaste hands of the bishop. Thus the nuptial blessing is given by a bishop, with a veil, and there hints of what that blessing might contain.

The presence of the Christ as the guest—that is, the spiritual presence—at the marriage at Cana in Galilee (John 2:1–11) provides for Christians the rationale for the nuptial blessing as the culmination of the wedding service. At this marriage Jesus Christ converted six stone jars of water into wine for the wedding guests, an act his disciples regarded as the first of his miraculous signs. As the mystics tell us, love is the wine, the intoxicating Spirit, so the Christ blessing at this wedding was a gift of exalted consciousness. We might take this interpretation one step further. The human body is in large part water; so when Christ transforms water into wine, the human organism of each wedding guest is permeated with the love and wisdom of the Christ, the awakener and quickener of eternal life. The Christ blessing transforms our ordinary, mundane, bodily consciousness into spiritual awareness.

Here we see the possibility of identifying the something that happens. It's a spiritual *presence*—be it the Christ, the angels, the Shekhinah, the Divine Sophia, the Buddha, the prophets, Allah, Hymen, Artemis, Hera and Zeus, the Great Mother Goddess, Agni the cosmic Fire God—the exact name, attribution, and precise identity are secondary to the fact that something ineffable is present that accomplishes the marriage, that literally *conjugates* the couple. Grace is bestowed. The "bishop"—the officiant in all its cultural and gender guises—is only the intermediary. As at the Cana wedding, Christ is the guest.

While the means of our joining may vary from crowning, to handfasting, to ring exchanges, what does not vary is the fact that it is Grace that conjugates us. The conjugation is the benediction; the beneficence is the verb, the act. The spiritual conjugation—the sacrament—remains like an irreducible pearl of great price, irradiating our world culture rituals long after the traditional rationale for marriage becomes irrelevant.

ROMANIA
TURKEY
RUSSIA
ARMENIA
SICILY
INDIA
CANADA
MALAYSIA
ECUADOR
KOREA
JAPAN
CHINA

The Nuptial Allegory of Reunion

With this insight in hand, we can now stage the next inquiry: Toward what end do we marry? When issues of independence, fertility, and familial continuity are no longer foremost, what is marriage? Why should we receive the grace, the blessing, the conjugal benediction? "The Holy Spirit can rest only upon a married man, for an unmarried man is but half a man, and the Holy Spirit does not rest on what is imperfect," says Jewish tradition. That's a bit severe and surely unfair (and probably incorrect) to unmarried but strongly spiritual individuals, as well as to gay and lesbian individuals who see the whole gender dance in entirely different terms. Still, there may be a kernel of wisdom in this rabbinical caveat.

Perhaps "dance" is the key here. Marriage is divinity's terpsichorean allegory. We dance the conjugation if we wish, swirling across the ballroom floor; but when we do, we are treading very old dance steps indeed. "The Rabbis playfully imagined the angels accompanying Adam and Eve, the first 'bride' and 'groom' at their wedding," notes Maurice Lamm in *The Jewish Way in Love and Marriage.* "The Midrash records that God appointed angelic escorts for Adam and brought ornaments for Eve at their wedding, and that He arranged seven *chuppot* set up in Paradise on which the Rabbis patterned the seven benedictions." In the Hebrew tradition, the wedding ceremony was called *kiddushin,* which means "sanctities," because matrimony was regarded as a sacred union in which the Jewish bride was consecrated to her husband and thereby made holy. The Jewish husband was held accountable to God and his community for his treatment of his wife, and was expected to conform to high marital standards. These "duties of the heart" included kindness, devotion, chaste conduct, and mutual respect.

Clearly the wedding rite, and marriage itself, was accorded high spiritual content among the Jews, certainly in comparison with the secularized *conjugium* of the Romans (and to some extent our Western Christian norm ever since), in which bride and groomed were joined together in a "marriage yoke."

What satisfies me—and perhaps the best we can expect is to find personally meaningful solutions—is that the marriage process redeems, in human, biological, individualized time, the primal sundering of the soul into two provisionally incomplete genders. Marriage is a redemptive act witnessed by our community. The wedding commemorates the successful, triumphant, and joyous reunion of the sundered halves; it relieves the agony of duality; it pleases the angels and vindicates God.

I don't mean we're all soulmates tearfully finding each other again in cloying New Age epiphanies. What fuels the wedding is that it's a spiritual allegory, a dramatic metaphor of our history and prospects as humans. And it's an allegory in we can *live,* in which we can actively participate.

Coronation with Wreaths of Myrtle and Gold

The Romanian ritual of *cununie,* or crowning, is staged in the church. All members of the bridal party take their prescribed place according to a hierarchy in relations in observance of the proprieties of *cinstea,* or family honor. The groom is the king, the *împarat,* and stands slightly forward of his bride, who is on his left; to her left is her chief bridesmaid. Behind them stand the *nanasi mari,* the "great godparents," as guardians and sponsors, because it's their responsibility to serve as usher for their godchildren when they marry. The flag-bearer stands behind them, giving honor to the godparents. During the ceremony the couple holds a long white banner and tall white candles given to them (and their godparents) by the sexton. The godparents are careful to not let their flames go out because this would portend grave misfortune for the bridal couple.

Now the priest lowers the wedding crowns on the heads of bride and groom, which they will wear for the remainder of the service. The priest will exchange the crowns on the head of the bride and groom three times, accompanied with a blessing. The couple exchanges wedding rings, then the groom, bride, bridesmaid, godparents, and flag-bearer follow the priest as he circles the altar three times. The priest, the bride, and the groom hold the white banner as they make their minute circumambulations. With everyone back in their original places, the priest offers a brief sermon and issues the marriage vows, beginning with the groom, who is expected to kneel. He vows, by the cross and Bible, that he will abide with his new wife peacefully and with understanding, that he will faithfully love her and not abandon her, regardless of good or bad times. He pledges his fidelity, support, and protection, kissing the Bible and the cross to seal his oath. The bride repeats this oath, pledging her husband fidelity, assurance, and obedience. At this point the couple is considered to be married before God.

Nuptial crowns also formed an integral part of Eastern Orthodox Turkish weddings, according to the English writer Miss Pardoe, who witnessed a ceremony of crowns in Turkey in 1836. The ceremony, conducted by the Archbishop of Nournaudkeüy and a party of priests, was held at a private home. The clergymen met the arriving bridal procession at the threshold with the formal chants of the marriage service. As the procession climbed the stairs to the second floor, where the marriage ceremony was to be held, they were showered with silver coins from people standing at the balcony. The parish rector, robed in brocaded yellow satin fringed with silver, offered a prayer, accompanied at intervals by a boys' chorus.

When the prayer was finished, the priests robed the archbishop in his vestments of violet satin embroidered with gold. He stood at a desk, which served as the altar, picked up the two diamond wedding rings, and used them to make the sign of the cross three times on the forehead, lips, and chest of the bride and groom. Then he gave them to the wedding "godmother," whose role here was similar to the traditional bridesmaid; she slipped rings on the fingers of the bride and groom, yet continued to hold them while the priest read a scripture. During the archbishop's recitation. she changed the rings three times, putting the bride's ring on the groom's finger, his ring on hers, and so forth. Then the archbishop placed the bride's hand in the groom's, and made the sign of the cross at their forehead, lips, and chest again, this time using the nuptial crowns, which were made of flowers, ribbons, and gold thread.

This invocation completed, he set the crowns on their heads; then he blessed a goblet of wine at his lips, handing it to the bride, groom, and godmother. Next the crowns were exchanged three times, just as the rings had been. Several wax candles were lit, and the priests began chanting as the bridal party walked in procession around the room under a shower of silver coins tossed by the wedding guests. The chanting stopped and the bride lifted her groom's hand to her lips, and kissed it; this was the signal for all the guests to approach the couple and kiss them on the forehead, completing the ceremony.

Kissing My Husband's Crown

Wedding crowns were used in the traditional Cossack ceremonials of Russians living in

ROMANIA
TURKEY
RUSSIA
ARMENIA
SICILY
INDIA
CANADA
MALAYSIA
ECUADOR
KOREA
JAPAN
CHINA

GAY HOLY UNIONS

Gay holy unions may not be quite as prevalent as lesbian joining ceremonies, explains James Mitulski, pastor of the Metropolitan Community Church of San Francisco, but each year he performs at least forty same-sex commitment ceremonies for men in this progressive church in the Castro district, the heart of San Francisco's gay and lesbian community.

The Metropolitan Community Church, which has three hundred members, is part of the Universal Fellowship of Metropolitan Community Churches, a worldwide network of two hundred churches. Like lesbian unions—Mitulski officiates at about sixty a year in his church—male marriages are a radical social statement, even if they are not legally binding. "These rites and sacraments don't reinforce the status quo; they challenge it," noted Mitulski in a special report in The Christian Century. "Whereas heterosexual marriage services are rites of passage into the mainstream, holy unions are rites of rebellion against a society that denigrates same-sex relationships."

The mainstream Christian church wrongfully abandons—and ostracizes—men and women because of their sexual orientation, comments Mitulski. "Following the example of Jesus at the wedding at Cana, the church is called to witness and support the love of all couples who seek a covenantal relationship," says Mitulski. Conventional, "straight" society may perceive gay marriages as rebellious, but they're primarily about publicly acknowledging commitment in a relationship, Mitulski comments. For many gay men—as for lesbians and heterosexual couples—it's important to "seek ritual affirmation of their love in the presence of God and community."

Mitulski asks gay couples to meet with him for two prewedding counseling sessions, in which they frankly discuss the quality of their partnership, societal attitudes about homosexuality, and the contents of their joining ritual. One gay couple presented Mitulski with a compendium of antigay quotations from the Bible; they devoted their pastoral sessions to clarifying their thoughts and feelings about these religious condemnations of their same-sex orientation. Further, they sought literary validation for their lifestyle from the works of Virginia Mollenkott, John Boswell, and Robin Scroggs.

Gay marriages have no legal status in most communities, but in San Francisco they are registered with the municipal government as "civil marriages" and "domestic partnerships." About twenty-five cities, states, or counties across the United States now legally acknowledge domestic partnerships; when New York City officially introduced the notarized "unmarried domestic partner affidavit" in February 1993, 109 same-sex couples queued in the city clerk's office with pink carnations or bouquets to receive their certificates.

Public and even quasi-legal recognition of same-sex marriages and homosexual families is important when it comes to spousal benefits, says Mitulski. Hospitals, for example, have visitation policies for family members, but these may not necessarily accept same-sex-constituted families; unemployment benefits for head-of-family is another inherently antigay and lesbian situation. But this is slowly changing, as a recent judicial precedent in Massachusetts indicates. In Reep v. the Department of Employment and Training (June 1992), the Massachusetts Supreme Judicial Court overturned the state's claim that only married people were legally entitled to benefits. Although this case wasn't specifically about gay and lesbian rights, it paved the way for spousal benefits for committed same-sex partnerships, even if they lack "legal" validation for their relationship.

Siberia, Kamchatka, and Northern Asia. In one late afternoon ceremony observed in Petropavlovski in the 1880s, the priest begins by handing the bride and groom each three lighted candles tied together with blue ribbon. He reads the marriage service to the "candidates for matrimony," which a deacon periodically punctuates with "doleful chanted responses," as George Kennan observed in his *Tent Life in Siberia*. His reading concluded, the couple crosses themselves six times, answers his queries about their intent to keep their marriage vows, then each accepts from him a silver ring. The priest reads more scripture, then offers them each a teaspoonful of wine from a cup. The priests continue their chanting and scripture reading while the couple crosses themselves and make prostrations, "and the Deacon closes up his responses by repeating with the most astounding rapidity, fifteen times in five seconds, the words, '*Gáspodi pomeelui,*' 'God have mercy upon us.'"

Now comes the crowning. The best man and chief groomsman sometimes hold the crowns a few inches above the heads of the bride and groom for fifteen minutes, until the priest sets these two large gilt crowns ornamented with medallions upon the heads of the couple and joins their hands. Then, clasping the groom's hands, he leads them in three circlings of the altar. The bride and groom kiss the crowns with reverence as they remove them from their heads, walk around the church, cross themselves, and bow before the various images of the saints on the church walls, then turn to the congregation to accept the congratulations of the audience.

In other parts of Russia, the bride wore a veil and crown of gilt silver or gold lined with silk. As the bridal couple sat at a wedding-eve feast table, women sang and strewed a fertility potpourri of hops, fragments of satin and taffeta, silver, barley, and oats on the heads of the couple and

ROMANIA
TURKEY
RUSSIA
ARMENIA
SICILY
INDIA
CANADA
MALAYSIA
ECUADOR
KOREA
JAPAN
CHINA

the party guests. In the church next day, the couple stood on a piece of crimson taffeta while the priest received oblations of bread, fish, and pastry from the congregation. He gave the couple his benediction, while holding above their heads the icons of their patron saints. Then he took the right hand of the groom and the left of the bride and asked them three times if they consented to marry each other and to be always loving and faithful. When they assented, he sang a psalm while the assembly joined hands in a solemn dance. The priest next placed a garland of rue or wormwood on the heads of the couple, drank their health with wine from a goblet, which they reciprocated three times, and then the groom smashed the goblet on the ground, stamping it with his feet while declaring: "Let them be so trampled upon and confounded who maliciously endeavor to create ill will between us!" The ceremony concluded when the entire company lit candles and the women strewed linseed and hempseed upon the crowned heads of the couple. The priest sprinkled hops on the bride's crown, wishing that she might be as fruitful as the hop plant, bearing as many children as hops were thrown.

Among the Georgians the wedding ceremony was performed in a private home. The bride literally kicked things off by formally kicking over a pitcher of wine and scattering with her hands a bowl of bread dough all over the apartment, as a communal fertility blessing. Bride and groom entered the next room, where they stood before a priest who read the marriage service to them by the light of a wax taper. The priest placed the veil over the groom's head, sewed the garments of the couple together, crowned them both with a garland of flowers, then exchanged them head to head several times. Next he gave bread to the couple three times, followed by an offering of wine, repeated three times. Each time he made his offering, laying the crowns on their heads, he said: "Let the servant of God (naming the bride or groom) be crowned by the servant of God (naming him-

self)." The priest ate the remaining bread, downed the wine, then severed the thread connecting the couple's bridal clothes, and with this he concluded the ceremony.

The old-fashioned Armenian ritual of crowning was part of a wedding ceremony that could last up to eight days. Before the ceremony begins, the wedding clothes are specially blessed by the priest to expunge any *djinns*, or evil spirits. The bride, clothed in red silk (sometimes she wears a blouse upon which flowers have been painted in blue), wears cardboard angel wings with feathers on her head; during the ceremony the priest ties a cross onto the forehead of bride and groom. The priest conjoins their hands while pronouncing a prayer; then, with his left hand, he gently knocks their heads together three times, while blessing them with his right hand. He joins their hands together a second time and queries the groom: "Will you be her husband?" The groom answers by raising the bride's veil then lowering it again. The priest now takes two wreaths of flowers, ornamented with dangling gold threads, and coronates the couple, exchanging them three times from bride to groom, while saying: "I unite you and bind you to one another—live in peace." He may also rest a sword and cross lightly on their heads. Finally the couple shares a cup of wine together, and in some cases a baby boy is laid upon the bride's lap to symbolize family good fortune and fertility.

There are many variations and nuances to the basic Eastern Orthodox ritual of crowning. In the Hungarian observance, six young girls clothed in white bear the nuptial crowns to the altar. The bride's crown is spangled, bears an ornamental mirror in its center, and its hues are the national colors of red, white, and green. Among Syrian Christians of the Coptic church, the priest, groom, and bride make three perambulations about the altar, then the couple exchanges their crowns three times. The Eastern church also knows this marriage crowning service as "the Ceremony of the Wreath." The crowns are wreaths made of olive sprays mixed with white and purple flowers and bands. As the priest places the wreaths upon the heads of the couple, he invokes a blessing that they may be crowned with honor and glory. The Polish bride was led to the church wearing a large silver-gilt crown, preceded by her bridesmaids in long mantles and red veils. She walked three times around a fire, sat down, and washed her feet, while her mouth was anointed with honey and her eyes covered by a thick veil. In Geoffrey Chaucer's England, crowning was still observed; Grisild wore "a coronne on hire hed" for her wedding in the "Clerk of Oxenford's Tale"; but a few centuries later, Henry VIII abolished the rite of crowning the bridegroom, only permitting a garland of flowers or corn-ears.

In the seventeenth-century Abyssinian (Ethiopian) ritual, the bride and groom sat on a couch outside the church entrance. Three priests encircled them three times, singing while they swung a censer and gestured with a cross. They cut off several locks of hair from the bride and groom, steeped them in honey and water, then fixed the bride's honeyed locks on the groom's head and his locks on her head. After this the priests sprinkled the couple with holy water, crowned and incensed them, and gave them communion and a blessing.

The Matrimonial Coronation

Crowns used in Greek marriages are made of orange-blossom wreaths, everlasting flowers, evergreens, myrtle leaves, roses, wild thyme, semi-precious stones, threads of gold and crimson, twigs of olive and vine wrapped in gold and silver paper, olive branches surrounded with white threads in-terwoven with purple, or tinsel. So prominent a place did the crown occupy in Greek weddings that the entire service was once described as "the matrimonial coronation."

In some modern instances, such as a Greek wedding witnessed in Palermo, Sicily, in the 1950s, the bride and groom each wore a crown of artificial white flowers; the two crowns were united in the back by trailing white ribbons. When the priest removed the crowns, the bride kissed her husband's crown and he kissed hers as a symbol that he would respect her as his "queen," and she would honor him as her "king." After this they each put a ring on the other's finger, drank wine from the same glass, then handed the goblet to the priest, who smashed it for good luck.

On Sunday morning before the wedding, the Greek groom leaves his home and walks along a path upon which his mother has sprinkled holy water and laid a sash. When the details of the marriage contract are settled, and rings exchanged, the groom's father is presented with a tray of sweet basil leaves by the bride's father, who says: "Accept this betrothal of my daughter." He presents the groom with a glass of wine, a ring-shaped cake, and a spoon. The groom drinks the wine, drops coins into the empty glass, then gives the spoon and half the cake to his best man to keep for the bride.

Meanwhile the best man helps the bride on with her wedding shoes. Her mother sprinkles water before her feet, and asks three times: "Bride, has thou thy shoes?" Candles are lit and the couple (now known as "neonymphs") exchanges their rings again, which they wear on the fourth finger of the right hand; the groom gives the bride a silver ring, she gives him a golden one. Now the priest lowers the crowns upon their heads, saying, "Crown thyself, servant of God, Beatrice, in the name of Demetrios" (these are their names). Alternatively he might say: "The servant of God, Demetrios, is crowned, that is, marries the handmaid of God, Beatrice."

The best man (known as the *paranymph*) or the priest now exchanges the crowns three times, moving them from the heads of the bride to groom and back again (the couple may at this point link the little fingers of their right hands) as he invokes the Holy Trinity, after which he conducts them in three circlings of the altar. When the priest removes the crowns and blesses them—he says, "Be thou magnified, O bridegroom," as he removes the crown—they're considered married. The priest blesses a cup of wine then hands it to the bride and groom three times; they drink it as a token of unity and a "pledge of community of possession," then are led around the church in a circular manner. The paranymphs (best man and groomsmen) carry the crowns; when the circling is completed, the crowns are tied together with a handkerchief. The best man kisses the bride, her mother places a loaf of bread on their heads, and the guests shower them in sweets.

In rural Greek weddings, a ritual called the Dance of Isaiah often follows next. The priest holds the Bible in one hand and the groom's hand in the other, the groom holds the bride's hand, and she clasps the hand of the *koumbaros* (the wedding sponsor, or godparent). Thus linked they circle the altar on which the crowns were laid before the ceremony began. They make three circuits around the altar, stopping at every quarter turn, as the guests shower them with bonbons and rice. Their circlings completed, they resume their original positions before the altar as the priest makes his final reading from scripture.

Crowned by the Glory of God

Why were crowns used as the central feature in so many wedding ceremonies? Folklore tells us the bridal couple was crowned in emulation of royalty, the imperial king and queen with their golden crowns. An early Christian Father suggests the rite of crowning was another aspect of the *imitatio Christi,* reminiscent perhaps of the thorn of crowns the Christ wore on Golgotha. John Chrysostom (347–407) invokes the marriage at Cana, at which the Christ was present as a guest who unobtrusively transformed barrels of water into wine; in the normal wedding, says Chrysostom, the Christ is present through the priest and the crowns represent the couple's "symbols of victory" over passion, a reward for continence. "Crowns are put on their heads as symbols of victory," wrote Chrysostom, "because, being invincible, they entered the bridal chambers without ever having been subdued by any unlawful pleasure." The text of a pontifical blessing from an eleventh-century Canterbury Benedictional explains that the couple is blessed by God "so that here and in eternity they may be *crowned* by God."

World folklore and wedding customs suggest another, more esoteric dimension to the origin of crowning. In the statement "*crowned* by God" we find a vital clue: crown as in *Sahasrara,* the crown chakra. The chakras (literally "spinning wheels"), according to spiritual teachers and psychics, are energy vortices arranged vertically along the human spine from groin to crown that receive, coordinate, and transmit subtle solar and cosmic energies to the physical organism. The seven primary chakras correspond to sequential stages in consciousness, interface with endocrine function, and mediate different stages in personal and spiritual development.

Hindu yogis describe the Sahasrara as a crown of flames, the thousand-petaled lotus energy and consciousness center at the top of the head, the seat of the "self-luminescent soul, or chitta, the essence of being," explains Tantric scholar Harish Johari in *Chakras: Energy Centers of Transformation.* "Here, chitta is like a screen upon which the reflection of the cosmic Self is seen, and through it the divine is reflected. In the presence of the cosmic Self it is possible for anyone to feel the divine and indeed to realize the divinity within himself." The experience of being "crowned by God" is well documented in Christian tradition as Pentecost, in which flaming tongues of the Holy Spirit—that same cosmic fire, *Esh,* which Hayyim Schneid talks about, and which is commemorated graphically in the flaming, coronal Hebrew letter *Sheen*—crowned the heads of the apostles and inspired them to independent experiences of the Christ and to speak on his behalf. The nuptial blessing by crowning has at least metaphorical origins in the experience of the Pentecostal flames under the auspices of the Christ.

Marrying Under a Crown of Silence

In the Quaker wedding ceremony, marriage happens "in the presence of God and these our Friends." The couple intending to marry has been interviewed by a "clearness" committee on behalf of the local Friends Meeting to make sure they are in fact clear about their marital aspirations.

The Quakers have always maintained that marriage is a deeply binding relationship entered into in a state of inner calm in the presence of divinity and of witnessing friends. So the context for the Quaker wedding is the standard meeting for worship, which is characterized by periods of prayerful silence out of which arise prayers and spoken messages by fellow members, as they feel inspired. Quakers insist on the freedom of the individuals to give themselves in marriage to each other without any intermediaries, either parents or clergy. "Friends believe that God alone can create

such a union and give it significance," explains *Faith and Practice,* the official Quaker handbook. "In an atmosphere of quiet and reverence, the promises of the bride and bridegroom are made to each other without the help of a third person."

The couple rises before the silent group. Then, holding hands, they state their promises and vows, saying, approximately: "In the presence of God and these our Friends I take thee to be my wife (or husband), promising with Divine assistance to be unto thee a loving and faithful husband (or wife) so long as we both shall live." Their vows committed, the couple sits down to receive the marriage certificate from a Friend for them to sign; another Friend reads the document aloud. The meeting continues in "silent waiting upon God" unless a Friend is moved to speak. When the wedding meeting finishes, the Friends present sign the marriage certificate to attest to their witnessing the union.

In the contemporary Quaker wedding of Scottie Mirviss and Paul Carvajal, held at the Friends Meeting House in Manhattan, the guests (not all Quakers) were initially counseled that silence isn't emptiness. The wedding ritual, which is inherently spontaneous, sprang into volubility as guests individually praised the couple, recounting personal anecdotes. The couple exchanged forty vows, which they had written themselves, expressing aspirations from the personal to planetary. Among Mirviss's vows was this caveat on arguing: "In absolute conflict, I promise to be humble enough to accept assistance to reach an understanding."

Circumambulating the Cosmic Fire

The variety and detail of Indian Hindu wedding rituals is prodigious. Their elaborate prep-

HOW TO DISPOSE OF YOUR WINE GLASS
AT A JEWISH WEDDING

During the Orthodox Jewish wedding service, in both the betrothal (erusin) and nuptial stage (nissu'in), the rabbi blesses a thin glass of wine then offers it to the bride and groom for a small sip. After the second wine offering has been drunk and the Seven Benedictions pronounced, the groom wraps the goblet in a napkin or cloth and smashes it under his foot. If the ceremony is held under a chuppah outdoors, the groom might fling the "cup of blessing" against the traustein, "the marriage stone," which is sometimes mounted—or even structurally built in—on the synagogue buttress. If there is no traustein, the groom throws the glass against the nearest northern wall of the building. As he smashes the goblet, he declares: "If I forget Thee, O Jerusalem, may my right hand fail at the height of my joy." This means the Jewish couple must not forget the fall of the Temple of Jerusalem and its implications for their own marriage, namely, that as the euphoria of the wedding day is not permanent, they should prepare themselves for life's exigencies. As they witness the groom smashing the cup, the audience shouts: "Mazel tov!" (originally "Good star," it means "Good luck!") or "Siman tov!" ("Good omen" or "Congratulations!").

The chastisement about forgetting Jerusalem is a reference to the destruction of the ancient Temple in Jerusalem in the first century, and the shattered glass represents the wreckage of Jewish former glory. That was the theory put forward in the fourteenth century by a prominent rabbi who wanted his people to see in the destruction of Zion a reminder that in life great joy can be canceled by sudden, unexpected grief. "Perhaps a deeper significance can be realized, if, as the groom's action recalls the demolished house of God," explains Maurice Lamm, "the now-married couple takes it as an obligation upon themselves to rebuild the Temple in their own lives by building in their own Jewish home, as every synagogue is, a mikdash me'at, a miniature temple."

The Talmud presents another origin for the glass smashing. There was once a wedding at which the rabbis became too boisterous in their joy, so Mar, the host, took a very expensive cup and suddenly and loudly smashed it before them. Everybody hushed up instantly in shock. The inference is that breaking the glass encourages sobriety, engenders a more "trembling" style of rejoicing, while keeping the general noise level down. Folklore appends this explanation by noting the prophet Jeremiah's comment that evil spirits come from the north; so if the groom smashes the wine glass against the synagogue's northern wall, presumably this sudden noisy act chases away malingering evil spirits who might otherwise seek to undermine the couple's happiness.

Jewish scholars provide yet another explanation. The fourth-century Babylonian Sage Ashi, concerned with the unbridled hilarity waxing strong at his son's wedding, smashed a glass. "And he brought a very fine glass and broke it, and they became sad," the Talmud records. "This ceremony goes back to very ancient times and has its origin in a heathen superstition," explains Jacob Lauterbach in his Studies in Jewish Law, Custom, and Folklore. It's those evil spirits, jealous demons, and "fallen angels of old" again who can't abide honest human joy at a wedding, says Lauterbach. The intention was to deceive the devils into thinking the wedding party was sad, because everyone grew still when the glass was broken; and, failing that, to scare them off with the explosive shower of glittering shards of glass.

Those familiar with the esoteric documents of the Jewish tradition, such as the Zohar and Qaballa, might read between the lines and put together an alternative and possibly more satisfying rationale *for smashing the glass. From the divine unmanifest, called* Ain Soph Awr, *precipitated the ten realms of cosmic existence, called* Sephiroth. *The Sephiroth each contained a quality or gradation of manifest light; as such they were light containers, or vessels; their totality was called the* Otz Chaim, *the Tree of Life. "The quality of each Sephirah is thought of as a translucent colored glass vessel," comments Charles Poncé in* Kabbalah. *"At the same time, the Sephiroth are themselves vessels made of light; that is, the quality of their light although originally derived from the Ain Soph is dynamically different." Qaballah suggests that the light was so intense it shattered each vessel in turn, fountaining out its sparks like a lava flow into the next lower shell; this primordial event was called the* shevirah, *"the breaking of the vessels."*

So why do they smash the wine glass? Obviously there wouldn't be a wedding if God hadn't smashed that first wine glass, the unity of the unmanifest, thereby precipitating the shattered vessels (the Sephiroth) and the glittering multiple realms of existence. As the bride and groom receive their nuptial blessing from the unbroken divine unity, allegorically embodying the primal couple reunited at last under the chuppah, so in counterpoint is the unity and source of all blessings shattered.

arations and meticulously orchestrated activities often occupy a week or ten days. At the heart of many of them is the ritual obeisance to the "sacred fire of the Fire God Agni" and its circumambulation; if not a living fire, the couple circles an outdoor altar or a nuptial pole.

Brahmins and other high-caste Hindus sometimes perform their joining ritual under a *bedi,* an outdoor shrine, a wooden structure that functions as a roof or rectangular canopy under which they light a small fire. Both the bride and groom are represented by a priest, who makes prayers and offerings. This marriage booth, also called the *marwa,* is erected around a green bamboo pole (known hereafter as the nuptial pole) set in the center of the family's courtyard. A *pandit* invokes Hindu spiritual beings when the nuptial pole is first established. The wedding ceremony culminates with *Bhanwar,* four circlings by the couple of the sacred fire and the nuptial pole. The first three times, the bride leads the groom, then on the fourth, the groom leads the bride; or they may circle the fire seven times, four times with the bride leading, then three times with the groom leading.

The circumambulation, so the Hindus believe, creates a sacred link between the bride and groom with Agni, the God of Fire, as witness. Agni, praised in more than two hundred hymns in the ancient Rig Veda liturgical texts, is the most important deity in the Hindu pantheon after Indra, revered as the ultimate fire-bringer, cosmic fire personified—"O Lord Fire, First Created Being." Agni represents fire in all its manifestations, whether earthly, meteorological (lightning), solar, or cosmic; Agni reigns with vitality over all the worlds, yet has his seat in every humble household at the hearth. It is Agni who sees into the hearts of all created beings, who bestows immortality, who purges the cankers of sin, burns off the residues of guilt, and transports the immortal aspect of the

ROMANIA
TURKEY
RUSSIA
ARMENIA
SICILY
INDIA
CANADA
MALAYSIA
ECUADOR
KOREA
JAPAN
CHINA

human to heaven after death. Agni is the god of priests and the priest of the gods, and thus the prime mediator between the heavenly and humanly realms.

The joining ritual itself is accomplished when the priest ties the groom's shoulder cloth or sash to the veil or sari of the bride. The bride and groom may feed each other curds as the Brahmin priest sits between them, reciting mantras. There is a brief ceremony in which seven lamps, seven coins, and a stone pestle are placed on a stone-grinding slab, before which the groom sits and the bride stands. The groom extinguishes the lamps with his bride's foot: he uses her foot to knock away the lamps and coins by sliding the pestle across the slab. The priest then leads the couple in making their seven matrimonial vows, which ends the formal parts of the ceremony.

Among the Tanners of India, the priest begins by reciting *mantar* (sacred chants) and a sacred fire is lit in a *chaunk,* a special small spot of ground selected by the priest. As the bride, groom, and their families sit about the fire, the fathers of the couple come forward and place a *mauli,* a small circle of multicolored cord, on their son's or daughter's head; then, with the cords in place, they exchange them four times from groom's head to bride's head. Then the bride's mother places her hands on the head of her new son-in-law and places sugar in the palms of his hands, seven times; this is intended as a welcoming, "sweetening" gesture, and completes the ceremony.

An important ceremony often performed before the joining and fire circumambulation is called *kankana,* "the tying of the wrist-thread." The bride and groom obtain two pieces of saffron-cloth, smear them with turmeric, and bind them in a double thread. They put two handfuls of rice on a metal dish, then put a coconut dyed yellow on top of the rice, then lay the two pieces of saffron on the top; this offering faces west, the direction of the god Varuna. They offer prayers to all the Hindu deities, imploring them to visit this kankana and

to reside with the bride during the five days of the marriage ceremony. The groom takes one strip of saffron and ties it around his bride's left wrist; she reciprocates, binding his right wrist.

In the typical Hindu wedding, the groom, his family, and their relatives arrive at the home of the bride for the wedding ritual. First they receive the ceremonial greeting, in which a relative of the bride marks the groom's forehead with a red paste, feeds him a sweet, and presents him with small gifts; a male relative washes his feet as a further sign of respect. Next they escort the groom to the wedding pavilion, where he sits facing east, directly across from the bride's family priest. The other members of his entourage sit adjacent a purified rectangle of ground (like the Tanner chaunk) upon which the ritual impedimenta necessary for the wedding (firewood, camphor, grain, grass, clarified butter, coconuts) have been set. This is done in the "seed pan ceremony." Four earthen pans are arranged to make a square, while a fifth is placed in the center; each pan represents one of a special quintet of gods: Indra (east), Varuna (west), Yama (south), and Soman (north).

Now the bride is led in and sits next to the groom. As the groom extends his hands palms upward, the priest slowly pours milk, water, and other liquids upon them; the groom is also fed honey and fruits. As he eats them, he declares: "I eat thee for the sake of brilliancy, power, and luck." The priest lights the fire, then the bride's father joins the hands of the couple, tying them together with a scarf. The bride's father may also wash the groom's feet as the couple sits before the sacred fire. The groom chants a verse: "O water, unite me with fame, splendor, and milk. Make me beloved of all creatures, the lord of cattle. May fame, heroism, and energy dwell in me. To the ocean I send you imperishable waters. Go back to your source. May I not suffer loss in my offspring. May my sap not be shed."

The tying of the scarf is a variation on a more central rite, "bestowing the *tali,*" the foremost act in a ceremony called *mangalashta.* Here

the bride and groom sit facing each other behind a suspended sheet of silk held by twelve Brahmins to keep them in seclusion from the guests. The groom fastens the tali around his bride's neck; this is a golden pendant on a cord dyed yellow with saffron and composed of 108 minute threads closely twisted together; there may also be flowers and tiny black seeds interwoven in the tali. The tali may be, variously, a turmeric-colored thread with a single golden jewel attached, an iron bracelet, or iron twined around a gold wire. The groom may also put rings on the second toes of both his bride's feet. The tali has already been sanctified in two ways. First it's set on a coconut dyed yellow, which sits on two handfuls of rice in a pot; to this the couple makes a sacrifice of sweet perfumes. Second the tali is born around the chamber, and each man and woman blesses it by touching.

As the bride receives the tali, the priests recite the "eight marriage verses," called the *mangala-ashtaka*, which invoke the gods, the saints, the trees, the hills and the rivers to bear auspicious witness upon the completion of the rite. Then the priests invoke a celestial roster of married couples: Vishnu and his wife Lakshmi, Brahma and Saraswati, Shiva and Parvati, the Sun and his wife Chhaya, the Moon and his wife Rohini, Indra and Sathi, Vasishta and Arundhati, Rama and Sita, Krishna and Rukmani. So as his bride sits facing east, the husband approaches her and, reciting mantras, fastens the tali about her neck securing it with three knots. He may sprinkle the tali (which sometimes—and perhaps originally was—is an oxen yoke containing a gold coin in its central hole) with water, saying: "May you become purified by the sun and water. May this water, which is the cause of the thunder and the lightning, bring happiness to you."

The tali ceremony symbolizes the achievement of married status. The tali is regarded as an emblem of the state of auspicious matrimony (*mangalyam*), a marriage badge; wearing the tali makes a Hindu woman out of a girl. Often the presentation of the tali is accompanied by a tray of eight auspicious objects (the *ashtamangalyam*, which includes coconut flowers); at the same time, paddy (unhusked rice) and cooked rice are placed near a lighted brass lamp to symbolize the wished-for prosperity of the new household. A freshly cut jasmine branch may be born in ritual procession as part of the tali rite. The groom now takes the bride's right wrist with his left hand, then passes his right hand over the united hands and wrist three times. This is considered a crucial phase of the binding ritual. As he crosses hands, his priest chants: "O Indra, cleanse and purify this girl, just as you did in the case of Abhala, by pouring water through the three holes. May this gold prove a blessing to you. May the hole of the yoke bring happiness to you."

Now comes the stage called *satapadi*, taking the "seven steps together." The couple rises and together circles the fire a number of times (typically four or seven). The priests have laid a stone sanctified by having been smeared with sandalwood oil along the circumabulatory path around the fire, and upon this stone the bride is careful to tred on each passage to symbolize her steadfastness in marriage. Her husband helps her in this observance; he takes her right foot in his right hand and makes it touch the sandalwood stone at the same time his foot touches it. He will lift her foot seven times, making this declaration:

One step for sap, may Vishnu go after thee. Two steps for juice, may Vishnu go after thee. Three steps for vows, may Vishnu go after thee. Four steps for comfort, may Vishnu go after thee. Five steps for cattle, may Vishnu go after thee. Six steps for wealth, may Vishnu go after thee. Seven steps for those who preside at sacrifices, may Vishnu go after thee. With seven steps we have become companions. May I attain to friendship with thee. May I not be separated from that friendship. Let us be united. Let us

ROMANIA
TURKEY
RUSSIA
ARMENIA
SICILY
INDIA
CANADA
MALAYSIA
ECUADOR
KOREA
JAPAN
CHINA

take counsel together. May we grow in strength and prosperity. Now we are one in minds, deeds, and desires. Thou art Rik and I am Samam. I am the sky, thou art the earth. I am the semen, thou art the bearer. I am the mind, thou art the tongue. Follow me faithfully, that we may have wealth and children.

While all this is happening, the priests are continually chanting mantras, adding more ghee to the sacred fire, pouring water, spilling milk, and the air is thick with purifying incense; at certain key moments of transition, women's voices or drumbeats enrich the aural atmosphere. Their fire circlings finished, the couple remains standing while the priest ends the ceremony by walking around them carrying a tray with a flaming lamp, to purge their auras of any evil influences. Rosewater, a liquor made from sandalwood, betel nut, and flower garlands, might be distributed to all the wedding guests at this time.

The wedding climax in the exhaustively detailed and procedurally intricate Bihar marriage ceremony (whose purificatory stages we reviewed in chapter 5) begins with the blessing of the groom. The family barber escorts the groom to his place under the wedding canopy, after which the bride's mother and relatives anoint his eyes with kohl, mark his forehead with curds, and present him a folded betel leaf in which the betel nut chewed earlier by his bride is deposited. She makes five circles around his head with her curry-roller, a gesture repeated by her female assistants. Now the groom takes his seat upon a sanctified stool; the priests of both families have blessed it with their pitchers. The bride's father sits by the groom's side, then his shawl is tied to a turmeric-colored string, which is itself tied to his wife's sari. The barber's wife escorts the bride into the chamber where she sits on her father's lap. The women sing:

On the thatching grass the father sits
The girl with loosened hair is in his lap,

O praise the thighs that bore a girl
Who holds her with a pearl in her hair.
O praise the thighs that bore a son
Who brings him in a golden litter
    to the wedding.

After the singing the party praises the divine couple Gauri and Ganesh, and invokes the blessings of the family ancestors.

Now the bride's youngest brother takes his position with a special pitcher of water. Her father places one of his hands on his daughter's hand, and puts the groom's hand on top of his. Then, as the priests recite protective charms and blessings, the bride's brother slowly pours water over their handclasp. For Hindus the act of pouring sanctified water makes a gift irrevocable, with the Lord Vishnu as witness. Now the father removes his hand and puts the hands of his daughter and son-in-law in a new handclasp. The priest asks the groom if he assents to take this woman as his bride; he affirms this, vowing by all the divinities that he will be faithful. The priest asks the woman if she will be a devoted wife; when she affirms this vow, she is put on her father's lap again while the groom is given a new turmeric-hued dhoti.

Next comes the ritual of *hathleva* ("hand-seizing"). The bride now stands directly in front of the groom; he stretches out his hands, linking all his fingers including the thumb, with all of hers in front of him; then with their hands clasped in this intimate way, the bride's brother sprinkles a small amount of parched, unhusked rice on them; finally the groom bends down to touch her toes with his hands. The bride and groom next circumambulate the perimeter of the wedding canopy seven times, while several men in the party pass the groom's shawl around the canopy in circles, too.

The culmination comes when the priest makes a mark with vermilion powder on the bride's forehead and knots the groom's shawl to the bride's sari, including a copper coin, rice, and a nut into the bind. The groom stands before his bride and makes the vermilion mark on the pitcher and the mud models of Gauri (one of the "seven ideal wives," who can endow her worshiper with unending good fortune) and Ganesh (bestower of good beginnings) used earlier in their worship; then he makes five vermilion dabs on her forehead. As the groom sits on the bride's left side, the priests utter protective charms and shower them with rice. The women in the audience file past the couple filling their hands with small quantities of rice and ornaments, making further vermilion marks on her forehead. These blessing gestures conclude when the priest sprinkles holy water on the couple.

A Wedding Blessed by Ganesh

The wedding ritual for those of the Jain religion in India centers around obeisance to Ganesh, the elephant-god who removes all obstacles and upholds righteousness. For Hindus Ganesh, the son of Shiva and Parvati, is the Lord of Hosts who generated the Buddha through coupling with the virgin goddess Maya; his image appears in Hindu and Buddhist temples throughout India, as well as over the doorway of many homes.

So for the Jaina, establishing the shrine for Ganesh is the first order of business in preparing for a wedding. They cover a stool with a white cloth, establish a small statue or image of Ganesh, then surround it with small mounds of rice, wheat, and other grains. They set twenty-five small grain heaps around the stool, in units of five, interspersed with twenty-five dates; then two women bring handfuls of cooked rice for worshiping Ganesh. The bride and groom sit on stools near the statue, as a "lucky woman" takes four pieces of wood, dips them in oil, and anoints

the foreheads of the couple. Next, the groom's paternal aunt steps forward, ties an iron ring to his *cotali* (an uncut portion of hair, that is, a ponytail), and gives him a few coins. Often seven auspicious women now approach the couple and present them with seven presents. During the evening of this prewedding day, young women sing auspicious songs outside the house and some distance from the Ganesh shrine, burying small coins and piles of grain, to invite prosperity and good fortune to the entire household and tomorrow's ritual.

The next day around sunset, the bride and groom again sit on their stools in the *mandapa,* the wedding booth erected three days earlier. Lucky women wash their toes, then the paternal aunt steps forward again and this time ties a silver ring to the grooms ponytail. The bride spits betel-nut juice at the groom, while her mother marks him with an auspicious herb called candalo, then sprinkles balls of rice and ashes over him, and waves a pitcher of water over his head. The bride and groom sit next to each other inside the mandapa, then after they shake hands, her sari is tied to his scarf and he presents her with rings and jewelry. Her father washes the groom's hand while his mother washes the bride's hand; then the mother places the bride's hand in the groom's. The couple stands and makes four clockwise circlings of a special fire lit in the center of the mandapa; as they circumambulate the fire, the groom offers handfuls of grain to women in the party. The wedding feast follows.

A Contemporary Vedic Marriage Ceremony

The following text, graciously provided by Ghanshyam Singh Birlaji, is taken from the actual thirteen-step program used at an April 1992 Hindu marriage performed in Montreal, Canada.

1. *Welcoming on Arrival of the Wedding Party:* The bride's parents and relatives greet and welcome the groom's parents and relatives.
2. *Welcoming the Bridegroom "Jaya Mala":* The bride greets and welcomes the groom on his arrival at the entrance of the Vedic ritualistic enclosures; they exchange garlands.
3. *Madhu Perka Vidhi (Ceremony to Ensure Affable Behavior):* As the bridegroom enters the place of marriage ceremony (*Pandal*), the bride, after according him proper reception, offers him *Madhu Perka* (*Amrit*, a beverage consisting of honey, curd, and ghee), which he tastes while reciting a mantra (hymn): "I will always cultivate in me the sweetness of Madhu Perka in all my dealings."
4. *Pani Grahan Vidhi (Giving Away of the Bride):* The father of the bride puts her right hand in the groom's hand and declares to the assembly that he, on this day and hour, of his own free will and that of the bride, hereby hands over his daughter to her man. The bridegroom takes the hand of the bride, and both of them take a solemn pledge keeping God as witness. They declare in the presence of all the men and women present to grace the occasion that their hearts have been united by God, that they have become one, and will love each other like the very air without which they cannot live. They promise to remain entirely devoted to each other.
5. *Pratigva (Sacred Vows Between the Bride and Groom Are Taken as Follows):* "I will always remember the Divine. I will always look upon the other with sympathy, love, and compassion. I will help in all good deeds of each of us. I will keep my mind pure and virtuous. I will be strong and righteous. I will show goodwill and affection to parents, brothers, sisters, and other

family members. I will bring up our children in such a manner that they are strong in mind and body. I will always welcome and respect guests."
6. *Shilarohan Vidhi (Rock Ceremony):* The brother of the bride requests his sister to place her foot on a piece of rock while reciting the hymn that indicates its significance: "Place your foot on this piece of rock and be strong like it, so as to resist the onslaughts in the world of wicked people."
7. *Laja-Huti (Offering of Puffed Rice in Sacred Fire for Shared Prosperity):* The bride and groom put parched rice, which is handed to them by brothers and cousins of the bride, in the sacred fire and recite a hymn praying for their prosperity.
8. *Gath Bandan (Tying of Knot):* The edges of the outer garments or the ends of the scarf of the bride and bridegroom are tied together, symbolizing their union. The bride and groom then walk around the sacred fire four times, the bride leading in the first three and the groom in the last circumambulation.
9. *Satapadi (Taking Seven Steps Together):* The couple then walks seven steps together reciting hymns that express the principal duties of householders: "Let us take the first steps to provide for our household a nourishing and pure diet, avoiding those foods injurious to healthy living. Let us take the second step to develop physical, mental, and spiritual powers. Let us take the third step, to increase our wealth by righteous means and proper use. Let us take the fourth step, to acquire knowledge, happiness, and harmony by mutual love and trust. Let us take the fifth step, so that we be blessed with strong, virtuous, and heroic children. Let us take the sixth step, for self-restraint and longevity. Finally, let us take the seventh step and be true companions and remain lifelong partners by this wedlock."
10. *Jalasinchana (Sprinkling of Water):* The groom's father sprinkles water on the couple

and blesses them with a prayer that they both be calm, cool, and pure like water.

11. *Ashirvad (Blessing by the Guests and Relatives):* The guests and the relatives recite a hymn, led by the priest, which means that all those who have assembled here wish the couple good luck, prosperity, and long life.

12. *Vadhu Satkar (Gift to the Daughter-in-Law):* The groom's grandfather puts a necklace around the bride's neck, symbolizing acceptance into their family.

13. *Shantipath (The Hymn of Peace):* This hymn is recited at the end of all ceremonies and functions that perfect peace and tranquility may reign throughout the Creation. "Let our hearts remain always united and full of love towards each other. Let us always hear in mind that God has brought about our union in His Infinite Grace. From today onward your heart is mine and my heart is yours. I bind your mind and your heart with the knot of health."

couple to invoke prosperity; he wrapped their wrists in red ribbon for protection as they began the "householder's journey"; to represent the desired "germination" (by pregnancy) of their union, the priest planted seeds in a silver urn filled with soil; finally, he applied a paste of honey and banana to the bride's lips as a preview of the sweetness of marriage. Before guests departed the temple for the reception, the priest and attendants offered them lentil doughnuts, candies, spiced cashew rice, coffee, fruit, rosewater perfume to fortify them for the symbolically arduous journey to the Tandoor Restaurant a few blocks away.

The wedding was both ecumenical and based on established traditions, one guest noted. "There was less emphasis on who the bride and groom were, or how they met, and more on the bond and all these mystical ways of bringing two people together."

ROMANIA
TURKEY
RUSSIA
ARMENIA
SICILY
INDIA
CANADA
MALAYSIA
ECUADOR
KOREA
JAPAN
CHINA

The Allegorical Wedding

Westerners can reasonably wonder why the wedding rituals in India are so ornately complex. An Indian bridegroom named Arun Alagappan, thirty-three, who married Francine Friedman, thirty, at the Hindu Temple Society of North America, in Flushing, Queens, New York, explained it this way: "I like symbolic and allegorical elements in weddings because allegory makes the intangible ideas of love, loyalty, and commitment accessible to everyone."

The couple sat cross-legged on the stage during the ceremony, as their Hindu priest performed a series of allegorical rituals during a two-hour ceremony. He threw curried rice at the

Announcing the Banns

The custom of publishing matrimonial vows and proclamations, called banns, is traceable to at least the third century. European Christians, who celebrated their weddings at church, preceded them with public announcements of their proposed unions, usually in church for three consecutive Sundays, but sometimes in the public market or local alehouse before a clutch of witnesses. Tertullian (160–230) contended that marriages were clandestine if not announced beforehand and publicly in church. Around 1200 the Synod of Westminster made the banns more official by ruling that under ordinary circumstances marriage ceremonies should be preceded by the publication—usually the reading aloud, but at least the posting of a printed notice—of the couple's banns.

ROMANIA
TURKEY
RUSSIA
ARMENIA
SICILY
INDIA
CANADA
MALAYSIA
ECUADOR
KOREA
JAPAN
CHINA

The banns were a way of ensuring community approval, of ascertaining if there were any impediments or objections to the union, not to overlook ecclesiastical confirmation: "If holy chyrche it wol ordeyne."

In today's Christian wedding format, in the query by the officiant if there are any people present objecting to the matrimony about to be ratified, we see a weak echo of the older banns. In effect announcing the banns made a couple's privately committed vows, the flower of their conjugal ardor and matrimonial intention, very public. It was potentially a moment both of vulnerability and ascendancy, as they stepped forward as "transfigured" individuals about to legitimize their relationship. Today we find the transformed spirit of the old banns in the form of the vows to which we publicly commit in the joining ritual. "The symbolism of divine marriage with its apparatus of incantation and magic is still with us," notes Eleanor Munro in her *Wedding Readings.* "Wedding vows in that sense are spells, invocations not so much to heaven as to a still-unrealized being in oneself who may grow to maturity to fulfill the promise."

The exchanging of personally developed vows formed the core of a joining ritual developed by Deborah L. Johnson and Zandra Z. Rolón. The ceremony begins with a welcoming statement presented by the couple and a consideration of the nuances of the word *tryst,* which they take to signify "a coming together in trust." A friend reads an excerpt from Kahlil Gibran's *The Prophet,* the minister discusses the meanings and responsibilities of commitment, and then performs a candle ceremony. Three unlit candles stand in a row; each member of the couple lights one candle, then they jointly light the "family candle" in the middle. The minister challenges them to blow out all three candles simultaneously, but this proves impossible (on purpose) due to their spacing and size. The minister reflects that their married life will be like this, that they could take solace in the likelihood that all

three candles could never be expunged; one or two of the unit would always remaining lit.

Now come the vows. For enhanced impact and reverence, the couple has not shown each other their statements before this public revelation; further, as a preface to their vows, they agree to repeat them aloud to each other on every subsequent anniversary. Among Deborah's vows:

I consider it both an honor and a privilege to be the one standing here with you today in love, mutual respect, and total honesty. Let us continue to build a relationship that suits our needs and never try to force our needs to fit any preconceived concepts. I support you in your intellectual, emotional, spiritual, and economic growth. I want to know of your changes and I promise to share mine with you. Never be afraid to tell me your thoughts. I believe it is the intensity of our intimacy that keeps us continually seeking the other for companionship. I will make myself a safe person for you to be around. I will provide a nurturing environment for your soul and care for the body in which it dwells. You are always welcome into my world. I place no limitations on the possibilities of our relationship. I hope we never truly discover just how high is high. As you go through life's ups and downs following your passions and your dreams, I want you always to remember that I believe in you and I'm rooting for you all the way.

Two women, Atimah and Aylana, describe a joining ritual they developed and performed "with the guidance of dreams" for the winter solstice, December 21. The ceremony begins outdoors, with the lighting of a large solstice fire. Wedding guests are invited to bring items (photos, clothes, objects, letters, poems, journals) from their lives they want to burn, to let go into the flames as an initial cleansing. Next the couple and all the guests are smudged with sage and cedar sticks. Starting at a person's feet, the "smudger" uses a feather to move the strong smoke up and around the body.

Then the ceremony moves inside the house to a specially prepared room. A circle of crystal clusters twelve feet in diameter has been erected on a floor rug laid on top of a king-sized bedspread; inside the crystal circle is another circle of twelve candles; in the center is a round, clear bowl, containing water from the Atlantic and Pacific oceans, set upon a mirror that rests on a round piece of oak. Eight lighted candles float in the seawater, producing the contiguity of fire and water and providing the room's only light.

The couple about to be joined sits within the circle, at opposite points on the perimeter, facing each other. Next to each is a personal "crystal medicine wheel," made of eight clear crystal balls surrounding a ninth larger one. A small bamboo tray serves as a food altar beside each, containing almonds (the seed of life), a Japanese pitcher filled with pomegranate juice (feminine associations with lushness and richness), and a cup. Guests are summoned by sounding several singing crystal bowls and tinkling a set of chimes. Welcoming prayers and invocations are offered, including this special request for beneficent spiritual agencies to be present:

> Today on this day of solstice we gather to witness and bless a joining of two life paths in One Spiritual Light! We call upon the powers of Heaven and Earth, the Ancestors and Angels of Light; and the keepers of the Sacred fire to give truth, Life, Love and Light to this union!
>
> *Ramahesh.*

Ramahesh, a Sanskrit word meaning "to be one with God," came to Atimah in a dream, as did "The Ancient River," a visionary prose poem about marriage, which a guest reads to the accompaniment of "the heartbeat of a drum." Chimes are rung again, many of the guests play the singing

crystal bowls together, Atimah and Aylana make an energy connection and inner visualization using the crystals from their individual medicine wheels, then more poems are recited.

Now the couple lights small pieces of sage to burn in smudge pots before them. Pouring a little quantity of pomegranate juice, they hold it above the sage smoke, then over the bowl of floating candles and seawater, for a blessing; they repeat the gesture with the dish of almonds, then offer the juice and almonds to each other. Next they rub frankincense oil on their hands, dip them in the seawater, and anoint each other's heart area and forehead.

Two guests discuss the themes of sun and moon as underlying energies in this relationship, relating insights drawn from meditation, dreams, and poetic reverie. Pendants and rings are exchanged, such that one partner accepts the sun jewelry and gives her moon energy.

For the "coming together ritual," the couple kneels with palms down; then, letting the palms lead them upward, they slowly rise until, facing each other, their hands are only one-quarter inch apart; they contemplate each other silently for several seconds, then allow the palms to meet; and, leaning over the bowl with floating candles, they kiss. The guests complement the joining with chanting *Om*, then offer a blessing prayer, another dream poem recitation, drum beats, crystal bowl ringings, and a final showering of the couple by a young girl with rose petals and corn kernels. The ceremony ends with a "pronouncement of union":

> We speak for the Circle—for the spirit of love in each heart gathered round you, seen and unseen. With the power of life invested in us—we pronounce you joined together as partners in Life, Love, and the Spiritual Path of Light! *Ho!*

In drafting their joining ritual, Marion Hansell and Barbara Hicks kept foremost the intention to do it all themselves, with "no doting

ROMANIA
TURKEY
RUSSIA
ARMENIA
SICILY
INDIA
CANADA
MALAYSIA
ECUADOR
KOREA
JAPAN
CHINA

mother to help with the outfits or make a wedding cake, no bridesmaids, no gifts from the family, and no honeymoon." They exchanged rings and vows, "using words that we scripted ourselves," casting a reasonable statement of commitment that honored and nurtured each other's growth but wouldn't indenture them "until death do us part," if maintaining the relationship proved to be a living death, "detrimental to our growth." Besides their own self-written texts, the ceremony included readings from Corinthians, Christopher Fry's *A Sleep of Prisoners,* Virginia Satir's *Making Contact,* a Jewish blessing, and the *Song of Songs.* One partner declares before the assembled guests:

> It is without fear or shame that I stand with you before our friends, declaring my love for you and my need of you. I open my hands to you as a symbol of what I offer you: freedom, not possession; openness, not restriction; honesty, fidelity, warmth, and gentleness; acceptance and respect. I have chosen to love you and give myself to you. I will contribute to the atmosphere of our relationship that allows you freedom and room for personal growth. Friends, by your presence here with us this evening, you show love and acceptance of us and good wishes for us.

As they exchange rings, each partner makes a public statement. One says: "I give you this ring so you may choose to wear it and in so doing be reminded and reexperience my deep love and regard for you." In response the other partner says: "I give you this ring: a dolphin ring—a symbol of health and right relationships between people as well as between humans and the creatures and all creation. A ring, I hope, of healing and joy. I give it to you so that you may choose to wear it and in so doing be reminded and know my deep love and regard for you and my wish that you may have a long life and a beautifully rich and creative one." To which the first partner replies: "I will wear this love

gift with honor and joy as a sign to others that I am committed to our union."

Handfasting—Wrists Joined, Hands in Fist

Several centuries ago Scotland and the north of England were rugged, independent districts of Britain that largely exempted themselves from ecclesiastical dictates surrounding marriage customs. There the ratification of vows, and technically the wedding too, was effected by a handfast: a clasping of hands, a joining of wrists.

Handfasting may have generated the word *wed,* which originally meant the pledge, nuptial promise, or sum of money (and later the ring) presented to the woman's father as a security deposit by the prospective groom. "Among the Anglo-Saxons, the first step involved obtaining permission from the bride's kinsmen," notes John R. Gillis in *For Better, For Worse.* "Once this was accomplished, the groom and his people offered to the bride's guardians a series of sureties called *weds* that guaranteed that the bride would be maintained and protected." The exchange of sureties on the bride's behalf, performed by handfasting of the couple before witnesses, thus constituted the first phase of the *beweddung,* as it was first called. Within handfasting rituals we note a continuum of rituals including the joining of hands, the tying together of garments, and the exchange of rings.

In the Sakai joining ritual in Malaysia, the handfasting is preceded by dancing accompanied by an orchestra of bamboo stampers. Several women squat before a log and strike it with bamboo sticks, producing a series of notes. The men form a long conga line with arms around the neighbor ahead of them; the women join the line, clapping, and they dance as a group for hours, in swaying and forward bowing movements, flexing their arms up and down. Then the *pungulu* (master of ceremonies) summons the group: "Harken, harken. Those who were at a distance are now together; they who were separated are now united." The couple getting married squats across from each other on a mat, joins hands, and feeds each other cooked rice, completing the ceremony.

The handfasting ritual among the Andaman Islanders of Polynesia illustrates a more comprehensive idea of joining. In the evening the bride sits on a mat at the edge of the dancing ground, accompanied by her friends and relatives, and illuminated by resin torches. The groom sits at the other end of the long mat, also among company. A village elder addresses the couple, admonishing them to be good, providing, faithful partners; then he leads the groom by the hand to where the bride sits, and gestures for him to join her on the mat. The elder takes the arms of bride and groom and places them like oval wreaths around each other's neck; then he makes the groom sit on his bride's lap, in which position they remain for several minutes, until the ritual concludes with dancing.

The contemporary Burmese joining ceremony adds lustration by water to the handfasting procedure. In Rangoon the wedding guests assemble in a large drawing room at the bride's home, men at one end, women at the other, while the presiding elders and the couple sit in the middle. A pair of lush cushions have been provided for the bride and groom, where they sit before a large bowl of carved silver filled with flower blossoms and other offerings. A man (the "panegyric reader") rises to chant the paean of praise for the couple, complimenting the young *tha-do-tha* (groom) "so blessed with virtues, complete with every manly quality," and the young *tha-do-thami* (bride), "so beautiful and full of womanly dignity." Both are of exemplary stock and "so great is their

merit," that they are hereby married auspiciously and surely shall have a good long life together, he concludes. Now the presiding elder (a woman) places the offerings in the silver bowl into the outstretched palms of the bride; she bows as she accepts each handful, knowing that through this *mingala*, she is auspiciously purified. The bridal pair rises from their cushions to take positions on the couch. Another presiding elder (male) takes the hands of the bride and groom, lays them upon each other, then dips them together into a golden bowl of water as the panegyric reader calls out his witnessing of the event. The elder concludes the ceremony by saying: "Maung Sett Khaing and Khin Khin Su, I pronounce you man and wife."

Eugene de Courcillon witnessed an old-fashioned church handfasting in the French village of Lammerville in the 1850s, which he recounted in *Le Curé Manqué*. A boy assisting the curé held a plate, onto which the groom placed a piece of silver and a gold ring and upon which the priest made a blessing. The priest read the marriage canons aloud, then put the customary query to the couple regarding their willing consent as they joined hands before him. When they assented, he said, "In the name of God, I pronounce you man and wife." The bride took the silver coin from the tray and pocketed it, while the groom placed the gold ring on her finger, saying, "I give you this ring as a pledge of the marriage contract." The bridal couple kneeled together beneath a white sheet, covering them from view, and the priest made a final blessing.

The core of the Cambodian joining ritual is the *can dai*, "the binding of hands." The ceremony takes place in a special shed roofed in foliage and draped within with red curtains on the bride's property. The groom and bride sit together on a mat, while the guests sit around them holding areca flowers in their hands. The groom bows three times to the assembled guests, then offers all guests older than him, beginning with those of the

ROMANIA TURKEY RUSSIA ARMENIA SICILY INDIA CANADA MALAYSIA ECUADOR KOREA JAPAN CHINA

ROMANIA
TURKEY
RUSSIA
ARMENIA
SICILY
INDIA
CANADA
MALAYSIA
ECUADOR
KOREA
JAPAN
CHINA

bride's family, an areca blossom. The guests lay their flower gifts on a tray, to which the groom's parents add a cash sum. Now both sets of parents take a bracelet woven of seven threads of untwisted cotton and pass it over the wrists of the couple; the relatives in both families repeat the gesture, passing the bracelet over the couple's fingers, then offering expensive gifts, such as jewels, land, cloths, and animals. The parents hold a lighted candle and circumambulate the seated couple three times; then they all proceed into the house to change from their gala clothes into something simpler for the wedding breakfast. Prayers to the ancestors and proferred samples of each dish are made before eating; after the meal the wedding ceremony concludes with the *phsàm damnek,* "the union in the same bed."

A Silken Cord of Infinity Shall Bind Them Fast

The traditional ceremony of binding observed in the Philippines actually derives from the Mozarabic Toledo rites introduced centuries earlier by Spanish missionaries. The bride and groom, dressed in white, stand before the altar with three sponsors. Their hands joined, they agree to marry, and the priest sprinkles their clasped hands with holy water. The priest puts a ring on the groom's left-hand finger, then gives him another ring for the bride; the priest prays aloud as the rings are presented. Next the bride cups her hands under the groom's cupped hands. The priest dribbles thirteen silver coins (from the Spanish *arras,* "earnest money") into the groom's open palms, and these trickle like a fountain into the bride's hands, and from her palms into a plate held underneath by an acolyte. The trickling of the arras is "a

sign of fidelity bestowed irrevocably" and completes the marriage contract. The priest recites prayers over the couple and may hold a nuptial Mass at this point. When that stage in the Mass called the Sanctus is reached, a bell rings and a veil is placed over the groom's shoulders and the bride's head. Now the priest entwines the *yugal* ("nuptial tie," a silken cord or string of flowers) around the necks of both bride and groom in the form of a figure eight, the sign of infinity, concluding the ritual.

In the Costa Rican wedding, the *padrinos,* an equal mixture of male and female witnesses, assemble at the back of the church in a double row. As the bridal music begins, the priest leads them down the flower-decked aisle, followed by the *porta arras,* a small girl bearing a tray with the rings and the arras, a bracelet of thirteen gilded *cincos* (coins), which the priest will present to the bride during the binding ritual. The padrinos form a semicircle about the bridal couple at the altar. The "yoke of matrimony" (reminiscent of the Hindu tali) is a white cord that the priest loops around the necks of the couple during the *velación,* or blessing of the future offspring.

The marriage rites of the Fellahin of Upper Egypt take place at night, as the procession approaches the church, the men carrying lanterns, the women trilling the *zagharit.* The priest, facing the bridal couple, takes a silken thread, passes it over the groom's right shoulder and under his left arm, then ties the thread into a knot with a loop; after making prayers, the priest unties the groom's knot, then binds the two engagement rings together with the silken thread. Then he queries the couple about their marital intentions, unbinds the rings, and puts the wedding rings on the fingers of the bride and groom.

In the original Roman handfasting ceremony, the *pronuba* (a married woman, acting as officiant) joined the right hands of the couple together in the presence of ten witnesses. Then the

Roman bride spoke the customary words: *"Quando tu Gaius, ego Gaia,"* "When (and where) you are, Gaius, then (and there) I am Gaia." The references to Gaius and Gaia were generic, possibly in commemoration of a forgotten couple or perhaps a more archetypal aspect of marriage, insofar as Gaia was the Greek name for the Earth Goddess. After making their oaths, the couple sat down on adjoining stools at the left of the altar; next came the offering of a wheat cake to Jupiter, of which bride and groom each ate a part.

The joining ritual for the Thai bridal couple is completed when, as the couple kneels together before a small shrine, their hands clasped together over a decorated silver bowl, the officiant unites them with a holy white cord wrapped conjointly around their heads. The wedding guests stand behind them and, while offering a blessing, sprinkle the couple with rice and lustral water poured from a conch.

The crux of the ancient Aztec wedding ritual was the "Tying of the *Tilmantli*," the hems of the outer cloaks of the bride and groom as they sat facing each other on a ceremonial mat. The *cihuat-lanque* (the presiding female elder) ties the man's cloak to the woman's blouse, thereby marrying them. Afterward the couple shares a dish of tamales, feeding each other morsels of the maize-cakes by hand.

In Mexican weddings the groom passes coins through the bride's hands, signifying she is to handle household finances. As the couple kneels before the altar holding lighted candles in their hands, the priest places a single silken scarf around their shoulders, then a single silver cord around their necks, which completes the ceremony.

In the Guatemalan joining ritual, the couple kneels before an altar with their marriage godparents before them, each holding a lighted yellow candle in their right hand. The marriage godfather takes a special cord in his hand, loops it around the groom's neck, and hands him a candle. The god-mother takes both ends of the cord, twists them once, and loops it around the bride's neck, giving the woman her candle. The priest pronounces Mass; then, after the benediction, he places the wedding ring on the bride's finger.

The Native American Ojibways join their couples by sewing together either the hems or sleeves of their garments to symbolize the permanence and indissolubility of their union.

"I Wed You with This Ring"

The joining ritual may concentrate its blessing through the ritual of exchanging rings, as this originally scripted wedding format, created by Martena and Randolph Sasnett of Santa Barbara, California, illustrates. It's not unusual to focus a wedding through the exchange of rings, but in this ceremony the ring ritual conveys a spirituality not often emphasized.

The minister addresses the assembled company by reviewing the nature of marriage. It is a relationship founded in nature, sanctioned by the state, consecrated by the church, and ennobled by the couple's adherence to its covenants, he explains. "As the bonds of the estate of matrimony depend upon a unity as of one heart and mind, a commitment to each other's interests and happiness, and a dedication to each other's self-fulfillment, they should be assumed only after prudent and reverent consideration." He next asks the couple if they stand before him with a sense of inner confirmation regarding these intentions of marriage. He asks the groom: "Will you love and cherish her with forbearance and understanding; will you endeavor to help her and satisfy her needs; will you share with her life's work and recreation, its chances and changes, its pleasures and adversities;

ROMANIA
TURKEY
RUSSIA
ARMENIA
SICILY
INDIA
CANADA
MALAYSIA
ECUADOR
KOREA
JAPAN
CHINA

and will you try to create between you a spirit of harmony and happiness?" He then asks the bride the same questions.

The exchange of rings comes next. The groom places his ring on a ritual cushion; the bride places her smaller ring inside his; the minister turns to the altar and lifts the cushion in a gesture of consecration. The groom takes the woman's ring, places it on her finger, and says: "I wed you with this ring, as a symbol of unbroken unity, everlasting devotion, and encircling love." He raises her hand to his lips and kisses the ring to seal the vow. The bride repeats this gesture, using the groom's ring. Then the couple recites this brief spiritual text together, making their pledges public while kneeling: "Supreme Giver of Life and Love, by Whose harmonious forces the universe is ordered, we kneel in gratitude for the guidance which has brought us to this union. We pray that we may adapt ourselves to the influences which will shape our lives for mutual service, and that in the years to come, we may give back to the world the beauty and inspiration which we achieve through each other." The minister closes the ceremony by reciting a poem appropriate to the subject of marriage; in the Sasnett's case it was a sonnet sestet from Robert Nathan's *A Winter Tide.*

"You Are Married Until the Tomb!"

On the eve of the wedding of Andean Indian couples in Peguche, Ecuador, the father and family of the groom visit the bride's home carrying *las cosas de mediano,* wedding foods including cooked guinea pigs and chicken in hominy, baskets of bread, ears of corn, peeled potatoes with sauce, hard-boiled eggs, and twenty bottles of rum. Both fathers declare over this agricultural bounty before them: "Let us marry our children with goodwill

and with affection! *"Hagamos palabray!"* "Let us go through with the words!" An altar table is set up in the middle of the room, overlaid with a fine cloth on top of which go a handful of carnations, the couple's individual rosaries, and two rings. The bride and groom kneel at opposite ends of the altar.

The *maytro* (master of ceremonies) asks the bride: *"Ahora si,* do you wish to marry this man?" She assents, he queries the groom, he assents, then he says, "Let us place the rosaries!" The groom lays his rosary around the bride's neck, she hangs her rosary around his neck. In some Indian communities, the maytro hangs a long rosary made of corals, copper beads, old silver coins, and a large silver crucifix first around the bride's neck then the groom's as the two kneel before him. The maytro blesses the couple, the bride's father blesses the groom, and the groom's father blesses the bride. As they did with their personal rosaries, now bride and groom exchange rings, fitting their own on their partner's finger. "Now it is not play, it is not joking, you are married until the tomb!" the maytro declares.

Then he addresses the guests and relatives: "You are witness that they have married of their own free will." The guests reply: "Good, this is no joke; they are married until the tomb." The groom asks the maytro to bless him; then both bride and groom kneel before him, kissing his hands; then the parents and guests give their blessings to the couple. The groom's father declares: "Now, my son, you have fulfilled your destiny. It was your destiny to be married. You and your wife are to become heads of a family."

The Fire in Your Eyes

For the Aranda tribe of Aboriginals in Australia's Central Desert, the joining ritual is disarmingly simple, certainly in comparison with their complex initiation rites. A couple announces their betrothal by appearing in public performing their daily tasks. Knowing they're being observed, the man hands the woman a small piece of wood shaped like a cup, which is part of the standard fire-making equipment. He spins a wooden rod inside the cup, which she holds close to a bundle of dried grass. The friction of the rod against the cup suddenly ignites into a spark and the grass bursts into flames. With the spurt of flames as a backdrop, the marriage is "made" when the couple gazes into each other's eyes.

A similar custom of producing sparks of fire from a flint was anciently practiced at home among the Laplanders of northern Scandinavia, "which was a symbol of the life latent within the sexes and which could be produced only by a conjunction of forces," explained Edward Wood, in *The Wedding Day in All Ages and Countries*.

P'yebaek—*The Great Kowtow*

In the traditional Korean wedding ceremony it's the formal bowing—the great kowtow—that completes the joining. The *p'yebaek* ritual preserves the concluding rite from the old Confucian wedding format, called the Rite of the Father-in-Law and Mother-in-Law; in this context p'yebaek's original function was to "make" the bride into a daughter-in-law and through this to knit the two families together.

An altar, established inside a special p'yebaek chamber, contains some representation of Korea's symbol for conjugal fidelity, the goose. It may be a gilded wooden goose or a live bird wrapped in cloth up to its head. Other altar items include *otsuka*, symbolic shapes and figures woven from

straw, dried pheasant, a gourd-bottle of rice wine tied in blue and red thread, rice-cakes, chestnuts, dates, and fruits. A series of reciprocal prostrations are the acts of mutual consent that compose the sacramental aspect of the joining ritual. The bride and groom bow to each other (the bride bows four times, the groom two or three), then sit down facing each other. The groom may also make several prostrations before the altar, including a dexterous genuflection in which he goes down to the floor holding the goose. A bridesmaid brings a bottle of rice wine, a bowl, and jujubes fruit, handing "the uniting wine cup" to the groom who drinks a little from the bowl; the bridesmaid offers the remaining wine to the bride, who finishes it. This ritual is repeated three times, after which the bride rises for more formal bowing.

The Korean bride offers a series of four deep formal bows and prostrations (kowtow) to her father-in-law, then three bows to her groom, then more bows to all the kin of her groom's family. Clothed in a white dress and veil, she raises her gloved hands to her face, then with a female assistant at each elbow, sinks to the floor in a profound genuflection, bending forward at the torso. The "great kowtow" is the subject of chapters in Korean etiquette books, and if large families are involved, the continual bowing can be a physical ordeal. "I was bobbing up and down all night," a contemporary Korean bride reported. The groom's kinsfolk, who have been bowed to, receive a cup of "bride's wine" (also called the "cup of the wine of mutual joy") and small portions of pheasant from the bridesmaids. The in-laws next politely pelt the bride on the long white sleeves of her wedding gown with dates and chestnuts, wishing her good fortune as a mother, and in effect welcoming her into the family as one worthy of continuing the family lineage; on leaving they may discretely deposit kowtow money for the bride in a white envelope on a tray. Today the groom joins his bride in making the prostrations before the families.

Sansankudo—*Nine Times Drinking Sake*

The central feature of the Japanese wedding ceremony is *sansankudo*, which means, literally, "three-three-nine times" and refers to a precise ritual of drinking sake. As with the Japanese betrothal ritual, the yuino, the seating arrangements for sansankudo are exceedingly precise and integral to the ritual itself. On one side of the room sit the *butsudan* (the family shrine), the groom's parents and grandmother, and the *shikaisha* (the go-between and master of ceremonies); on the other side, first there is the *tokonoma* (the display of yuino presents), then the bride's parents and her elder brother; at the head of both sides sit the bride and groom.

Once seated, the two families exchange formal bows. A girl carries in a small table of *noshi* (dried abalone wrapped in red and white paper), sets it before the couple, and bows. Next two older girls enter carrying a nest of three sake cups, each one smaller than its neighbor, and two fancy sake pourers, which, respectively, bear images of male and female butterflies (or paper origami butterflies attached with *mizuhiki*, strings of colored paper). One girl presents the cups to the bride, while the other fills the top cup with sake. The bride's elder brother leaves the room to sing a *kageutai*, a wedding song, on the other side of the sliding rice paper door. The girl and bride bow to each other, then the bride drinks the cup of sake when her brother finishes his song; now the girls move the sake tray before the groom, exchange bows with him, and repeat the ritual; again the elder brother makes a kageutai, and this time the groom drinks a cup of sake. The girls return to the bride and repeat the sake offering again. Sake is then served, in this order, to the groom's father, mother, the bride's father, then mother; after which, all the guests proclaim, *"Omedeto gozaimasu!"* "Congratulations!"

Thus the bride and groom have sipped sake together nine times in three rounds: (1) bride, groom, and bride drink from the first cup; (2) groom, bride, and groom drink from the second cup; (3) bride, groom, and bride drink from the third cup. Why? Presumably the couple drinks from the same cup as a symbolic agreement that they will share a lifetime of joy and sorrow. The Japanese regard three (*san*) as an extremely auspicious number; in earlier days there were three people present at the wedding ritual, a fire was maintained for three nights, and three trays of food were served. *Sakazukigoto*, the ritual sharing of sake, is an old custom (codified as early as the fourteenth century in the "Samurai Rules of Etiquette," but it was in use at weddings even earlier in the Heian period, 794–1185) and is used in many Japanese functions to create or reinforce social bonds.

The traditional Chinese wedding ritual similarly turns on the sharing of wine by the couple, but without the meticulous orchestration of the Japanese sansankudo. But before they share the wine, they pay obeisance to the gods of heaven and earth, kowtowing to each other before an altar on which stand two red candles and three incense sticks. On their way to the *hsi-fang*, or marriage room, the bride, heavily veiled and escorted by two women, receives a square piece of sweet cake wrapped in red cloth; then she has to step over a saddle laid in her path to represent evil spirits that might try to block the couple's union. In the hsi-fang bride and groom sit on separate beds, and the groom removes the bride's red veil. Now, the bride and groom drink wine (sometimes mixed with honey) out of two gilded cups that are tied together with a red silken thread. This ceremony is sometimes called *T'wan Yuan*, meaning "to make a perfect circle," because after the groom has sipped a little wine from his cup, the contents are emptied into the bride's cup, which she then drinks.

Next, a brass basin is brought into the room and set upside down before them on the altar. Underneath the basin are two apples and a small box with the ideograms for "Harmony" inscribed. The basin serves as a table for the couple's first food-taking together, taken in (and over) harmony; traditionally this inaugural food will be thirty-two meat-dumplings prepared at her parent's home. The wine sharing ritual is followed by their mutual veneration by kneeling of the groom's parents, the spiritual powers of heaven and earth, and the solemn presentation of the bride before the white tablets of the ancestors and household gods.

The Benediction—Blessings from Above

As the sixth-century Gregorian Sacramentary puts it, "O God, you have hallowed marriage by a mystery so excellent." The culminating stage of the joining ritual is the benediction, in which the priest, minister, or officiant makes a nuptial blessing on the couple. The blessing can be a formal liturgy from the particular religious canon informing the ceremony or an inspired reading, drawn from poetry, literature, or even an extemporaneous oration. But in whatever format it assumes, the intention here is to transmit a *spiritual* blessing to the bridal couple.

In the Hebrew wedding ritual, the *Sheva Berakhot* (Seven Benedictions) offered by the officiating rabbi derive from the Talmud, a compilation of centuries of rabbinic commentary and law. For Christians the source of the blessing and the canonical legitimacy a priest might reasonably claim derive from the "miracle" performed by

Master Jesus, his first of seven, at the famous marriage at Cana in Galilee. According to Christian interpretation, Jesus Christ's presence itself was what *married* the bride and bridegroom, irrespective of what ritual gestures the officiating rabbi might have made.

As the Gospel According to John informs us (2:1–11), Jesus, his mother, and his disciples were guests of a wedding at Cana. The nuptial sponsors suddenly realized they had run out of wine—well before the feasting would be completed. Jesus, who wasn't well known at this point, and was an inconspicuous guest at the ceremony, directed that six stones jars, each capable of holding about twenty gallons, be filled with water and that a cupful be presented to the wedding steward. The steward was surprised to find that such "good wine" had been kept in reserve; it was customary to serve the good wine first, then move on to the poorer vintages. "This, the first of his signs, Jesus did at Cana in Galilee, and manifested his glory; and his disciples believed in him," comments the author of John.

What was Jesus' blessing at the Cana wedding? It wasn't just the gracious favor of providing a lot more wine on the quick; the transformation of water into wine, as far as we're concerned today, is of greater allegorical than practical value. "The chance wedding guest becomes the central figure," comments Gerhard Wehr in *The Mystical Marriage*. The attention of the guests may be drawn to the bridal couple, but "the real action emanates from the man who sits inconspicuously at one side. A gentle gesture of blessing is hinted at; his presence is everything, the 'real presence' at that holy meal."

Why should Jesus the Christ be the source of the nuptial blessing? "He" is just the sacrificial son of a patriarchal, power-hungry ecclesia, or so many feel. Because, says the esoteric side of Christianity, the Christ is the alpha and omega, the beginning and end, the scarlet blush of unconditional universal Love from Above, the male and the female, Eesh and Esha perfectly integrated as Esh— as cosmic fire, as Logos. As such, the spiritual, supersensible, atemporal being known as Christ (who is neither solely owned nor represented by any church or institution, but is a cosmic fact like the sun and the stars) is the perfect exemplar of the wine-soaked and wedded human.

Wine-soaked: in the sense of being inebriated with God. As the late Turkish Sheikh Muzzafer Ozak said, "Love is the wine. The sheiks are the pourers of the wine and the dervish is the glass." Fermentation, after all, is an ancient symbol for human transformation; each of us can emulate the Winemaker: take the ego, crush it, inoculate it with Love, incubate it in a stone jar, and it turns into a delicious, intoxicating wine. And who drinks wine at the "tavern"? The cosmos of saints, gods, goddesses, and angels all potentially present as guests at our wedding, if we wish it. One day before the marriage, Jesus said to his apostle Nathanael, by way of preparing him for the first miracle at Cana: "Truly, truly, I say to you, you will see heaven opened, and the angels of God ascending and descending upon the Son of Man."

We get a little taste of this heavenly largess in the final stage of the world culture wedding, the opulence of recessional, banquet, and honeymoon, which we will explore in our next and final chapter. The couple is now blessed, transfigured, and married, as witnessed by the families and community. In a consummate expression of matrimonial enthusiasm, the families and the wedding guests celebrate the pristine union with a lavish (if not in material goods, always in good cheer and fellowship) nuptial feast, which we will highlight by way of the Roman *confarreatio,* in which the wedding cake (or marriage loaf, shower of grains, confetti, garlands, speeches of praise, music, toasts—seeds of opulence in whatever guise) represents the community's wishes to the couple for fertility, abundance, and unceasing spiritual presence.

8

THE

CONFARREATIO

THE OPULENCE OF RECESSIONAL, BANQUET, AND HONEYMOON

Taking its name from the cake of far and mola salsa that was broken over the bride's head, *confarreatio* was attended with an incident that increases its resemblance to the way in which our ancestors used at their weddings objects symbolical of natural plentifulness. Whilst she gave her right hand to her spouse, the ancient Roman bride, married in accordance with the practices of confarreation, held in her left three wheat-ears, just as the English bride in later centuries bore in her hand or on her head a chaplet of bearded spikes of wheat.

—*John Cordy Jeaffreson*, Brides and Bridals

During the reception for a recent Chinese wedding in Manhattan, the bridegroom's friends subjected the thirty-year-old man to a barrage of games intended variously to humiliate, entertain, confuse, intoxicate, or generally humor him. Nine women, including his wife, kissed white paper napkins, which were then displayed on a string; he had to identify which lipstick imprint represented his bride's kiss. Fortunately for him, he got it right, for which he earned the guests' accolade: "The man knows his bride."

Another couple, both of whom worked in TV or radio, organized an extravagant reception that was a blend of cabaret, matrimonial celebration, and political fund-raiser. Their reception displayed all the style and panache of a theatrical production, including printed program, a long queue to get into the Algonquin Hotel lobby in Manhattan, and a title: "Our Love Is Here to Stay." Professional singers and cabaret stars performed songs about love and marriage, and the $12,000 contributed by the four hundred guests was donated to an AIDS activist group.

An American couple in their late twenties traveled to Pamplona, Spain, where they got married in a Catholic church on the first day of the

Feast of San Fermin, in July, which is a time of bullfights and all-night street parties. Only the couple and two relatives were present in the huge church, but afterward they staged a unique reception. The groom donned white clothes with a red sash and neckerchief, the traditional fiesta outfit, and ran through the Pamplona back streets, followed (or perhaps chased) by six bulls, four cows, and about a hundred Spanish partiers.

A New York couple, both twenty-six, who had known each other since high school, invited their oldest friends (some of whom had known them since kindergarten) to a reception based on the ties of old friendships. Bridesmaids fed cake to the ushers, who fed pieces to the bride. "That was the most spiritual moment of the wedding for me," commented the bride. "We've known these friends for so long."

A Piece of Wedding Cake

The recessional is a shower of seed—of confetti, rice, wheat, dates, almonds, crushed pomegranates, broken vases of scent, sweetmeats, garlands, coins, hurrahs, songs, epithalamiums—an ejaculation of praise and abundance by an admiring, celebratory community. Emerging from the sanctum of their matrimonial blessing, bride and groom are accorded the flawless opulence of Eden, a mythopoeic taste of that prodigal *fête champêtre* once lavished upon their archetypal forebears, that primal couple Adam and Eve, setting forevermore the fecund ambiance of reception. Newly formed, this pristine couple will be generously supported, endowed by spirit and nature, at least for one epiphanous day—that's what the postnuptial rites of recessional, banquet, and honeymoon so unreservedly declare. Every marriage is a reaffirmation of the unfathomable potentiality of being launched

human with a celestial imprimatur in hand upon a virginal, opulent world.

Among patrician Romans that imprimatur was granted by the god Jupiter, the deity of good faith in all alliances, at the conclusion of their *confarreatio* rites of marriage. The Roman couple sat with veiled heads in flame-colored head scarves called *flammeum*, on stools carpeted in sheepskin, attended by two quasireligious dignitaries, the Pontifex Maximus and the Flamen Dialis, ten witnesses, the pronuba (a matron), and the *camillus*, a young boy who holds the wheaten offering in the *cumerus*, a covered basket. The Flamen Dialis ceremonially offers a round salted cake of *far* (Latin for a coarse Italian wheat, also known as spelt, *Triticum spelta*; also called *panis farreus*) first to Jupiter Farreus, Juno the goddess of marriage, and the local deities of the country and its fruits, and then to the bride and groom, who share it as a sacrament while holding hands. The understanding was that something of the supersensible potency of the god Jupiter dwelt in the far and was assimilable by the couple upon eating the sanctified loaf. Scholars believe that the Flamen Dialis then crumbled the far loaf over the heads of the couple as an evocation of fertility and abundance.

Why Jupiter? For one reason, Jupiter was the Roman name for Zeus, for the Greeks, the chief of the Olympian gods, equipped with thunderbolt and staff. Astrologers tell us that Jupiter, as a planet, is exalted (or most comfortable) in Cancer, the sign of the home, domesticity, the family. Just as Jupiter/Zeus presides over the family of gods and goddesses, so he benignly oversees affairs of the human household. Jupiter is also the planet of good fortune, the bestower of material gifts and worldly gain, generally exhibiting a spirit of munificence, expansiveness, and philanthropy, in both a material and spiritual sense.

So with this symbolic gesture, the ubiquitous wedding cake was born, evolving over the centuries from dry cake to honeyed biscuit, to small buns (made of flour, sugar, eggs, milk, and spices)

TURKEY
ROMANIA
HUNGARY
YUGOSLAVIA
GREECE
ITALY
CORSICA
RUSSIA

iced in almond paste and comfits, to the ornate, outrageous, and calorically prodigious confections we're familiar with in the late twentieth century. The guests must have their token morsel of the nuptial culinary opulence, too. "A cake being broken over the head of Mrs. Tabitha Lismahago, the fragments were distributed among the bystanders," wrote Tobias Smollett in his *Expedition of Humphrey Clinker* (1771), "according to the custom of the ancient Britons, on the supposition that every person who ate of this hallowed cake should that night have a vision of the man or woman whom Heaven designed should be his or her wedded mate."

Pieces of cake the size of the bride's little finger were threaded through the wedding ring (ideally nine times, the luckiest number for matrimony) "for the dreaming Emolument of many Spinsters & Batchelors," explained Lady Alice Houblon in *The Houblon Family* (1907). This dreaming emolument was like a tacit fertility "charm," an act of sympathetic magic the bride performed for her guests; later discrete slices of cake were packaged up in little white boxes for distribution to guests who never made it to the reception. The poet of *Progress of Matrimony* encapsulated the custom in 1733 in this way:

> But, madam, as a present take
> This little paper of bride-cake;
> Fast any Friday in the year,
> When Venus mounts the starry sphere,
> Thrust this at night in pillowbeer;
> In morning slumber you will seem
> T' enjoy your lover in a dream.

A Dughun *for the Newlyweds*

For Osmanli women of Turkey, their postnuptial celebrations, called *dughun*, begin when the bride temporarily returns to her parent's home. She removes her formal wedding clothes, then seats herself in the middle of the apartment. Her mother paints her right hand with henna paste, onto which the groom's mother affixes a gold coin; her female companions repeat the gesture. They cover this hand with a silken bag that she holds across her eyes, then they plaster and gild her left hand then her feet in the same manner. While the henna dries and stains to its characteristic ruddy orange, a troop of entertainers perform the *Sakusum,* a pantomimic dance with somewhat ribald, "immodest" inferences. Then the henna paste is removed so the bride's hands and feet won't turn black from overstaining.

The next day the bride is conveyed to the groom's home, accompanied by a great host of women in carriages and men on horseback and musicians walking along ahead on foot. She has already taken her ritual, teary leave of her father, in which he tied her bride's sash about her, hugged her, and received her kisses on his feet and hands. The groom welcomes her at the door of his house, escorts her to the bower in the bridal chamber, where the *koulavouz* (the attending matron) raises her veil after the groom departs. At prayer time the Imam adds a benediction for the newlyweds.

The groom now hurries back to the bridal chamber, as his friends pound him on the back and throw old shoes at him. He finds his bride standing on the edge of her veil, which has been laid on the floor as a delicate silken carpet. With her behind him, the groom kneels and makes a prayer. They move to the divan, sitting next to each other as the koulavouz holds a mirror before them, showing them for the first time the reflection of their united faces; she offers them her best wishes for a harmonious married life together. She takes a lump of sugar and puts it first in the bride's mouth, then the groom's, to remind them of the shared sweetness of their relationship. This sugar-sharing is succeeded by coffee, supper, and their first night together in the "bridal bed." The next

TURKEY
ROMANIA
HUNGARY
YUGOSLAVIA
GREECE
ITALY
CORSICA
RUSSIA

morning the couple enters the reception room hand-in-hand as the family members are eager to discern "whether their stars have met," namely, whether their union was sexually consummated. The couple tries to dissemble the truth as long as possible; they salute the groom's parents, enjoy a grand reception and meal at midday, and basically spend the next two days, well-fed and appreciated, sitting in array and taking congratulations from visitors.

Tipatul Grîului—
The Throwing of the Grain

After the crowning ceremony, the Romanian recessional begins when the groom's flag-bearer first steps out of the church, filled with wedding guests eager to welcome the newlyweds. The village women will scrutinize the precise manner in which the couple emerges from the church; if the bride steps across first, she will undoubtedly rule the household. In earlier days the godparents would stand before the couple holding up the *colac,* a circular loaf of bread with a hole in its middle. The couple would gaze at the sun through the colac's hole, then break it in half; whoever retained the larger piece would emerge as household authority. From here the wedding recessionals of the groom and bride proceed independently—with music, shouts, and vigorous flag-waving, of course—to their respective homes.

The family cook greets them at the front steps of their home by pelting the bride and groom with wheat grains. This is called tipatul grîului, the "throwing of the grain" as an expression of *belciug,* or bounty, the blessing of the hearth, symbolizing family, prosperity, and warmth made on behalf of the family and community by the one who epitomizes nurturance—the cook. She calls out verses

like these as she throws the wheat (*grîu,* the symbol of abundance and fertility):

I throw the wheat from this plate:
The groom is quite handsome
And the bride is also beautiful.
I throw the wheat from this plate:
The groom is a decent person
And the bride should be like him.
I throw wheat red as fire:
Beautiful may their luck be.
I throw flowers of wheat:
The groom's family is good.
I throw wheat, I don't throw rye:
The groom is the leader of the land.
I throw wheat beside the breads,
Over the groom, over the wedding guests,
And over the dear godparents.
God bless them with luck!

At the bride's house, her companions jest that the number of wheat grains she collects in her apron will be the number of her future offspring.

The wedding party now enters the house, where they find the musicians are seated on side benches around a series of feast tables laid out in a U formation, with places set on both sides of all tables. Each table displays its ritual ornaments and symbolic magical tokens of fertility: grains of wheat, a spindle of wool, colac with basil in its center. The wheat signifies abundance, the wool prosperity, and the colac holiness, all of which are present here to invoke positive, generous, supportive results for the newlyweds. The *paharnici* (glass-tenders) begin serving drinks, the musicians strike up a tune, and the protracted wedding feast begins. During the meal the groom dispatches emissaries (a male and female relative) to the bride's home, bearing gifts of food and drink, such as plum brandy and colac. This ritual exchange of nuptial foods is called giving *pominoc,* and is a central facet in the Romanian concept of social sustenance. The emissaries are graciously welcomed, then, forming a circle with the rest of the bride's party, they toast the bride and shout *strigaturi*, poetic declamations spoken to music. They return home to the groom's house and, while awaiting the reciprocal arrival of the bride's delegation, they shout more self-adulatory strigaturi about their journey and the bride's qualities:

I traveled well, I returned well
And was pleased by what you bargained for
Well I went, well I entered
And I was pleased by what you bought.
The road is long and muddy
I did it for love.

The Romanian postnuptials are lengthy and dramatic. At least two more major rituals—the *Cererea Mniresii*, "Asking for the Bride," and the *Horea Gainii*, "Song of the Hen," which concern the groom's acquisition of a comely bride and her incontestable virginity—complete with strigaturi, music, drama, and ribaldry, must be enacted at the groom's house before they can formally toast the bride. The groom's party escorts her to her new home's courtyard where she is greeted and honored by her new mother-in-law:

Long life to you because you are beautiful.
You speak well with your mouth,
You are lovely and decent:
Exactly what I like.
Green, green leaf—
Long life to my darling daughter-in-law.
If she'll be lovely and well behaved,
Everything will go forward.

Concluding her accolades, the groom's mother presents her daughter-in-law with two ritual breads, one on each arm, and two bottles of horinca (a fermented beverage), then kisses her on the cheek. Feasting, drinking, and continual toasting of the bride by the various family members will occupy everyone for three days. The wedding celebrations can be an exhausting ordeal for the couple, and they can hardly wait for the final postnuptial ritual, "Asking for the Bride," around

Monday midday, when family members and friends arrive from the bride's home. Basically they are here to steal her back, an intention that is acted out through a highly scripted dance in which members of both families form dancing circles and try to appropriate the bride into their circle. Eventually the bride's party admits defeat, they're feasted, and then depart, consoled to their loss.

The final stage of the wedding, the *Dezbracarea Mniresii*, Undressing of the Bride, is a parallel inversion of the earlier stage of dressing the bride before the wedding. Then they coached her with songs of separation, but now the matrons prepare the new wife for her marital consummation and the donning of the married woman's scarf around her head by singing strigaturi of incorporation. The matrons tell her to leave her wedding crown at her mother's house because she has joined the ranks of the matrons. The crown is placed on the head of a girl about four years old to ensure that one day she will legitimately wear the bride's crown too. The bride's mother will bury the crown in her garden where basil (a holy plant) and *tamîita* (an aromatic medicinal plant) will sprout in its memory. "You will no longer be a girl on the path. You won't go and come, for your husband will make love to you."

A Lakodalam *in the Hills and Valleys*

The word most frequently associated with Hungarian weddings is *lakodolam*, which means banquet, feasting, and carousing. The most exquisitely entertaining lakodolam is one "in the hills and in the valleys," which means a celebration that is gay, well-provisioned, amply toasted, and virtually endless.

TURKEY
ROMANIA
HUNGARY
YUGOSLAVIA
GREECE
ITALY
CORSICA
RUSSIA

TURKEY
ROMANIA
HUNGARY
YUGOSLAVIA
GREECE
ITALY
CORSICA
RUSSIA

After the church ceremony is finished, the wedding party leaves for the groom's home. The dowry cart, which bears the bride's "bed" (which is to say, her entire trousseau), the horses and their harness, are adorned with garlands of flowers and tinkling bells. As they pass through the village, somebody might smash a ceramic pot against the cart wheel, making the wish: "May this married couple part when this broken potsherd grows together." The groom's mother receives his new wife at the doorstep with lumps of sugar, declaring: "God brought you to us! May your life be as sweet as this sugar!" Next, she escorts the wife into her house, whereupon a series of dances begin immediately.

In the evening a banquet is staged, and the bride's entire family and household—called *hérész*—is invited; with her mother at the rear of the procession, they arrive bearing sweets, nuts, apples, a stuffed chicken, and a bottle of very sweet wine. The groom and his best man, the bride and her bridesmaids, stand on the porch holding lighted candles as they welcome the hérész. The feasting continues until midnight when the hérész departs, accompanied by the bridal couple. When the bride is at her parents' home again, her hair is put up, then the best man presents her formally to the groom, who kisses her; this is the signal for the Gypsy band to begin playing.

Around three o'clock in the morning, it's time for the Bride's Dance. To participate, every guest has to put money on a tray, all of which accrues to the bride afterward. The vigor of wine, song, and dance are intimately interdependent, as every Hungarian knows. "We have had a good wine harvest; it will give us full strength and a great wish for dancing!" proclaims the old folk poem. A sixteenth-century Hungarian nun once outlined the essentials for dancing the renowned *kállai kettős*: "The space shall be beautiful, wide, light, and peaceful; there shall be an abundance of food and strong liquor, the bodies of the dancers shall be beautiful, light, elegant, and strong."

The Buklijas *Renames the Wedding Guests*

Feasting surrounds the traditional wedding of Yugoslavian Krusevacs at both ends, before and after the church ceremony. Before the joining ritual, wedding guests drink *rikija* and other liqueurs at the bride's home in the morning. The *dever* (best man) holds out the *pogaca*, a large, round, flat, unleavened loaf of bread, for the guests to throw money on; he collects the money, pockets it, then holds the pogaca over the head of the bride, now kneeling. Now all the guests break off a piece, a formality called *grabite pogacu*, "grabbing the loaf."

After the ceremony the wedding party journeys on foot to the house of the groom's father accompanied by bagpipers. They're greeted at the gate by the *buklijas*, a young man with a wooden wine flask, flanked on either side by another man. The buklijas offers the wine first to the bride's father, who crosses himself then takes three drinks; then he offers it to the chief wedding guest (*stari svat*) and the chief male sponsor (*kum*). As the three men take their drinks, the rest of the party toasts and celebrates them. However, a fair number of rituals must be performed before anybody will enter the house.

Now the buklijas leads the bride and her wedding party up to the house through an archway of entwined flowers. Just before they enter, he picks up a sieve that contains an apple, maize, and a posy of flowers, and hands it to the groom's mother, who presents it to the bride. She scatters the maize kernels among the guests, flings the posy, and tosses the apple, then she throws the sieve onto the roof, where it will remain for a couple of months. In some instances the bride may do this while standing on a sack of grain. As the bridal couple and *dever* advance to the front door, a woman steps forward before them carrying her three-year-old son; she presents the male child to the groom, who foists him up in his arms three times, kissing him, then hands him to the bride, who repeats his gesture, gives him a shirt, and returns him to his mother. Through a kind of sympathetic magic, it's hoped that the handling of a young male child will lead to the birth of their own son in about a year.

Next the groom's mother presents the groom with a little pot of honey. He scoops some up with the middle finger of his right hand and puts it to his wife's lips. Then his mother hands the bride two loaves and two liters of wine, putting them under her arms; she enters the house alone and sets her bread and wine down on the kitchen counter, then the groom follows. When all the guests have entered, the bride sits on her mother-in-law's lap on a stool as the buklijas scatters water from a pitcher on the floor, saying: "Make water, O mother-in-law!" The bride stands up, kisses her mother-in-law, and gives the buklijas a pair of socks.

With all these formalities of greeting and gift-giving completed, the wedding guests sit down for a big meal, as a *cigani* band plays in the background and people break into song. After dinner the younger members of the party dance the *kolo* with the bride, while the older folk drink wine and sing songs—all of which can easily last until dawn. It's the stari svat's responsibility to announce the end of festivities. He gestures for the buklijas to bring a sieve containing a little maize. Standing with the bride before the stari svat, the buklijas gives each guest a new nickname, honorific nuptial names they must use in the future.

As each guest accepts his nuptial nom de plume, he puts a coin in the sieve while the buklijas chants: "Six hundred, five hundred, and the bride! I hail thee by the new name of . . . !" Finally the buklijas adds his own dinar to the hoard in the sieve, then knocks the bride and groom three times

on the forehead with it, to settle the matter. Now the groom presents all the guests with small gifts: blouses or scarves for the women, toys for the children, and pointed caps of black sheep's wool for the men. The stari svat bundles up the dinars in a handkerchief and presents it to the bride. With the cigani band in tow, the bridal couple escorts the stari svat and guests to the courtyard gate and bids them goodnight.

Wedding Feast as Family Communion

For the Sarakatsani shepherds of rural contemporary Greece, the wedding feast is an expanded version of the family communion of bread and wine, both of which have strong symbolic content among most Mediterranean cultures. Bread is more than a symbol of life. It is a composite of many grains, molded and baked to form one substance; so when it's broken into pieces, it symbolizes the sharing of life, a community at peace, and a family bound together by common principles. Wine symbolizes the blood, the life-fluid— "To your wedding! To the marriages of your sons!" declare the toasters. In recognition of this, each guest brings a round loaf of bread, a wooden bottle of wine, and some roasted lamb to the wedding feast. There they will eat, drink, toast, and dance, with the uninhibited wail of the clarinets of the gypsy band in the background.

In some instances the bride and groom may sit on an elevated wooden platform as the jubilant wedding guests toast their health and prosperity, and throw rice and cotton seed at them. When the bridal couple first arrives at the house of the groom's mother, she may present the bride with a glass of honey and water. The bride sips this

TURKEY
ROMANIA
HUNGARY
YUGOSLAVIA
GREECE
ITALY
CORSICA
RUSSIA

TURKEY
ROMANIA
HUNGARY
YUGOSLAVIA
GREECE
ITALY
CORSICA
RUSSIA

so that the words from her lips may sound as sweet as honey; her mother-in-law smears the lintels of the doorway so strife will never enter their married home; another of the wedding party will smash a pomegranate on the threshold as a token of the prolific seeds for future progeny; or the couple may share a quince, to ensure that their conversation would forevermore be as sweet as the taste of this fruit; the quince's bittersweet taste also reminds them that they have taken each other "for better, for worse, the bitter with the sweet." In Kilkis, Macedonia, the bride's brother breaks a large round pie on her head (painlessly, one hopes) as she stands on the threshold, then distributes the pieces to all the guests.

We see many of these elements dramatized in the postnuptial celebrations in Rhodes. Celebratory exchanges precede and succeed the actual joining rituals in the church. First comes mutual gift-giving: the groom sends his bride a skirt, braided jacket, shoes, and a gold-embroidered veil, while she gives him a silken shirt and an embroidered tobacco pouch. When she is dressed in her full nuptial costume, her palms are anointed with cinnamon. Musicians enter her chamber and make pantomime gestures, passing their instruments over her head as a kind of musical blessing.

After the joining ritual, the couple is conducted to their new home, the dowry gift of the bride. The husband dips his finger in a honey pot and makes a cross in honey over the door, while his companions cry out: "Be good and sweet as this honey is!" Next he trods a fresh pomegranate on the doorstep, a gesture his wife repeats. As they enter the home, the wedding guests shower them with corn, cotton-seeds, and orange-blossom water. Once inside, the couple takes their seats and the musicians repeat their musical blessing pantomime. The bride kneels and kisses the hands of her husband's parents, then is led to a neighboring house for a private meal. All the guests receive a honeyed sesame-cake. At dusk the dancing and festivities begin, and they may last for two full

days. The home's patron saint is honored, too: the water on which floats the oil in the lamp before his icon is replaced by wine.

A Cluster of Bridal Confetti

In Italian hill town weddings, the banquet is held at the bride's home, but the high spirits begin the moment the new married couple steps out of the church. Guns may be fired in the air, almonds thrown at the children, flowers and corn kernels thrown at the bridal couple, and plates smashed. As the guests wait for dinner to be announced, they admire the display of the numerous wedding gifts, flower bouquets, telegrams, nuptial cards received from well-wishers throughout the community. A customary wedding gift is a basket of ripe corncobs with a bottle of wine festooned with flowers, and the salutation: "As many grains, so many good wishes for your happiness." Mothers of the couple may give them several nuptial baskets: one basket has nine loaves of bread, whose crusts are ornamented with sesame seeds in figures of birds and doves; another basket contains nine candies of almond paste in the form of doves, hearts, rings, and chains, four of which are set in pairs to symbolize the couple's freshly completed union. The mother may write or tell her daughter directly: "I bless you for every drop of my milk that I have given you. Be happy!"

The wedding meal is sumptuous to excess, guaranteed to render everyone more than happy, as if the intent were to provide more courses than even the stoutest eater could pack away in a night's work with knife and fork. When the *spumante* (a foamy dessert) is served, this signals the most distinguished men to offer their formal but sometimes hilarious nuptial toasts. Then the bridal couple tours the banquet hall, greeting each guest with

WHAT THEY THREW AT THEM—VARIATIONS ON A CONFETTI THEME

Bridal couples have been perennially subjected to having things thrown at them. And for couples around the world, rice is the least of their worries:

- The English interpreted the spirit of confetti broadly, fashioning mixed bags of paper symbols, such as horseshoes, slippers, and hearts, or simply minute circles and streamers of multicolored tissue paper. English bridal couples might be pummeled with paper rose petals, lucky horseshoes, silver satin slippers, or old boots.
- "The English, when the bride comes from church, are wont to cast wheat upon her head," noted Thomas Muffet in *Health's Improvement* (1665).
- Among affluent Persians earlier in the twentieth century, it was customary for the groom to throw fistfuls of *noql* (little pieces of sugar-coated almonds) and silver coins to the admiring crowds lining the streets after the service, symbolically sharing his nuptial opulence with the community.
- In Tibet, by way of commencing the three days of wedding celebration, the officiating lama would put the ceremonial rice-cake on the heads of the couple and through this confer his blessings for a long life, health, wealth, and progeny. The bride, about to cross the threshold of her new home for the first time, is given a cup filled with flour and butter and an arrow festooned with silken streamers. The lama performs a purificatory exorcism on her by hitting her head with a stack of sacred texts; in retaliation the leader of her bridal party taps the lama with a stick; after this everyone laughs, and presumably the bride doesn't have a headache.
- One Korean groom no doubt wished his well-wishers would only throw confetti at him. In one instance observed in the 1960s, male friends of the groom seized the newly minted and somewhat inebriated husband, bound his feet together, and strung him upside down from a beam. Even then they didn't ply his palate with sweet confections; no, they beat the soles of his feet with a stick, demanding him to sponsor another great feast for them very soon.

Confetti may also be offered as a way of influencing, by sympathetic magic, the couple's future food supply or affluence.

- Couples in the Duke of York islands stood together as well-wishers opened a coconut over their heads and dribbled the rich milk over their bodies.
- In Andrja, Morocco, the groom's mother throws bread and dried fruit over the couple's *ammariya*, or "bridal box," to ensure the couple will always have plenty to eat.
- Among certain clans in the Philippines, the bridal couple performs a stylized wedding dance called *ado*, during which their guests throw money at their feet, an act known as *gala*.
- Vietnamese wedding feasts were more straightforward: a collection of cash gifts was taken from the guests for the bridal couple.

TURKEY
ROMANIA
HUNGARY
YUGOSLAVIA
GREECE
ITALY
CORSICA
RUSSIA

a cluster or tiny box of bridal confetti. We normally think of confetti as shredded pits of colored paper, but when the Italians invented it, it wasn't paper they used, but sugared almonds. Technically the small disks of paper, distributed with abandon at carnivals, are called *coriandoli*, "coriander seeds"; but whether it's sugared almonds, coriandoli, or spring almond blossoms spontaneously whipped by the wind "into a shower of white petals, confetti for Carnival and for weddings, [it's] a symbolic sowing that links field and family in a prayer for fertility, for new crops and new generations," explains Mary Taylor Simeti in *On Persephone's Island: A Sicilian Journal.*

Corsican wedding feasts offer an array of confetti pastries and cakes, such as macaroons, delicate cheesecakes baked on grapevine leaves, and sometimes an elaborate confection made of spun caramel sugar, twisted and baked into a pyramid of spirals. As daunting to the Corsican teeth and gums as such a confection might be, it's not meant to be sliced anyway. Wedding guests pulverize it with hammers, then scoop up the tiny pieces in bowls for a light dessert. The day after the wedding, guests may be sent mementos of the celebration, in particular, elaborate arrangements of confetti, such as an ornate ashtray bearing five white candies, wrapped with ribbons and flowers and a gift card from the bridal couple.

The Zolochenie—*Gilding the Bride and Groom*

When Vladimir and Marfa came home from the church after their wedding ritual in 1860, his parents greeted them with ceremonial bread and salt, recounts Mary Matossian in *The Peasant in Nineteenth Century Russia.* Vladimir's

parents bless them both, sprinkling them with hops and kernels of grain; Vladimir's father removes the bride's veil, then escorts them to their special seat at the table beside the family icons.

As a variation sixteenth-century couples, upon stepping out of the church, were presented a loaf of bread by the bride's father; they gave it to the priest, who broke it into pieces eaten by the couple as a declaration of their sincere agreement and to symbolize that they would be like pieces of a single loaf. Among the Usviats, the groom's father greets the arriving couple with a cloth-covered tray with bread, salt, and two wine glasses. The groom's mother clasps an icon in one hand, the hem of her skirt with the other. The husband and wife drink part of the wine, then toss the remainder over their shoulders and smash the goblets against the porch "for good luck." Then the mother sprinkles them with grain, candy, and coins she had tucked up in her skirt, "so they will be healthy, happy, and have many children." They're offered a slice of bread "so they will be well-fed all their lives." As they enter the house, they tred upon a thick winter coat (or rug or blanket) "so they will be rich."

During the wedding feast, Marfa and Vladimir will take their meal privately, behind a partition or in another room. After eating they rejoin the wedding party in full celebratory throttle; everyone of course is singing, drinking, dancing, and with the arrival of the bridal couple, toasting. The toasters wax eloquent with their superlatives, comparing Vladimir and Marfa to a white swan and falcon, a duck and drake, a pair of doves, the moon and sun, a pearl and *iakhoni* (ruby, sapphire, or amethyst), a marten and a hunter, a grape vine that entwines a post or oak tree. No doubt blushing from the encomiums, Marfa presents her guests with little sweets (desserts of roasted almonds, pistachios, and fruits possibly with wine and honeyed cake), and they in turn give her and Vladimir money—a friendly "gilding" rite called *zolochenie,* as a gesture of gilding their marital life now beginning with the wealth of gold and silver.

Vladimir and Marfa might also discover their shoes have been filled with poppy seeds.

At the close of the feast, Vladimir's best man and his *svakha* (married aunt) lead the couple to their bedroom, as the inebriated guests burst forth into bawdy songs and ribald anecdotes. In the morning the best man and svakha wake the couple to collect their bedsheet or Marfa's shift, which presumably is stained red with hymeneal blood, as proof of her virginity and "innocence." They parade this marital document around the house while beating earthen pots, a ritual sometimes called "breaking pots."

Vladimir and Marfa take a cleansing steam bath together, then travel to her parent's home for the *chuloba* ritual. During a breakfast of omelettes, Vladimir drops a couple of coins into a glass of wine and hands it to his wife, a sign everyone understands as his acknowledgment that his wife is "honorable"—she was a virgin until her wedding night. As an alternative he might tie a red flower to a bottle of wine—or a white flower, if his wife had proved to be sexually experienced. There will be two more days of serious celebration, including skits by mummers, dressed in drag, or as hunchbacks, gypsies, or bears, who enact scenes, often erotic, from family and social life. On the third day, Marfa will finally remove her scarf, dance, and make merry with the guests.

The Yichud: *Post-Wedding Seclusion*

The epithalamium is more than a serenade by friends before the bedroom door as the virginal bride and groom discover each other's sexual and relational depths. In a sense it's a farewell, a discrete leave-taking, a respect for the bridal cou-

ple's profound need at this point for intimacy, privacy, and seclusion. The community has brought them safely, generously, triumphantly to the *thalamus,* the nuptial bed, ushering them graciously through a mythopoeic sequence of rituals, confirmations, and acclaims known as the wedding process. So here they reside, together, yet another living, precious example of the archetypal human couple launched on the "month of honey," the first blissful days of married life.

The moment of consummation isn't necessarily a sexual joining. Rather, as the Hebrew postwedding custom of *yichud* has it, it's a moment of silent communion, of resting, residing in the silence together apart from the clamor and demands, even the good wishes of one's family, friends, and wedding guests. The yichud is the final act that seals the marriage, and it begins immediately after the formal joining ceremony in the synagogue.

Yichud is the quiet moment, the calm interlude between days of preparation past and hours of joyous partying to come. It's a moment during which these two profound "solitudes" can acknowledge each other, as Rainer Maria Rilke would say, and through this gesture of acknowledgment forge a sustainable spiritual connection. "I'll pursue solitary pathways through the pale twilit meadows, with only this one dream: You come too," Rilke says.

A private chamber is provisioned with food near the chuppah; as the couple has been fasting for close to a day, this will be their first food taken together on their wedding day. Here they spend at least ten minutes in seclusion having their first food, as two members of the wedding party bear witness outside the door. Jewish spiritual law requires the married couple to reside together in seclusion for a week—not to work or separate from each other. Friends of the couple recite the Sheva Berakhot every day on the couple's behalf as they "rejoice one another." Only after a week has passed should the couple contemplate taking a

MAIDENHOOD,
O MAIDENHOOD

*T*he practice of presenting the stained bedsheet as proof of virginity, which strikes our "sexually liberated" American sensibility as rude and invasive—was widespread and unquestioned among Mediterranean, Slavic, and Islamic cultures, and in fact continues today. The custom originates perhaps not so much from a prudish, puritanical reserve, if not prohibition, about sexuality as from a reverential attitude that sees sexual intercourse as a sacramental experience most honored by saving it for the nuptial evening.

"When we truly understand our sexuality, we come face-to-face with the mystery of the spirit," observes Georg Feuerstein in Sacred Sexuality: Living the Vision of the Erotic Spirit. Our times are marked not so much by unlicensed sexual freedom and mature expression as by sexual malaise, argues Feuerstein, which itself is rooted in a "deeper spiritual dilemma: the obscuration of the sacred dimension."

One antidote, Feuerstein suggests, is the reintegration of sexuality with spirituality in the Western psyche as sacred sexuality, which is about "recovering our authentic being, which knows bliss beyond mere pleasurable sensations. It is a special form of communication, even communion, that fills us with awe and stillness." Traditional cultures seem to have recognized this to some degree, as witnessed by the widespread custom of singing epithalamia (by children, maidens, or bachelors) before the bridal chamber on the night of the wedding, such as this Greek epithalamium written by Sappho:

> Maidenhood, O Maidenhood
> Where art thou flown away from me?
> Never again shall I come back,
> Never again back to thee.
> Bridegroom dear, to what shall I compare thee?
> To a slim green rod best do I compare thee.

honeymoon, in the sense of traveling away from their new home.

Allowing this space for uninterrupted meeting is the spirit behind honeymoon, the last act in this majestic nuptial drama. Newly married Bulgarian couples are required to observe a week of seclusion in their home during which time they don't receive visitors or go out. At the end of the *solitude à deux,* matrons arrive at the house to conduct the bride to the well; she walks with them carrying two water-pails slung yoke-fashion around her neck. She circumambulates the well three times, making an offering to the *genii loci,* the presumed water spirits of the well. She fills her pails with well water, then the matrons empty their contents all over her in a matronly shower. She kisses their hands and they each give her a fig.

From this moment forward, as she shakes off the rivulets of water from her hair and dress and tastes the sweet juicy fig, this Bulgarian matron, as all married women—and men—is now launched, chastened and fortified, into what the American poet Wendell Berry calls "the country of marriage." In that matrimonial land there is "a forest in which there is a graceful clearing and in that opening a house, an orchard and garden, comfortable shades, and flowers." The forest is mostly dark, but it's a gleaming dark that's "richer than the light and more blessed," provided one has the bravura to keep on going in, the bravery to keep renewing, and the fortitude to make "a new day after day."

I'd like to think that these qualities properly describe the aspirations of the world culture wedding, the fruit of our weddings by design. Because the wedding, despite all its possibilities for imaginative design, is only the beginning of the encounter between two human beings. Looked at in this new light, the design of your wedding—from betrothal to honeymoon—will resemble a kind of matrimonial architecture, in which stable and spiritually meaningful foundations are likely to produce a durable, satisfying, and illuminating marriage.

TURKEY
ROMANIA
HUNGARY
YUGOSLAVIA
GREECE
ITALY
CORSICA
RUSSIA

Abrahams, Israel. *Jewish Life in the Middle Ages.* London: The Macmillan Company, 1897.

Abrahams. I. "Marriage (Jewish)." In *Encyclopaedia of Religion and Ethics,* vol. 8, edited by James Hastings. New York: Charles Scribner's Sons, 1916.

Aglarov, M. A. "Forms of Marriage and Certain Features of Wedding Ceremonial Among the 19th Century Andii." *Soviet Anthropology and Archaeology* 3, no. 4 (Spring 1965).

Amegah, Shell Slaton. "Weddings with Personality." *Bride's* (December 1991/January 1992).

Ames, Katrine, with Kendall Hamilton. "For Better, for Worse." *Newsweek* (February 15, 1993).

Ammar, Hamed. *Growing Up in an Egyptian Village: Silwa, Province of Aswan.* London: Routledge & Kegan Paul Ltd., 1954.

Anesaki, Masaharu. "Japanese." In *The Mythology of All Races,* vol. 8, edited by Canon John Arnott MacCulloch. Boston: Archeological Institute of America, Marshall Jones Company, 1928.

Archer, William G. *Songs for the Bride: Wedding Rites of Rural India.* New York: Columbia University Press, 1985.

Arisian, Khoren. *The New Wedding: Creating Your Own Marriage Ceremony.* New York: Vintage/Random House, 1973.

Ausubel, Nathan. *The Book of Jewish Knowledge.* New York: Crown Publishers, 1964.

Aziz, Barbara Nimri, translator. "A Pillar So Straight." *Parabola* 7, no. 3 (1982).

Babeva, R. "Materials for the Study of Marriage Ceremonies on the Apsheron Peninsula in the Past." *Soviet Anthropology and Archaeology* 6, no. 2 (Fall 1967).

Bacon, George B. *Siam: The Land of the White Elephant, As It Was and Is.* New York: Charles Scribner's Sons, 1893.

Barber, Benjamin R. "Jihad Vs. McWorld." *The Atlantic* 269, no. 3 (March 1992).

Barclay, Harold B. *Buurri Al Lamaab: A Suburban Village in the Sudan.* Ithaca: Cornell University Press, 1964.

Barringer, Felicity. "Rate of Marriage Continues Decline." *The New York Times* (July 17, 1992).

Bastien, Joseph W. *Mountain of the Condor: Metaphor and Ritual in an Andean Ayllu.* St. Paul: West Publishing Co., 1978.

Batchelor, Rev. John. *The Ainu of Japan: The Religion, Superstitions, and General History of the Hairy Aborigines of Japan.* New York: Fleming H. Revell Company, 1943.

Beardsley, Richard K., John W. Hall, and Robert E. Ward, *Village Japan.* Chicago: The University of Chicago Press, 1959.

Beauchamp, Henry K. *Hindu Manners, Customs, and Ceremonies.* London: Oxford at the Clarendon Press, 1928.

Bell, Sir Charles. *The People of Tibet.* London: Oxford at the Clarendon Press, 1928.

Belshaw, Cyril S. *Under the Ivi Tree: Society and Economic Growth in Rural Fiji.* Berkeley: University of California Press, 1964.

Belshaw, Michael. *A Village Economy: Land and People of Huecorio,* New York: Columbia University Press, 1967.

Benedict, Ruth. *The Chrysanthemum and the Sword: Patterns of Japanese Culture.* Boston: Houghton Mifflin Company, 1946.

Bennett, J. G. *Gurdjieff: Making a New World.* London: Turnstone Books, 1973.

Berreman, Gerald D. *Hindus of the Himalayas.* Berkeley: University of California Press, 1963.

Biesanz, John and Mavis. *Costa Rican Life.* New York: Columbia University Press, 1944.

Blackman, Winifred S. *The Fellahin of Upper Egypt.* London: Frank Cass & Co., 1968.

Boner, Charles. *Transylvania: Its Products and Its People.* London: Longmans, Green, Reader and Dyer, 1865.

Bord, Janet and Colin. *The Secret Country: More Mysterious Britain.* St. Albans: Paladin/Granada Publishing, 1978.

Bowers, Alfred W. *Mandan Social and Ceremonial Organization.* Chicago: The University of Chicago Press, 1950.

Bradburd, Daniel. "The Rules and the Game: The Practice of Marriage among the Komachi." *American Ethnologist* 11, no. 4 (November 1984).

Brady, Lois Smith. "Vows—Adrienne Thomas and Steven Harper." *The New York Times* (October 18, 1992).

———. "Vows—Amelia Marshall and Daryl Waters." *The New York Times* (December 6, 1992).

———. "Vows—Andrea Marcovicci, Daniel Reichert." *The New York Times* (February 7, 1993).

———. "Vows—Angela Gomez, Wayne Sinhart." *The New York Times* (December 13, 1992).

———. "Vows—Annette Andrada, Robert Babich." *The New York Times* (August 2, 1992).

———. "Vows—Annie Towe and George Egan." *The New York Times* (May 17, 1992).

———. "Vows—Brunilda Burgos and Adalberto Rodriguez." *The New York Times* (May 3, 1992).

———. "Vows—Candice Solomon, Louis Michel Doyon." *The New York Times* (February 21, 1993).

———. "Vows—Cynthia Rhea and Harry Woods." *The New York Times* (September 20, 1992).

———. "Vows—Elizabeth Egan and Emanuel Stern." *The New York Times* (June 28, 1992).

———. "Vows—Francine Friedman, Arun Alagappan." *The New York Times* (September 13, 1992).

———. "Vows—Glynis Karp and Scotty Greenberg." *The New York Times* (September 6, 1992).

———. "Vows—Joan Hardy, Stephen O'Brien." *The New York Times* (August 8, 1992).

———. "Vows—Joanna Romano and Joe Restuccia." *The New York Times* (May 31, 1992).

———. "Vows—Josefa Mulaire and William Tester." *The New York Times* (June 7, 1992).

———. "Vows—Julie Halston, Ralph Howard." *The New York Times* (August 16, 1992).

———. "Vows—Kathy Phillips and Jake Daehler." *The New York Times* (May 24, 1992).

———. "Vows—Kyoko Soda and Shuji Nakano." *The New York Times* (May 10, 1992).

———. "Vows—Leslie Montana and David Joseph." *The New York Times* (November 8, 1992).

———. "Vows—Linda Harris, Michael Paolillo." *The New York Times* (January 31, 1993).

———. "Vows—Lucie Pastoriza and Ken Sharples." *The New York Times* (April 11, 1993).

———. "Vows—Lucy Schulte and James Danziger." *The New York Times* (September 27, 1992).

———. "Vows—Marily Foo and Gary Au." *The New York Times* (January 10, 1993).

———. "Vows—Mary Beth Love, Michael Russom." *The New York Times* (July 26, 1992).

———. "Vows—Mary Lou Hotesse and Norberto Delgado." *The New York Times* (August 30, 1992).

———. "Vows—Maryanne Blacker, Nicholas Baker." *The New York Times* (January 24, 1993).

———. "Vows—Melissa Burtt and Allan Smith, Jr." *The New York Times* (December 27, 1992).

————. "Vows—Mimi Lister and Sheldon Toney." *The New York Times* (August 23, 1992).

————. "Vows—Scottie Mirviss and Paul Carvajal." *The New York Times* (October 11, 1992).

————. "Vows—Shayna Hendel, Chaim Meiseles." *The New York Times* (December 20, 1992).

————. "Vows—Steven Holl and Janet Cross." *The New York Times* (November 22, 1992).

————. "Vows—Tracy Horton and Jon Leshay." *The New York Times* (October 4, 1992).

Braha, James T. *Ancient Hindu Astrology for the Modern Western Astrologer.* North Miami: Hermetician Press, 1986.

Brand, John. *Observations on the Popular Antiquities of Great Britain.* London: George Bell and Sons, 1882.

Brandes, Stanley H. "Wedding Ritual and Social Structure in a Castilian Peasant Village." *Anthropological Quarterly* 46, no. 2 (April 1973).

Brochner, Jessie. *Danish Life in Town and Country.* New York: G. P. Putnam's Sons, 1903.

Brooks, Andrée. "Wedding Bells, Dotted Lines." *The New York Times* (December 19, 1992).

Brubach, Holly. "For Better or for Worse?" *The New Yorker* (July 10, 1989).

Bunzel, Ruth. *Chichicastenango: A Guatemalan Village.* Seattle: University of Washington Press, 1959.

Burkhardt, V. R. *Chinese Creeds and Custom,* vol. 1. Hong Kong: South China Morning Post, 1953.

Butler, Becky, editor. *Ceremonies of the Heart: Celebrating Lesbian Unions.* Seattle: The Seal Press, 1990.

Caico, Louise. *Sicilian Ways and Days.* New York: D. Appleton and Company, 1910.

Campbell, Joseph, and Henry Morton Robinson. *A Skeleton Key to Finnegans Wake.* New York: Penguin Books, 1977.

Campbell, J. K. *Honour, Family, and Patronage: A Study of Institutions and Moral Values in a Greek Mountain Community.* Oxford: Clarendon Press, 1964.

Caplan, Lionel. "A Himalayan People: Limbus of Nepal." In *South Asia: Seven Community Profiles,* edited by Clarence Maloney. New York: Holt, Rinehart and Winston, 1974.

Chandruang, Kumut. *My Boyhood in Siam.* New York: The John Day Company, 1938.

Christiano, Donna. "The New Look of African American Weddings." *Glamour* (May 1993).

Cocks, Jay. "Scenes From a Marriage." *Time* (July 7, 1986).

Cohen, David, editor. *The Circle of Life: Rituals from the Human Family Album.* San Francisco: HarperSanFrancisco, 1991.

Cole, Hariette. *Jumping the Broom: The African-American Wedding Planner.* New York: Henry Holt & Company, 1993.

Collier, John, Jr., and Anibal Buitron. *The Awakening Valley.* Chicago: The University of Chicago Press, 1949.

Cook, Anthony. "The $60,000 Wedding." *Boston* (May 1990).

Crawley, Ernest. *The Mystic Rose: A Study of Primitive Marriage and of Primitive Thought in Its Bearing on Marriage.* New York: Meridian Books, 1960.

Dan, Nguyen Trieu. *A Vietnamese Family Chronicle: Twelve Generations on the Banks of the Hat River.* Jefferson, North Carolina: McFarland & Company, 1991.

Das, Sarat Chandra. *Journey to Lhasa and Central Tibet.* New Delhi: Manjusri Publishing House, 1970.

Davis, William Stearns. *Life on a Mediaeval Barony.* New York: Harper & Brothers, 1923.

Deane, Shirley. *In a Corsican Village.* New York: The Vanguard Press, 1965.

de Bunsen, Victoria. *The Soul of a Turk.* London: John Lane/The Bodley Head, 1933.

de Courcillon, Eugene. *Le Curé Manqué, or, Social and Religious Customs in France.* New York: Harper & Brothers, 1855.

De Pina-Cabral, Joao. *Sons of Adam, Daughters of Eve: The Peasant Worldview of the Alto Minho*. Oxford: Clarendon Press, 1986.

deYoung, John E. *Village Life in Modern Thailand*. Berkeley: University of California Press, 1963.

Diamant, Anita. *The New Jewish Wedding*. New York: Summit Books, 1985.

Dillard, Annie. *Holy the Firm*. New York: Harper & Row, 1977.

Doolittle, Rev. Justus. *Social Life of the Chinese*, vol. 2. New York: Harper & Brothers, 1865.

Dreyer, Ronnie Gale. *Indian Astrology: A Western Approach to the Ancient Hindu Art*. Wellingborough, England: Aquarian Press/Thorsons, 1990.

Driver, Tom F. *The Magic of Ritual: Our Need for Liberating Rites that Transform Our Lives & Our Communities*. San Francisco: HarperSanFrancisco, 1991.

Dube, S. C. *Indian Village*. New York: Harper Colophon Books, 1967.

Duby, Georges, editor. *A History of Private Life, II: Revelations of the Medieval World*. Cambridge: Belknap Press of Harvard University Press, 1988.

du Chaillu, Paul B. *The Viking Age: The Early History, Manners, and Customs of the Ancestors of the English-Speaking Nations*, vol. 2. New York: Charles Scribner's Sons, 1890.

————. *The Land of the Midnight Sun: Summer and Winter Journeys Through Sweden, Norway, Lapland and Northern Finland*. New York: Harper & Brothers, 1882.

Dumezil, Georges. *Archaic Roman Religion*, vol. 2. Chicago: University of Chicago Press, 1970.

Eberhard, Wolfram. *Chinese Festivals*. New York: Henry Schuchman, 1952.

Edwards, Walter. *Modern Japan Through Its Weddings: Gender, Person, and Society in Ritual Portrayal*. Stanford: Stanford University Press, 1989.

Eliade, Mircea. *Cosmos and History: The Myth of the Eternal Return*. New York: Harper Torchbooks, 1959.

Elwell, Dennis. *Cosmic Loom: The New Science of Astrology*. London: Unwin Hyman, 1987.

Embree, John F. *Suye Mura: A Japanese Village*. Chicago: University of Chicago Press, 1939.

Emmett, Isabel. *A North Wales Village: A Social Anthropological Study*. London: Routledge & Kegan Paul, 1964.

Evans, M. Filmer. *The Land and People of Korea*. London: Adam and Charles Black, 1962.

Fakhouri, Hani. *Kafr El-Elow: An Egyptian Village in Transition*. New York: Holt, Rinehart and Winston, 1972.

Farnell, Lewis Richard. *The Cults of the Greek States*, vol. 5. London: Oxford at the Clarendon Press, 1909.

————. *The Cults of the Greek States*, vol. 3. London: Oxford at the Clarendon Press, 1907.

————. *The Cults of the Greek States*, vol. 1. London: Oxford at the Clarendon Press, 1896.

Fei, Hsiao-Tung. *Peasant Life in China: A Field Study of Country Life in the Yangtze Valley*. New York: E. P. Dutton & Company, 1939.

Fenner, Kay Toy. *American Catholic Etiquette*. Westminster, MD: The Newman Press, 1962.

Feuerstein, Georg. *Sacred Sexuality: Living the Vision of the Erotic Spirit*. Los Angeles: Jeremy P. Tarcher, 1992.

Fitzwalter, Bernard. *The Complete Sun Sign Guide*. Wellingborough, England: The Aquarian Press, 1987.

Foster, George M. *Tzintzuntzan: Mexican Peasants in a Changing World*. Boston: Little, Brown and Company, 1967.

Fowler, W. Warde. "Marriage (Roman)." In *Encyclopaedia of Religion and Ethics*, vol. 8, edited by James Hastings. New York: Charles Scribner's Sons, 1916.

Frederic, Louis. *Daily Life in Japan at the Time of the Samurai 1185–1603*. New York: Praeger Publishers, 1972.

Freedman, Maurice. *Chinese Family and Marriage in Singapore.* Colonial Research Studies, no. 20. London: Her Majesty's Stationery Office, 1957.

Fried, Martha Nemes, and Morton H. Fried. *Transitions: Four Rituals in Eight Cultures.* New York: W. W. Norton & Company, New York, 1980.

Gamble, Sidney D. *Ting Hsien: A North China Rural Community.* New York: International Secretariat Institute of Pacific Relations, 1954.

Garnett, Lucy M. J. *The Women of Turkey and Their Folk-Lore: The Christian Women.* London: David Nutt, 1890.

———. *Turkey of the Ottomans.* New York: Charles Scribner's Sons, 1911.

———. *The Women of Turkey and Their Folk-Lore: The Jewish and Moslem Women.* London: David Nutt, 1891.

———. *Turkish Life in Town and Country.* New York: G. P. Putnam's Sons, 1904.

Gennaro, Gino. *The Phenomena of Avalon.* London: Cronos Publications, 1979.

Gernet, Jacques. *Daily Life in China on the Eve of the Mongol Invasion 1250–1276.* Stanford: Stanford University Press, 1962.

Gies, Frances and Joseph. *Marriage and the Family in the Middle Ages.* New York: Perennial Library, Harper & Row, 1987.

Gifford, Rev. Daniel L. *Every-Day Life in Korea: A Collection of Studies and Stories.* Chicago: Fleming H. Revell Company, 1898.

Gillis, John R. *For Better, For Worse: British Marriages, 1600 to the Present.* New York: Oxford University Press, 1985.

Ginzberg, Louis. *The Legends of the Jews,* vol. 1. Philadelphia: The Jewish Publication Society of America, 1909.

Graves, Robert. *The White Goddess.* New York: Farrar, Straus & Giroux, 1948.

Grayzel, Solomon. *A History of the Jews.* Philadelphia: The Jewish Publication Society of America, 1947.

Greene, Liz. *Astrology for Lovers.* York Beach, ME: Samuel Weiser, 1989.

Greenglass, Esther R. "A Social-Psychological View of Marriage for Women." *International Journal of Women's Studies* 8, no. 1 (January/February 1985).

Griffis, William Elliot. *Korea: The Hermit Nation.* New York: Charles Scribner's Sons, 1882.

Guggenbühl-Craig, Adolf. *Marriage, Dead or Alive.* Dallas: Spring Publications, 1977.

Guppy, Shusha. *The Blindfold Horse: Memories of a Persian Childhood.* London: Heinemann, 1988.

Hall, Florence Howe. *Social Customs.* Boston: Dana Estes & Co., 1911.

Halpern, Joel M. *A Serbian Village.* New York: Harper & Row, 1956.

Hamlin, Cyrus. *Among the Turks.* New York: Robert Carter and Brothers, 1878.

Harding, Michael, and Charles Harvey. *Working with Astrology: The Psychology of Harmonics, Midpoints, and Astro-Carto-Graphy.* London: Arkana/Penguin, 1990.

Harris, Lis. *Holy Days: The World of a Hasidic Family.* New York: Summit Books, 1985.

Hart, Donn V. *Compadrinazgo: Ritual Kinship in the Philippines.* De Kalb: Northern Illinois University Press, 1977.

Hazlitt, W. Carew. *Faiths and Folklores: A Dictionary.* London: Reeves and Turner, 1905.

Headland, Isaac Taylor. *Home Life in China.* New York: The Macmillan Company, 1914.

Heindel, Max. *The Message of the Stars: An Esoteric Exposition of Natal and Medical Astrology,* 16th ed. Oceanside, CA: Rosicrucian Fellowship, 1973.

Helias, Pierre-Jakez. *The Horse of Pride: Life in a Breton Village.* New Haven: Yale University Press, 1978.

Hendry, Joy. *Marriage in Changing Japan: Community and Society.* New York: St. Martin's Press, 1981.

Hershman, Paul. *Punjabi Kinship and Marriage.* New Delhi: Hindustan Publishing Corporation, 1981.

Hickey, Gerald Cannon. *Village in Vietnam.* New Haven: Yale University Press, 1964.

Hicks, Jonathan P. "A Legal Threshold Is Crossed by Gay Couples in New York." *The New York Times* (March 2, 1993).

Hodge, Lieutenant General John R. *Korea.* Korea: Troop Information & Education Section Headquarters XXIV Corps, 1948.

Hole, Christina. *English Custom & Usage.* New York: Charles Scribner's Sons, 1942.

Homans, George Caspar. *English Villagers of the Thirteenth Century.* Cambridge: Harvard University Press, 1941.

Howard, George Elliott. *A History of Matrimonial Institutions.* New York: Humanities Press, 1964.

Howard, Michael. *Incense and Candle Burning.* London: The Aquarian Press, HarperCollins Publishers, 1991.

Hsu, Francis L. K. *Under the Ancestors' Shadow: Chinese Culture and Personality.* New York: Columbia University Press, 1948.

Huc, M. *A Journey Through the Chinese Empire,* vol. 2, New York: Harper & Brothers, 1857.

Huddleston, Sidney. *Between the River and the Hills: A Normandy Pastoral.* Philadelphia: J. B. Lippincott Company, 1930.

Ivashnea, L. L., and E. N. Razumovskaia. "The Usviat Wedding Ritual in Its Contemporary Form." *Soviet Anthropology and Archaeology* 20, no. 1 (Summer 1981).

Jackson, A. V. Williams. *Persia Past and Present: A Book of Travel and Research.* London: The Macmillan Company, 1909.

Jeaffreson, John Cordy. *Brides and Bridals.* London: Hurst and Blackett, 1872.

Jeremy, Michael, and M. E. Robinson. *Ceremony and Symbolism in the Japanese Home.* Honolulu: University of Hawaii Press, 1989.

Johari, Harish. *Breath, Mind, and Consciousness.* Destiny Books, 1989.

———. *Chakras: Energy Centers of Transformation.* Rochester, VT: Destiny Books, 1987.

Johnston, Miss Ann C. *Peasant Life in Germany.* New York: Charles Scribner, 1858.

Johnston, Basil. *Ojibway Heritage.* Lincoln: University of Nebraska Press, 1976.

Jordan-Smith, Paul. "The Teasing of the Bride." *Parabola* 8, no. 3, 1982.

Joseph, Frank, editor. *Sacred Sites: A Guidebook to Sacred Centers & Mysterious Places in the United States.* St. Paul: Llewellyn, 1992.

Jyoti, Surinder K. *Marriage Practices of the Sikhs: A Study of Intergenerational Differences.* New Delhi: Deep & Deep Publications, 1983.

Kawaguchi, The Shramana Ekai. *Three Years in Tibet.* Benares: Theosophical Publishing Society, 1909.

Keightley, Thomas. *World Guide to Gnomes, Fairies, Elves, and Other Little People.* New York: Avenel Books, 1978 (reprint).

Keith, A. Berriedale. "Marriage (Hindu)." In *Encyclopaedia of Religion and Ethics,* edited by James Hastings, vol. 8. New York: Charles Scribner's Sons, 1916.

Keller, Bill. "Nongoma Journal: Zulu King Takes a Bride, the Xhosa Tribe's Juliet." *The New York Times* (July 28, 1992).

Kelsey, Vera, and Lilly de Jongh, Osborne. *Four Keys to Guatemala.* New York: Funk & Wagnalls Company, 1939.

Kendall, Ann. *Everyday Life of the Incas.* New York: Dorset Press, 1973.

Kendall, Laurel. "Ritual Silks and Kowtow Money: The Bridge as Daughter-in-Law in Korean Wedding Rituals." *Ethnology* 24, no. 4 (October 1985).

———. "'A Noisy and Bothersome New Custom': Delivering a Gift Box to a Korean Bride." *Journal of Ritual Studies* 3, no. 2 (Summer 1989).

Kennan, George. *Tent Life in Siberia and Adventures Among the Koraks.* New York: G. P. Putnam's Sons, 1886.

Khaing, Mi Mi. *Burmese Family.* Bloomington: Indiana University Press, 1962.

Kligman, Gail. *The Wedding of the Dead: Ritual, Poetics, and Popular Culture in Transylvania.* Berkeley: University of California Press, 1988.

Kolenda, Pauline. "Woman as Tribute, Woman as Flower: Images of 'Woman' in Weddings in North and South India." *American Ethnologist* 11, no. 1 (February 1984).

Krader, Lawrence. *Peoples of Central Asia.* Bloomington: Indiana University Press, 1966.

Kunio, Yanagida. *Japanese Manners & Customs in the Meiji Era.* Tokyo: Obunsha, 1957.

Lacy, Peter. *The Wedding.* New York: Grosset & Dunlap, 1969.

Lambek, Michael. "Virgin Marriage and the Autonomy of Women in Mayotte." *Signs: Journal of Women in Culture and Society* 9, no. 2 (Winter 1983).

Lamm, Maurice. *The Jewish Way in Love and Marriage.* San Francisco: Harper & Row, 1980.

Landor, A. Henry Savage. *In the Forbidden Land,* vol. 1. London: William Heinemann, 1898.

Lane, Edward William. *An Account of the Manners and Customs of the Modern Egyptians,* vol. 1. London: Charles Knight and Co., 1842.

Lang, Olga. *Chinese Family and Society.* New Haven: Yale University Press, 1946.

Lauterbach, Jacob Z. *Studies in Jewish Law, Custom, and Folklore.* KTAV Publishing House, 1970.

Lawlor, Robert. *Voices of the First Day: Awakening in the Aboriginal Dreamtime.* Rochester, VT: Inner Traditions, 1991.

Leathley, Rev. S. A., translator. *The Roman Family, and De Ritu Nuptiarum: Title XXIII (2) from the Digest of Justinian.* London: Oxford University Press, 1922.

Lees, Dorothy Nevile. *Tuscan Feasts and Tuscan Friends.* New York: Dodd, Mead and Company, 1907.

Leonard, Linda Schierse. *On the Way to the Wedding.* Boston: Shambhala, 1987.

Levin, Laurie, and Laura Golden Bellotti. *You Can't Hurry Love: An Intimate Look at First Marriages After 40.* New York: Dutton, 1992.

Little, Mrs. Archibald. *Intimate China: The Chinese as I Have Seen Them.* London: Hutchinson & Co., 1899.

Lobacheva, N. P. "On the Shaping of New Marriage Ceremonial Among the Peoples of Uzbekistan." *Soviet Anthropology and Archaeology* 7, no. 4 (Spring 1969).

Lodge, Oliver. *Peasant Life in Jugoslavia.* London: Seeley, Service & Co., 1945.

Machal, J. "Marriage (Slavic)." In *Encyclopaedia of Religion and Ethics,* vol. 8, edited by James Hastings. New York: Charles Scribner's Sons, 1916.

Madsen, William. *The Virgin's Children: Life in an Aztec Village Today.* Austin: University of Texas Press, 1960.

Mahaffy, John Pentland. *The Silver Age of the Greek World.* Chicago: University of Chicago Press, 1906.

Makal, Mahmut. *A Village in Anatolia.* London: Valentine, Mitchell & Co., 1954.

Manuel, E. Arsenio. *Manuvu' Social Organization.* Quezon City: Community Development Research Council, University of the Philippines, 1973.

Marano, Hara Estroff. "The Reinvention of Marriage." *Psychology Today* (January/February 1992).

Markides, Kyriacos C. *The Magus of Strovolos: The Extraordinary World of a Spiritual Healer.* London: Arkana/Routledge & Kegan Paul, 1985.

Marques, A. H. de Oliveira. *Daily Life in Portugal in the Late Middle Ages.* Madison: The University of Wisconsin Press, 1971.

Martin, Judith. *Miss Manners's Guide to Excruciatingly Correct Behavior.* New York: Atheneum, 1982.

Mathews, Anna. *The Night of Purnama.* London: Jonathan Cape, 1965.

Matossian, Mary. "The Peasant Way of Life." In *The Peasant in Nineteenth-Century Russia,* edited by Wayne S. Vucinich. Stanford: Stanford University Press, 1968.

Mayer, Adrian C. *Peasants in the Pacific: A Study of Fiji Indian Rural Society.* Los Angeles: University of California Press, 1961.

Michell, John. *The New View Over Atlantis.* London: Thames and Hudson, 1983.

Miles, Arthur. *The Land of the Lingam.* London: The Paternoster Library, no. 9, 1933.

Mindell, Arnold. *The Dreambody in Relationships.* New York: Routledge & Kegan Paul, 1987.

Mitulski, James. "Committed Couples in the Gay Community." *The Christian Century* (February 28, 1990).

Monsarrat, Ann. *And the Bride Wore: The Story of the White Wedding.* New York: Dodd, Mead, 1973.

Montet, Pierre. *Everyday Life in Egypt.* London: Edward Arnold, 1958.

Moore, Melinda A. "Symbol and Meaning in Nayar Marriage Ritual." *American Ethnologist* 15, no. 2 (May 1988).

Munro, Eleanor. *Wedding Readings: Centuries of Writing and Rituals on Love and Marriage.* New York: Viking, 1989.

Murphy, Brian. *The World of Weddings: An Illustrated Celebration.* New York: Paddington Press Ltd., 1978.

Musil, Alois. *The Manners and Customs of the Rwala Bedouins.* New York: Czech Academy of Sciences and Arts and Charles R. Crane, 1928.

Nash, Manning. *The Golden Road to Maturity: Village Life in Contemporary Burma.* New York: John Wiley & Sons, 1965.

National Center for Health Statistics. Quoted in *Nation's Business* (June 1990).

Nayagam, X. S. Thani. *Tamil Culture and Civilization, Readings: The Classical Period.* New York: Asia Publishing House, 1970.

Nelson, Peter. *Marry Like a Man: The Essential Guide for Grooms.* New York: Plume/New American Library, 1992.

Nevadomsky, Joseph. "Wedding Rituals and Changing Women's Rights Among the East Indians in Rural Trinidad." *International Journal of Women's Studies* 4, no. 5 (November/December 1981).

Nilson, Lisbet. "A Funny Thing Happened on the Way to the Altar." *Boston* (February 1989).

Noble, Barbara Presley. "Legal Victories for Gay Workers." *The New York Times* (June 21, 1992).

Osgood, Cornelius. *Village Life in Old China: A Community Study of Kao Yao, Yunnan.* New York: The Ronald Press Company, 1963.

———. *The Koreans and Their Culture.* New York: The Ronald Press Company, 1951.

Owen, G. Dyfnallt. *Elizabethan Wales: The Social Scene.* Cardiff: University of Wales Press, 1962.

Parsons, Elsie Clews. *Peguche: Canton of Otalvo, Province of Imbabura, Ecuador: A Study of Andean Indians.* Chicago: University of Chicago Press, 1947.

Pears, Sir Edwin. *Turkey and Its People.* London: Methuen & Co. Ltd., 1911.

Philadelphia Yearly Meeting of the Religious Society of Friends. *Faith and Practice: A Book of Christian Discipline.* Philadelphia: Philadelphia Yearly Meeting, 1972.

Phillips, Arthur, editor. *Survey of African Marriage and Family Life.* London: Oxford University Press, 1953.

Pierce, Joe. E. *Life in a Turkish Village.* New York: Holt, Rinehart and Winston, 1964.

Poncée, Charles. *Kabbalah: An Introduction and Illumination for the World Today.* Wheaton: Quest Books, Theosophical Publishing House, 1973.

Oken, Alan. *Alan Oken's Complete Astrology,* revised edition. New York: Bantam Books, 1988.

Pardoe, Miss. *The City of the Sultan; and Domestic Manners of the Turks in 1836.* London: Henry Colburn, 1837.

Perrot, Michelle, editor. *A History of Private Life, IV: From the Fires of Revolution to the Great War.* Cambridge: Belknap Press of Harvard University Press, 1990.

Quain, Buell. *Fijian Village.* Chicago: University of Chicago Press, 1948.

Rabinovich, M. G. "The Wedding in the Sixteenth Century Russian City, Part 1." *Soviet Anthropology and Archaeology,* 18, no. 4 (Spring 1980).

———. "The Wedding in the Sixteenth Century Russian City, Part 2." *Soviet Anthropology and Archaeology,* 20, no. 1 (Summer 1981).

Radford, E. and M. A. *Encyclopedia of Superstitions,* edited and revised by Christina Hole. Chester Springs, PA: Dufour Editions, 1961.

Radha, Swami Sivananda. *From the Mating Dance to the Cosmic Dance: Sex, Love, and Marriage from a Yogic Perspective.* Spokane: Timeless Books, 1992.

Rauf, Mohammad A. *Indian Village in Guyana: A Study of Cultural Change and Ethnic Identity.* Leiden: E. J. Brill, 1974.

Reed, Julia. "Wedding Bells—and Bills—are Ringing." *U.S. News & World Report* (June 16, 1986).

Rees, Alwyn, and Brinley Rees. *Celtic Heritage: Ancient Tradition in Ireland and Wales.* New York: Thames and Hudson, 1961.

Rees, Alwyn D. *Life in a Welsh Countryside: A Social Study of Llanfihangel yng Ngwynfa.* Cardiff: University of Wales Press, 1961.

Rhys, John. *Celtic Folklore, Welsh & Manx,* vol. 1. London: Wildwood House, 1983 (reprint).

Robinson, C. E. *Everyday Life in Ancient Greece.* London: Oxford at the Clarendon Press, 1933.

———. *The Days of Alkibiades.* London: Longmans, Green and Co., 1916.

Rodd, Rennell. *The Customs and Lore of Modern Greece.* London: David Stott, 1892.

Rops, Henri Daniel. *Daily Life in the Time of Jesus,* translated by Patrick O'Brian. New York: Hawthorn Books, 1962.

Rose, H. J. *Primitive Culture in Greece*. London: Methuen & Company, 1925.

Rotundo, E. Anthony. *American Manhood: Transformations in Masculinity from the Revolution to the Modern Era*. New York: Basic Books, 1993.

Roy, Sarat Chandra. *The Mundas and Their Country*. Calcutta: Asia Publishing House, 1970.

Sanders, Irwin T. *Balkan Village*. Lexington: The University of Kentucky Press, 1949.

————. *Rainbow in the Rock: The People of Rural Greece*. Cambridge: Harvard University Press, 1962.

Schneid, Hayyim. *Marriage*. New York: Leon Amiel Publisher, 1973.

Scott, Stephen. *The Amish Wedding, and Other Special Occasions of the Old Order Communities*. Intercourse, PA: Good Books, 1988.

Seligson, Marcia. *The Eternal Bliss Machine: America's Way of Wedding*. New York: William Morrow, 1973.

Service, Elman R. *Profiles in Ethnology*. New York: Harper & Row, 1958.

Sharp, Daryl. *Getting To Know You: The Inside Out of Relationship*. Toronto: Inner City Books, 1992.

Shen, Tsung-Lien and Liu, Shen-Chi. *Tibet and the Tibetans*. Stanford: Stanford University Press, 1953.

Silverman, Sydel. *Three Bells of Civilization: The Life of an Italian Hill Town*. New York: Columbia University Press, 1975.

Simeti, Mary Taylor. *On Persephone's Island: A Sicilian Journal*. New York: Alfred A. Knopf, 1986.

Smith, William, William Wayte, and G. E. Marindin, editors. *A Dictionary of Greek and Roman Antiquities*, 3rd edition, vol. 2. London: John Murray, 1891.

Soustelle, Jacques. *The Daily Life of the Aztecs on the Eve of the Spanish Conquest*. New York: The Macmillan Company, 1962.

Stein, William W. *Hualcan: Life in the Highlands of Peru*. Ithaca: Cornell University Press, 1961.

Steinberg, David J. *Cambodia: Its People, Its Society, Its Culture*. New Haven: HRAF Press, 1959.

Stevenson, Kenneth. *Nuptial Blessing: A Study of Christian Marriage Rites*. New York: Oxford University Press, 1983.

Stevenson, Mrs. Sinclair. *The Heart of Jainism*. London: Oxford University Press, 1915.

Stewart, Martha. *Weddings*. New York: Clarkson N. Potter, 1987.

Sumner, William Graham. *Folkways: A Study of the Sociological Importance of Usages, Manners, Customs, Mores, and Morals*. Boston: Ginn and Company, 1906.

Sur, A. K. *Sex and Marriage in India: An Ethnohistorical Survey*. Bombay: Allied Publishers, 1973.

Swan, James. *Sacred Places: How the Living Earth Seeks Our Friendship*. Santa Fe: Bear & Company, 1990.

Szyliowicz, Joseph S. *Erdemli: Political Change in Rural Turkey*. The Hague: Mouton & Co.,1966.

Tagore, Rabindranath. "The Indian Ideal of Marriage." In *The Book of Marriage*, edited by Count Hermann Keyserling. New York: Harcourt, Brace & Company, 1926.

Tapper, Nancy. *Bartered Brides: Politics, Gender, and Marriage in an Afghan Tribal Society*. Cambridge: Cambridge University Press, 1985.

Teitell, Beth. "Priscilla's Brides." *Boston* (June 1991).

Thompson, Roger. "Romancing a $30 Billion Market." *Nation's Business* (June 1990).

Thornton, Penny. *Synastry: A Comprehensive Guide to the Astrology of Relationships*. Wellingborough, England: Aquarian Press/Thorsons, 1982.

————. *Romancing the Stars: The Astrology of Love and Relationships*. Wellingborough, England: Aquarian Press/Thorsons, 1988.

Tissot, Victor. *Unknown Hungary.* London: Richard Bentley and Son, 1881.

Tomasic, Dinko. *Personality and Culture in Eastern European Politics.* New York: George W. Stewart, 1948.

Toor, Frances. *Festivals and Folkways of Italy.* New York: Crown Publishers, 1953.

Trumbull, H. Clay. *Studies in Oriental Social Life.* Philadelphia: John D. Wattles & Company, 1894.

Tucker, T. G. *Life in Ancient Athens.* New York: The Macmillan Company, 1906.

Turney-High, Harry Holbert. *Chateau-Gerard: The Life and Times of a Walloon Village.* Columbia: University of South Carolina Press, 1953.

Uhl, Sarah. "Making the Bed: Creating the Home in Escalona, Andalusia." *Ethnology* 28, no. 2 (April 1989)

Urlin, Ethel L. *A Short History of Marriage.* London: William Rider and Son, Ltd., 1913.

Vaughan, J.D. *The Manners and Customs of the Chinese of the Straits Settlements.* Kuala Lumpur: Oxford University Press, 1971.

Veyne, Paul, editor. *A History of Private Life, I: From Pagan Rome to Byzantium.* Cambridge: The Belknap Press of Harvard University Press, 1987.

Vincent, Frank, Jr. *The Land of the White Elephant: Sights and Scenes in South-Eastern Asia.* New York: Harper & Brothers, 1874.

Viski, Karoly. *Hungarian Peasant Customs.* Budapest: Dr. George Vajna & Co., 1932.

von Hagen, Victor Wolfgang. *The Ancient Sun Kingdoms of the Americas.* Cleveland: World Publishing Company, 1957.

Vorren, Ornulv, and Ernest Manker. *Lapp Life and Customs: A Survey.* London: Oxford University Press, 1962.

Vuillier, Gaston. *The Forgotten Isles: Impressions of Travel in the Balearic Isles, Corsica, and Sardinia.* New York: D. Appleton and Company, 1896.

Walker, Barbara G. *The Women's Encyclopedia of Myths and Secrets.* San Francisco: Harper & Row, 1983.

Walsh, William S. *Curiosities of Popular Customs, and of Rites, Ceremonies, Observances, and Miscellaneous Antiquities.* Philadelphia: J. B. Lippincott Company, 1914.

Walters, Derek. *The Chinese Astrology Workbook: How to Calculate and Interpret Chinese Horoscopes.* Wellingborough, England: Aquarian Press/Thorsons, 1988.

————. *Chinese Astrology: Interpreting the Revelations of the Celestial Messengers.* Wellingborough, England: Aquarian Press/Thorsons, 1987.

Wehr, Gerhard. *The Mystical Marriage: Symbol and Meaning of the Human Experience.* Wellingborough, England: Crucible/Aquarian/Thorsons, 1990.

Wells, Linda. "The Wedding: Stretching the Rules." *The New York Times Magazine* (January 29, 1989).

————. "The Wedding: Formalities." *The New York Times Magazine* (January 28, 1990).

————. "The Wedding: Traditional Celebrations are Taking on Modern Twists." *The New York Times Magazine* (February 14, 1988).

Westermarck, Edward. *Marriage Ceremonies in Morocco.* London: Macmillan and Co., 1914.

————. *Ritual and Belief in Morocco.* London: Macmillan and Co., 1926.

————. *Wit and Wisdom in Morocco: A Study of Native Proverbs.* London: George Routledge & Sons, 1930.

Whetten, Nathan L. *Guatemala: The Land and the People.* New Haven: Yale University Press, 1961.

White, Suzanne. *The New Chinese Astrology.* New York: St. Martin's Press, 1993.

Whyte, Martin King. "Choosing Mates: The American Way." *Society* (March/April 1992).

Wilhelm, Richard. *The Soul of China.* New York: Harcourt, Brace and Company, 1928.

————. "The Chinese Conception of Marriage." In *The Book of Marriage,* edited by Count Hermann Keyserling. New York: Harcourt, Brace & Company, 1926.

Williams, Lena. "Women Ponder the Rodham Question." *The New York Times* (March 18, 1993).

Williams, Mary Wilhelmine. *Social Scandinavia in the Viking Age.* New York: The Macmillan Company, 1920.

Williams, Monier. *Religious Thought and Life in India, Part I: Vedism, Brahmanism, and Hinduism.* London: John Murray, 1883.

Williams, Thomas, and James Calvert. *Fiji and the Fijians,* edited by George Stringer Rowe. New York: D. Appleton and Company, 1859.

Winnington, Alan. *Tibet: Record of a Journey.* New York: International Publishers Inc., 1957.

Wood, Edward J. *The Wedding Day in All Ages and Countries.* London: Richard Bentley, 1869.

Woodhouse, W. J. "Marriage (Greek)." In *Encyclopedia of Religion and Ethics,* vol. 8, edited by James Hastings. New York: Charles Scribner's Sons, 1916.

Worcester, Dean C. *The Philippine Islands and Their People.* New York: The Macmillan Company, 1899.

Wylie, Laurence. *Village in the Vaucluse.* Cambridge: Harvard University Press, 1974.

Yang, Martin C. *A Chinese Village: Taitou, Shantung Province.* New York: Columbia University Press, 1945.

Zabilka, Gladys, compiler. *Customs and Culture of the Philippines.* Tokyo: Charles E. Tuttle Co., 1963.

Zhirnova, G. V. "The Russian Urban Wedding Ritual in the Late Nineteenth and Early Twentieth Centuries." *Soviet Anthropology and Archaeology* 14, no. 3 (Winter 1975–76).

Zimmern, Alice. *The Home Life of the Ancient Greeks.* New York: The Cassell Publishing Co., 1893.